MANAGING A HEDGE FUND

MANAGING A HEDGE FUND

A Complete Guide to Trading, Business Strategies, Operations, and Regulations

KEITH BLACK, CFA, CAIA

McGraw-Hill

New York   Chicago   San Francisco   Lisbon
London   Madrid   Mexico City   Milan   New Delhi
San Juan   Seoul   Singapore   Sydney   Toronto

3 4 5 6 7 8 9 0   DOC/DOC   0 9 8 7 6 5

ISBN 0-07-143481-X

McGraw-Hill books are available at special discounts to use as premiums and sales promotions, or for use in corporate training programs. For more information, please write to the Director of Special Sales, Professional Publishing, McGraw-Hill, Two Penn Plaza, New York, NY 10121-2298. Or contact your local bookstore.

This book is printed on recycled, acid-free paper containing a minimum of 50% recycled de-inked paper.

Library of Congress Cataloging-in-Publication Data

Black, Keith H.
  Managing a hedge fund : a complete guide to trading,
  business strategies, operations, and regulations / by
  Keith H. Black.
     p. cm.
  Includes bibliographical references.
  ISBN 0-07-143481-X (hardcover : alk. paper)
  1. Hedge funds. 2. Risk management. I. Title.
HG4530.B58 2004
332.64'5—dc22

                          2003027121

CONTENTS

ACKNOWLEDGMENTS

Any project of this effort has to be supported by many friends and colleagues, and this book is no exception. Of course, my primary thanks are offered to my wife, Melissa, and my children Tricia and Parker, who heard too often in recent months that their father was too busy to play.

This book started out as the class notes for an Internet-based course on hedge funds offered by the Illinois Institute of Technology. Many thanks to Audrey Gramstad and her I-course team at IIT, who are able to make financial topics come alive online while allowing students around the world to access the course content on a wide variety of computing platforms. Without Audrey, this book and this course never would have come to fruition. Special thanks go to I-team members, Chetan V. Patel, Shobhna A. Tattamangalam, and Bilyan Belchev, who illustrated this project. Mike Jawor, CFA, from Glenwood was influential in designing the outline for the course and the book.

Many thanks also go to the Chartered Alternative Investment Analyst Association, which has built an impressive study program and examination process. The curriculum for the CAIA exam was very influential in the design of this book, as can be seen from the bibliography. I appreciate the friendship that I have developed with Dr. Kathryn Wilkens from Worcester Tech, who introduced me to the CAIA program.

I am especially grateful to those who took the time to thoroughly read the book at various stages of completion. Those who offered especially helpful comments during the writing process include Jeff Levitt, Rob Schulte-Albert, Dr. Steve Moffitt, students in my hedge fund classes at IIT, and my friends at Cabrera Capital Markets. Of course, any errors that remain in this project are my own. I also value the friendship of Jerry Laurain, director of Alternative Investments at ABN Amro–LaSalle Bank Wealth Management, as he has always grounded our discussions in the relevance of the real world.

Given that the hedge fund world can be very secretive and data can be expensive or hard to find, I must acknowledge those who were instrumental in providing data for this project. Without Dan Coker from MSCI, TASS, CSFB/Tremont, Undiscovered Managers and Van Hedge Fund Advisers International, this book would be much shorter and much less relevant. In fact, without their help, this book might never have been a viable project.

Keith H. Black, CFA, CAIA
Assistant Professor of Investments
Stuart School of Business
Illinois Institute of Technology
565 West Adams #643
Chicago, IL 60661
Kblack@stuart.iit.edu
312-906-5146

This project started as class notes for the Hedge Funds course in the M.S. Financial Markets program of the Stuart Graduate School of Business at the Illinois Institute of Technology. When this course was first taught in the fall of 2002, I could not find one book that covered all the topics necessary to teach a comprehensive graduate course on hedge funds. This book is an attempt to summarize research from all areas of the industry, allowing readers one-stop access to hedge fund information.

Therefore, it is my hope that more M.B.A. and M.S. programs will start to include courses on hedge funds, and that this book will be very helpful in their teaching process. This book is written at an intermediate level, presuming prior knowledge of options and futures markets as well as Markowitz-style investment theory.

Professionals from all areas of the alternative investment arena may also find this project helpful. Regulators, brokers, and bankers may have advanced knowledge of standard financial products but may have been unable to keep up with the phenomenal growth of the opaque hedge funds industry.

Perhaps the most important audience could be those who currently manage, or aspire to manage, hedge funds or funds of hedge funds. Hedge fund managers may find new ways of analyzing the risk and reward of their trades or may be able to offer new funds in another style area. Funds of funds managers need to understand all styles of trading. It is hoped that this book will allow these managers to become fluent in all strategies.

Finally, this project hopes to demystify hedge funds for investors. Hedge funds should be seen as a way to diversify a portfolio, reducing risks and offering investors returns that can offset losses in their traditional investment portfolio. Investors should learn the reasons for the lack of transparency of hedge funds and should come to recognize that hedge funds don't have to be seen as an inherently risky investment style.

The hedge fund industry is so diverse, so young, and moving so fast that it is important to try to summarize the current status. Because regulations and strategies change so quickly, it is important to use the most current information possible. This project is designed to get readers up to speed on the hedge funds industry, but should be used for educational purposes only. The author and publisher are not in the business of giving investment or legal advice and cannot be responsible for the results of investment or business decisions made by readers of this book. Before making any investments or designing any business strategies, the reader is referred to competent brokers and attorneys, who make it their business to have access to the most accurate and current information available in the industry.

CHAPTER 1

Introduction to Hedge Funds

Hedge funds, by design, often have very different characteristics from the standard long-only stock and bond investments that are the dominant asset classes in most portfolios.

This first chapter will draw three contrasts between the world of hedge funds and the more familiar world of long-only investing.

First, most individual investors only invest in mutual funds, as hedge funds have long been the secret investments of the wealthy. What are the regulatory differences between hedge funds and mutual funds? Why don't mutual funds implement the same strategies as hedge funds?

Second, we will consider the difference between alternative and traditional investments. Traditional investment classes, such as long-only investments in stocks and bonds, hold the vast majority of investor assets. Alternative investments are rapidly gaining assets, and taking portfolio share, from traditional investments, especially among institutional investors. Alternative investment asset classes include hedge funds, venture capital and private equity, real estate, managed futures, and commodity funds, among others.

Finally, we will address the different mindset of investors in traditional investments relative to that of investors in alternative assets. Investors in traditional stock and bond funds attempt to beat the market, focusing on relative returns or the standing of their fund in relation to the level of market returns. Mutual fund managers can be rewarded for losing 15 percent of their client funds in a year when the stock market declined 25 percent. Similarly fund managers who gain 20 percent could be viewed as a disappointment in a year when the market grew by 25 percent.

Many managers in alternative investments, especially those that hold both long and short positions, focus on absolute returns. These managers strive to earn 5 to 20 percent each year, regardless of market direction. Often these returns are less volatile than the returns to traditional asset classes because many alternative investment strategies have the ability to profit when stock and bond prices are declining.

MUTUAL FUND CHARACTERISTICS

Mutual funds have a long history of pooling investor funds and offering professional investment management to investors who decide to place funds in a specific asset class. In fact, mutual funds existed before the Investment Company Act of 1940 was designed to regulate these investments. This act requires that funds publish a prospectus, which states the investment objective of the fund. Once published, the investment objective and operating procedures of the fund can only be changed with appropriate notice to, and voting by, the fund shareholders. Most funds will have a specific objective, investing client assets in categories such as short-term U.S. government bonds or large-capitalization value stocks. Mutual funds have diversification requirements, which cause the funds to invest their assets in a large number of liquid securities. Returns of mutual funds, by design, offer very high correlations to the returns of the asset class in which they invest.

Most mutual funds are available to all investors, offering minimum investment sizes that can be as low as $1000. Most mutual funds will accept thousands of investors, as long as each investor chooses the fund and deposits funds that exceed the minimum required investment. Many mutual fund companies advertise heavily by purchasing advertisements on television or in mainstream financial publications.

Mutual fund prices are widely disseminated on a daily basis. Investors can buy or sell shares on a daily basis. Mutual fund investment strategies are disclosed in the prospectus, and the holdings of the funds are fully disclosed on a quarterly basis.

Mutual funds are divided into actively and passively managed funds. Passive funds take a buy-and-hold approach to investing, assuming that it is difficult to beat a market in which assets are efficiently priced. Passive funds largely trade only to meet investor buy and sell orders or to rebalance to their target index. Passive funds typically market themselves as cost-efficient, charging annual management fees of less than 0.5 percent of assets.

Managers of active mutual funds believe that it is possible to beat market indices, and their fees and trading strategies reflect that belief. Most active funds will charge an annual fee of 0.75 percent to 2.25 percent of assets and justify the higher fee as the cost of investment research. Active managers trade much more often than passive managers, typically owning each security between three months and three years. The more frequently an active fund manager trades, the greater the tax consequence for his or her investors.

Many equity mutual funds are allowed to trade stock index futures, while many bond funds trade futures on fixed-income securities. The use of these futures allows the funds to facilitate quick investment and liquidation of investor positions and to help the fund more closely track market indices. A small but growing number of mutual funds allow a limited ability to short securities and the use of leverage. However, most funds use only a small amount of leverage, options, futures, and short positions to better serve their investors in their search for relative returns. Mutual funds are generally designed to be conservative, buy-and-hold investment funds that seek to have a high correlation to market benchmarks. An increased use of derivatives would reduce this correlation, which modifies the investment objective of the funds.

HEDGE FUND CHARACTERISTICS

Hedge funds were little known before the late 1980s. The first funds were started by traders with significant experience trading for mutual funds, currency desks, or proprietary trading firms. Often these traders made significant fortunes in their careers and would leave the large firm to start their own fund. These managers invested their personal assets and traded using strategies refined over the course of their institutional career. Hedge funds experienced dramatic growth during the 1990s, increasing in number from fewer than 2000 in the late 1980s to over 6000 in March 2003. TASS estimates that the number of hedge funds rose from an estimated 4850

FIGURE   1–1

Growth in number and asset size of hedge funds. *(TASS, CSFB/Tremont, www.hedgeindex.com.)*

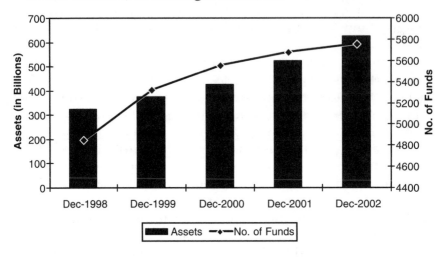

in December 1998 to 5750 at the end of 2002. (See Fig. 1-1.) Industry assets grew faster than the number of funds, rising from $325 billion to $625 billion over the same time period. Hedge funds generally attract new assets at a faster rate when stock prices are falling, so it is no surprise that these funds attracted $200 billion in 2001 and 2002, twice the rate of the prior two years. If equity markets return to the negative returns experienced in 2001 and 2002, new investments in hedge funds can be expected to grow at a rapid rate.

Hedge funds escape the regulation of the Investment Company Act of 1940 through a section 3(c)1 exemption. In order for a fund to be exempt from the regulations and disclosures required by this act, it must meet several requirements. The fund is limited to 99 accredited investors, and is not allowed to actively market its investment products. The National Securities Market Improvement Act of 1996 offers a more liberal exemption under section 3(c)7, which increases the number of qualified purchasers to 500. As a trade-off for the increased number of investors, the fund is only allowed to accept investments from "qualified purchasers," such as families with assets over $5 million or institutions with over $25 million in assets. Many funds are only available to "accredited investors" who have a minimum of $1 million in liquid assets, or an annual individual income in excess of $200,000, or an annual family income of $300,000.[1]

The 2003 World Wealth report by Cap Gemini Ernst & Young and Merrill Lynch estimates the number of millionaires worldwide.[2] Nearly 90 percent of millionaires worldwide have a net worth between $1 million and $5 million U.S. dollars, making them eligible to invest in accredited investor funds but not qualified purchaser funds. Of course, non-U.S. investors who invest in offshore funds are not required to follow the accredited investor and qualified purchaser restrictions, or any other regulations of the U.S. government. Offshore investors are required to follow the rules of their home country. Many countries, especially in the Caribbean, have little to no financial regulation.

Given that individual investors worldwide own a combined net worth of $27.2 trillion, hedge funds have a large base of potential investors among high-net-worth individuals. As the number of individual qualified purchasers is only 800,000 worldwide, hedge fund marketers have a relatively short list of marketing leads to find new investors for their qualified purchaser funds.

Net Worth	Est. Investors Worldwide
$1 million to $5 million	6,500,000
$5 million to $10 million	446,000
$10 million to $20 million	166,000
$20 million to $30 million	44,000
Over $30 million	58,000

Source: Cap Gemini Ernst & Young, Merrill Lynch.

While the majority of hedge funds are focused on the U.S. market, Americans own only 27 percent of this worldwide wealth. Hedge funds increasingly are marketing to Asian and European individuals, where the number of millionaires grew twice as fast as those in the rest of the world during 2002.

Hedge funds desire to be governed by a minimum of regulation, so they find these registration exemptions extremely valuable. Because they are only allowed to accept up to 99 investors per fund, the funds require very large minimum investments, often $500,000 to $1 million, or more. These large investment sizes and lack of advertising by funds have led to an exclusive environment where only wealthy individuals with good advisers and institutional investors have access to hedge fund investments.

Obviously a minimum investment size of $10,000 would make these funds uneconomical for the investment manager, as 99 investors with $10,000 stakes only allows a manager to run $990,000. A large minimum investment is required to ensure that the manager can gather a significant level of assets. A fund with a minimum investment requirement of $500,000 and 99 investors could manage nearly $50 million, which makes the fund large enough to be economically viable. Most fund managers require at least $10 million in assets under management to ensure the long-term success of their fund. Below these levels, the fee income of the fund is unlikely to support the income requirements of the manager or the fixed costs of running an investment management firm.

The median hedge fund now manages only $33 million. Figure 1-2 shows the size distribution of hedge funds at the end of 2002, as estimated by Van Hedge Fund Advisers International. Some funds are extremely small, with 15.9 percent of funds holding less than $5 million in assets and 29.1 percent of funds holding $5 million to $25 million under management. The most populated category of funds, 32.4 percent, manages assets of between $25 million and $100 million. A few funds are extremely large, with 19.1 percent of funds managing between $100 million and $500 million, while only 3.5 percent of funds are larger than $500 million. With 45 percent of fund managers having less than $25 million in assets, we may find that a large percentage close their doors each year, unable to earn enough in asset management fees to justify their existence. In fact, a fund is just as likely to cease operations from the failure to attract investors as from poor investment performance.

While mutual funds are designed to have a stable investment strategy in a given asset class, hedge funds are much more flexible. Managers of hedge funds have the ability to frequently change their investment strategies and the types of assets that they trade. In fact, one might determine that mutual funds are investors, while hedge funds are much more likely to act like frequent traders.

Hedge funds offer minimal liquidity and transparency. Many funds will only allow investors to redeem shares during limited monthly or quarterly withdrawal windows. Hedge funds are not

FIGURE 1–2

Size distribution of hedge funds as of December 31, 2002. *(Van Hedge Fund Advisors International, 2003.)*

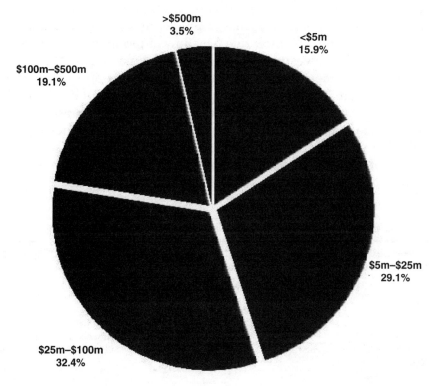

required to disclose their positions or trading strategies, so investors rarely see the types of portfolio detail that are regularly available from mutual funds. Some hedge funds will publish their returns in hedge fund publications and databases, while other funds will only provide their return history when requested by qualified investors.

Hedge funds often do not attempt to match the return to market indices, but instead hope to profit in all market environments. If a hedge fund has both long and short positions, or positions in different markets, it is not feasible to measure its performance relative to one market. In fact, the search for absolute returns often demands that fund returns are not highly correlated to movements in the stock or bond markets.

The fee schedule of hedge funds explains why many fund managers and traders at large funds would leave that secure world to start their own fund. Fees charged by hedge funds are much larger than those levied by mutual funds. Standard fees for hedge funds include a 1 percent management fee in addition to a 20 percent incentive fee. The incentive fee allows fund managers to keep 20 percent of all investment gains, giving the managers a virtually unlimited income if they attract significant assets and earn large returns. Figure 1-3 shows the detailed characteristics of hedge fund structures. The incentive fee is only paid when the fund profits exceed some threshold amount, most typically zero (82 percent of funds) or some higher hurdle rate (18 percent of funds). The risk-free interest rate is the most frequently used hurdle rate. The annual management fee is paid regardless of fund returns.

FIGURE 1-3

Global hedge fund characteristics as of first quarter 2003.
(Van Hedge Fund Advisors International, 2003.)

	Mean	Median	Mode	
Fund size	$120 million	$33 million	$3 million	
Fund age	6.3 years	5.5 years	3.0 years	
Minimum investment required	$630,414	$500,000	$1,000,000	
Number of entry dates	27	12	12	
Number of exit dates	22	4	4	
Management fee	1.3%	1.0%	1.0%	
Performance allocation ("fee")	16.8%	20.0%	20.0%	
			Yes	
Fund has hurdle rate			18%	
Fund has high-water mark			89%	
Fund has audited financial statements or audited performance			90%	
Manager has $500,000 of own money in fund			82%	
Fund can handle "hot issues"			56%	
Fund is diversified			51%	
Fund can short-sell			87%	
Fund can use leverage			74%	
Fund uses derivatives for hedging only in or none			66%	
Level of turnover	Low (0–25%) = 21%	Medium (26–75%) = 26%	High (>75%) = 53%	
Capitalization of underlying investments	Small ($1–$500m) = 11%	Medium ($500–$1000m) = 4%	Large (>$1000m) = 9%	Mixed = 76%

Hedge funds often have much more aggressive trading strategies than mutual funds. We can see that 87 percent of hedge funds have the ability to take both long and short positions in equity and fixed-income securities. Some funds will also trade in extremely illiquid areas, such as nontradable private placements or private equity investments. Other funds will directly invest in cash commodity markets or the direct purchase of real estate.

The vast majority of hedge funds, 74 percent, have the ability to use leverage, borrowing money to increase the size of their investments. In extreme cases, funds may be able to borrow and invest an amount that exceeds 20 times their investor capital. This leverage causes funds to become volatile, which creates the opportunity for large positive returns to the fund. However, leverage works both ways. We have seen numerous cases when an extreme level of leverage combined with small nominal losses have caused the demise of hedge funds.

MANAGED FUTURES FUNDS

Managed futures funds offer a different yet more highly regulated way of increasing exposure to alternative investments. Managed futures funds operators are registered as commodity pool operators (CPOs) or commodity trading advisers (CTAs) and invest in physical commodities, futures, and futures options. CTAs are single-manager funds that may offer separate accounts management, where investors have their positions managed in separate personal accounts held in their own name at a brokerage firm. CPOs place all investor funds in a commingled account, similar to the way mutual funds manage all client funds in one account. CPOs typically invest in a number of CTAs, increasing investor diversification across managers and trading styles.

Due to their investments in the futures markets, these funds are more highly regulated than hedge funds that only invest in fixed-income and equity securities. Any fund that trades futures must register as a commodity pool operator with the National Futures Association (NFA). The Commodity Futures Trading Commission (CFTC) may also regulate these funds.

There are several reasons for this increased regulation. When a fund invests in fixed- income and equity securities, the amount of margin used is often limited to 50 percent, which means that the fund must prepay at least half of the investment amount. Higher levels of leverage are available, but are limited to the amount of credit extended by the prime broker. The risk of failure of the fund impacts the prime broker, who can lose the entire amount loaned to a fund. As long as your broker will allow you to implement your trades, there are often no other regulations.

When trades are placed in the futures markets, the amount of natural leverage is much higher. When futures are traded, the required amount of margin can be 10 percent or lower. This means that the fund must place only 10 percent of the notional amount of the trade into a collateral account to repay future potential losses. This higher level of natural leverage can create larger gains and larger losses for a given amount of fund capital. Futures trades are guaranteed by a clearing firm, which is backed by the assets of all market participants. The risks of a failing fund can be passed on to all other market participants, so the regulatory agencies have an incentive to monitor and limit the risks of funds with large positions in the futures and futures options markets.

Managed futures funds trade in a variety of liquid worldwide futures markets. Many managers will trade in a variety of markets, while others may focus specifically on a single market. Futures markets can be divided into several areas, including energy, metals, or agricultural commodities; currencies; and financial futures, including those based on interest rates or stock market indices.

Managed futures funds typically trade in reaction to price patterns, either in a trend-following or in a countertrend fashion. Trend followers trade in the direction of a trend, assuming that the trend will continue. Trend followers may choose to buy futures when they predict that a market will continue to increase in price. Countertrend trading assumes that prices will remain in a range rather than a trend, where the trader will sell at the higher end of the range and buy at the lower end of the range.

CPOs can have very simple accounting, especially if all of their investments are exchange-traded futures and options, and the amount of margin is that limited to exchange rules. CPOs have a special tax treatment, which vastly simplifies the accounting relative to hedge funds. While hedge funds have to keep meticulous track of each trade and borrowing transaction, CPOs only need to report the annual change in the value of each account. Sixty percent of the fund's profit and loss is treated as long-term under the tax code, which allows the investor a lower tax rate. Forty percent of the fund's profit and loss is treated as short-term under the tax code, which is taxed at the investor's marginal tax rate. Hedge fund profits are taxed based on the holding period of the investments, with investments held longer than one year paying capital gains taxes based on lower long-term rates, while positions held less than one year are taxed at the higher short-term rate.

Managed futures funds can be extremely lucrative for a manager. They can earn a 2 percent management fee in addition to a 20 percent incentive fee. Investors must be very careful when investing in managed futures funds, as fees can be extremely high. The fund manager may also own a futures commission merchant (FCM) that executes the fund trades. The owner of the FCM can earn a commission on each trade executed by the fund manager; this can give the manager an incentive to overtrade the account to earn extra commissions, which is often not in the best interest of the investor.

TRADITIONAL VERSUS ALTERNATIVE INVESTMENTS

Traditional investments include widely held liquid investments in equity and fixed-income securities. These investments can attract trillions of dollars in assets and directly finance the operations of corporations and governments worldwide. At times these investments can be quite volatile, as the returns to these securities are correlated to the business cycle.

The three main criteria for choosing investments are the annual return, the risk as measured by the standard deviation of annual returns, and the correlations to other asset classes. U.S. Treasury bills are often referred to as the risk-free asset, as U.S. government debt is assumed to have no credit risk. However, most fixed-income investments have a risk to inflation, where the future purchasing power of the investment declines as inflation increases. As interest rates and inflation increase, the present value of the face value of the bond declines, sending the bond price lower.

Investments in large U.S. stocks have average annual returns around 14 percent, with an annual standard deviation exceeding 15 percent. Small-capitalization stocks or international stocks can have slightly higher returns, but with risk levels exceeding 20 percent. Investment-grade bonds will have average returns of 6 to 9 percent over long periods of time, with volatility levels often under 10 percent.

A typical institutional portfolio may invest 60 percent in equity securities and 40 percent in fixed-income securities. A diversified portfolio may be allocated 40 percent in large stocks, 10 percent in small stocks, 10 percent in international stocks, 20 percent in government bonds, and 20 percent in corporate bonds. Over the last 30 years a portfolio with this asset allocation, rebalanced annually, has had an average annual return of around 13 percent, with an annual standard deviation of 12 percent.

Notice that the standard deviation of this diversified portfolio is significantly smaller than the average standard deviation of the individual asset classes. Diversification among asset classes reduces risk when the correlation of returns between asset classes is less than 1. The long-term correlation between the returns of stocks and bonds is approximately 25 percent.

This diversified portfolio of traditional assets had an average annual return of 11 percent and a risk of 12 percent between 1994 and June 2003. From January 1994 to June 2003, the funds included in the CSFB/Tremont Hedge Fund Index, published by Credit Suisse First Boston, had an average annual return of 11.35 percent and a risk of 8.69 percent. We can see that hedge funds and managed futures funds have a much lower volatility of returns than traditional investments.

Traditional asset classes have much larger capacity than alternative investments. At the end of 2002, North American listed equity markets, most notably the S&P 500 and the NASDAQ composite index, had a market capitalization of over $11.5 trillion, dwarfing the total amount invested in the alternative investment universe. U.S. government bonds outstanding exceed $3 trillion, while U.S. mortgage-backed securities total $7 trillion. The amount of mortgage-backed securities outstanding has more than doubled since 1996. One of the largest U.S. equity mutual funds, Fidelity Magellan, held over $63 billion in assets in September 2003.

The amount of assets that can be invested in alternative asset strategies is limited. In 2002, managed futures funds had over $50 billion in assets, while hedge funds were estimated to manage $600 billion in assets. Hedge fund investments are growing rapidly, increasing assets by two-thirds from 2000 to 2003. Before hedge funds became more popular, the category of alternative investments generally referred to private equity, venture capital, private debt, and real estate investments. In 1995, private equity investments were around $150 billion, while private debt investments exceed $250 billion. Real estate investments are much larger than any other alternative investment category. The *Wall Street Journal* quotes a 2003 Prudential Real Estate Investors study that the investable U.S. commercial real estate market is valued at over $4 trillion.[3]

Many alternative investment funds will limit the amount of assets under management. Depending on the style and trading strategy of the fund manager, they may decide to close the fund, which means that they stop accepting new investments once the size of the fund exceeds some threshold, such as $100 million or $500 million.

CNN estimated that the 10 largest hedge fund companies had combined assets of only $34 billion in 2000. The largest hedge fund organization is George Soros's macro funds, which had $8.2 billion invested in 2000. When Soros reached $10 billion in assets under management, he stated that the funds were too large to be managed effectively.[4]

HEDGE FUND STYLES

There are many organizations that track the returns to different styles of hedge funds. Each analyst describes hedge fund categories in slightly different ways. In later chapters, we will discuss the various hedge fund benchmarks, and their impact on portfolio construction techniques. We will also discuss the specifics of a number of these strategies so that you will be able to create and analyze your own hedge fund trades and strategies.

Figures 1-4 and 1-5 illustrate the hedge fund categories tracked by Morgan Stanley Capital International (MSCI). Approximately 25 percent of hedge fund assets are in the directional trading area. These managed futures can be divided into discretionary and systematic trading, while market-timing funds are included in the tactical allocation category. Global macro funds may also be included in the discretionary trading category.

Relative-value funds are typically the least volatile hedge fund category, as these managers typically match the size and risk of their long and short positions. Over 20 percent of hedge fund assets are managed in the arbitrage, merger arbitrage, and statistical arbitrage categories.

FIGURE 1-4

Hedge fund categories tracked by Morgan Stanley Capital International. *(Reprinted by permission of MSCI.)*

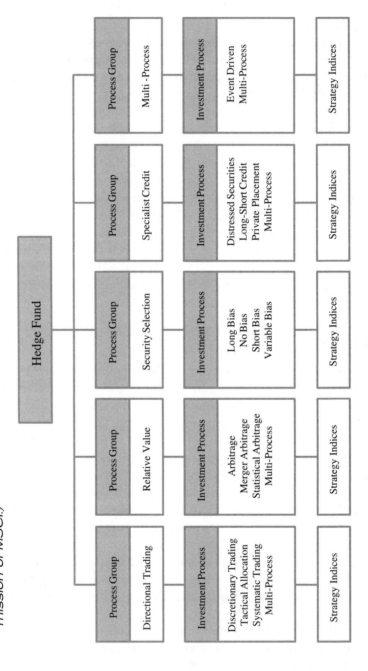

FIGURE 1–5

Investment process asset distribution in hedge funds tracked by Morgan Stanley Capital International. *(Reprinted by permission of MSCI.)*

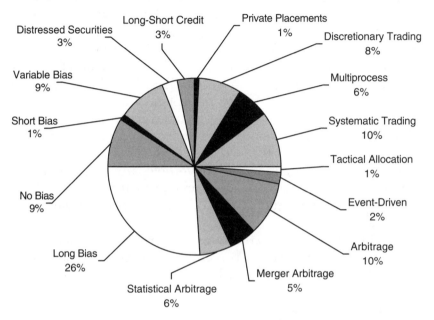

The largest category of hedge funds, with over 45 percent of assets, is security selection funds. These funds both buy long and sell short securities, but they are not always hedged. Long-bias funds will typically have larger long positions than short positions, while short-bias funds will keep larger short positions. No-bias funds take little directional exposure, while variable bias funds can switch between net-long and net-short positions based on the manager's view of market direction.

Specialist credit and multiprocess funds control less than 10 percent of hedge fund assets. These funds can take directional bets on changes in the debt or equity structure of a firm or hedged bets on the yield spreads between different types of fixed-income securities.

The two parts of Figure 1-6 demonstrate the dramatic changes in the hedge fund industry over the last decade, as reported by

Undiscovered Managers, LLC. Notice that this firm classifies hedge funds into dramatically different categories than MSCI. In 1990, 71 percent of funds were categorized as global macro funds, which take concentrated and risky bets on the impact that political and economic changes can have on the volatility and direction of worldwide currency and bond markets. By 2001, global macro managers' share of the hedge fund world had fallen to only 15.4 percent, as the market share of lower-volatility funds and equity markets funds increased. Funds based on equity securities, including long-short equity, risk arbitrage, and equity market–neutral, grew from 21.7 percent of assets in 1990 to 54.4 percent of assets in 2001.

The CSFB/Tremont Hedge Fund Index includes nine categories, which are different than the two classification systems previously discussed. These categories are convertible arbitrage, dedicated short bias, emerging markets, equity market–neutral, event-driven, fixed-income arbitrage, global macro, long-short equity, and managed futures.

Most mutual fund fee structures are fairly simple, charging an annual management fee of 0.1 percent to 2.5 percent. Fee structures of hedge funds are typically much more complicated than those of

FIGURE 1−6A

Absolute-return industry composition in 1990. *(Undiscovered Managers, LLC.)*

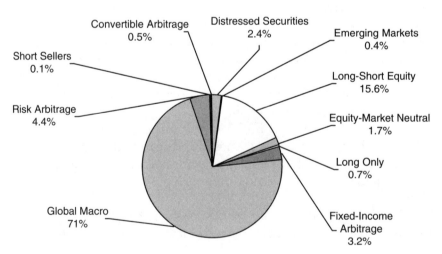

mutual funds. Hedge fund fees can far exceed the total fees charged to mutual fund investors; this has led to a rapid exodus of mutual fund managers to the hedge fund world.

Similar to mutual funds, most hedge funds charge an annual management fee of 1 percent of assets. Many managed futures funds, or funds of hedge funds, may charge a management fee of 2 percent. This fee is typically paid monthly, and is required regardless of the profitability of the fund. This fee allows the fund to stay in operation and is intended to pay for salaries, office space, and the research infrastructure.

What makes hedge funds so attractive to new managers is the incentive fee. A typical incentive fee allows the manager to keep 20 percent of all gains in the fund above the hurdle rate. The hurdle rate is the minimum return the fund needs to earn before the incentive fee is earned. The hurdle rate is often set near the risk-free rate or at a higher annual level between 5 percent and 10 percent. The total fees paid to hedge fund managers increase when the hurdle rate is reduced or eliminated. Investors pay a lower incentive fee when they demand a higher hurdle rate, such as 5 percent to 10 percent.

FIGURE 1 – 6 B

Absolute-return industry composition in 2001. *(Undiscovered Managers, LLC.)*

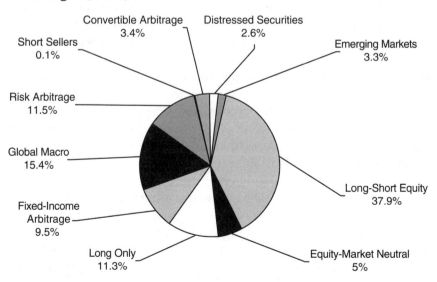

Obviously the incentive fee is often a vital part of the negotiations between hedge fund managers and new investors in the fund.

What is the total fee potential of a hedge fund manager? Figure 1-7 presents the fees due on a fund that starts operations in 1995 with $100 million in assets and earns gross returns averaging 9.1 percent per year. The management fee is 1 percent and the incentive fee is 20 percent of all gains in excess of the hurdle rate, if any. In the first example, the fund earns incentive fees on all gains, as the investor has not demanded a hurdle rate. The average annual fee on this fund is 2.8 percent of assets, leaving investors with a net return of 6.3 percent and the manager with average annual fee income of $3.6 million. Note that the fund manager earns incentive fees in every year except 1998, when the fund lost 3.3 percent of investor capital.

The second example introduces a hurdle rate, where the manager is required to earn a higher return than Treasury bills before earning any incentive fees. The average annual fee on this fund is only 2.0 percent of assets, leaving investors with a net return of 7.2 percent and the manager with average annual fee income of $2.5 million. Notice that this fund doesn't earn any incentive fees in 2000, 2001, and 2002, as the cumulative performance in these three years is lower than the returns to the risk-free asset. At the end of this eight-year period, the investor in the fund with the hurdle rate has $9.4 million more assets than the investor in the fund without a hurdle rate.

Typically the incentive fee is paid in any month where the net asset value (NAV) of the fund makes a new high. After an incentive fee is paid for a given month, that month-end NAV price is saved as the high-water mark. Future incentive fees are only paid in months where the NAV is higher than the previous high-water mark. The reason that this rule exists is to make sure that fund managers only earn an incentive fee when making new gains. The fund manager is unable to earn an incentive fee for simply recouping previous losses. This guarantees that each dollar of gain is assessed an incentive fee only one time.

Calculation of incentive fees using a high-water mark can be illustrated using the first scenario in Figure 1-7. At the end of 1997, the fund's ending assets, and high-water mark, were $136.2 million in assets. The high-water mark is typically computed at net asset value (NAV), but we will assume that this fund simply has one

FIGURE 1-7

Potential fee income for hedge fund managers.

Start with $100 Million in Assets, Average Performance
No Hurdle Rate

	Million $ Total Assets	Gross Return	Risk-Free Hurdle Rate	Return over Previous High-Water Mark	Management Fee %	Incentive Fee % (20% of Gains)	Total Fee %	Net Return	Million $ Ending Assets	Total Fee $ Millions
1995	100.0	12.8%	0.0%	12.8%	1.0%	2.6%	3.6%	9.2%	109.2	3.6
1996	109.2	15.1%	0.0%	15.1%	1.0%	3.0%	4.0%	11.1%	121.3	4.4
1997	121.3	16.7%	0.0%	16.7%	1.0%	3.3%	4.3%	12.4%	136.3	5.3
1998	136.3	-3.3%	0.0%	0.0%	1.0%	0.0%	1.0%	-4.3%	130.5	1.4
1999	130.5	22.3%	0.0%	19.0%	1.0%	3.8%	4.8%	17.5%	153.3	6.3
2000	153.3	3.7%	0.0%	3.7%	1.0%	0.7%	1.7%	2.0%	156.3	2.7
2001	156.3	2.8%	0.0%	2.8%	1.0%	0.6%	1.6%	1.2%	158.3	2.4
2002	158.3	2.8%	0.0%	2.8%	1.0%	0.6%	1.6%	1.2%	160.2	2.5
Average		9.1%					2.8%	6.3%		3.6

Start with $100 Million in Assets, Average Performance
Risk-Free Hurdle Rate

	Million $ Total Assets	Gross Return	Risk-Free Hurdle Rate	Return over Previous High-Water Mark	Management Fee %	Incentive Fee % (20% of Gains)	Total Fee %	Net Return	Million $ Ending Assets	Total Fee $ Millions
1995	100.0	12.8%	5.6%	7.2%	1.0%	1.4%	2.4%	10.4%	110.4	2.4
1996	110.4	15.1%	5.1%	10.0%	1.0%	2.0%	3.0%	12.1%	123.7	3.3
1997	123.7	16.7%	5.2%	11.5%	1.0%	2.3%	3.3%	13.4%	140.3	4.1
1998	140.3	-3.3%	4.9%	0.0%	1.0%	0.0%	1.0%	-4.3%	134.3	1.4
1999	134.3	22.3%	4.8%	9.3%	1.0%	1.9%	2.9%	19.4%	160.4	3.8
2000	160.4	3.7%	6.0%	0.0%	1.0%	0.0%	1.0%	2.7%	164.7	1.6
2001	164.7	2.8%	3.5%	0.0%	1.0%	0.0%	1.0%	1.8%	167.7	1.6
2002	167.7	2.8%	1.6%	0.0%	1.0%	0.0%	1.0%	1.8%	170.7	1.7
Average		9.1%					2.0%	7.2%		2.5

large investor account with no contributions other than the original $100 million. In 1998, the fund had a negative return of -3.3 percent, ending below the high-water mark, so no incentive fees were earned in that year. In 1999, the fund returned 22.3 percent, but incentive fees are only paid on the 19 percent of gains above the high-water mark. The fund, then, earns no incentive fees for the first 3.3 percent of gains earned in 1999, as the investor already paid incentive fees on this gain in 1997.

There can be conflicts between the investors and the fund manager. Fund managers would like to earn extremely high returns in order to increase their incentive fee. Investors may not approve of this extra risk, especially if they are investing in hedge funds to reduce their portfolio risk or preserve their capital. Fund managers can double their fee income by doubling the assets under management or by doubling the return to the fund, which may necessitate significantly higher levels of return volatility.

Some investors can negotiate an even better fee arrangement, including a look-back period. If the manager grants the investor a three-month look-back period, the incentive fees will be rebated if the fund loses value within three months of a new high-water mark. This ensures that investors only pay incentive fees for lasting gains and that managers don't value the portfolio at unsustainable prices just to increase their fees.

Small funds may struggle for revenue if their returns do not exceed the hurdle rate. If the fund is only yielding a 1 percent management fee on $50 million in assets, the revenue of the fund is only $500,000. This does not go far if there are office and data expenses, as well as a few salaried employees. In order to be successful and earn significant revenue, a fund should attract at least $20 million in assets. Most funds will close within two years if they are unable to raise this minimum amount of capital. Obviously, hedge fund managers need to earn significant incentive fees to earn a good living.

There are a number of other fees that some funds will charge. A surrender fee may be charged to encourage investors to keep their investments in the fund for long periods of time. If you sell your stake in a hedge fund in a short period of time, you will be asked to pay a fee. If the fee is paid to the fund, you are simply compensating other investors in the fund for your use of liquidity. If the fee is paid to the manager, this is yet another source of fee income for the fund manager. Some funds may charge financing fees when they arrange for loans to facilitate levered investments in the fund. Other funds may charge a trading commission or keep a portion of the commissions generated by the trading of the fund. This can create a conflict of interest, as the fund's profits will rise as investor expenses increase. As investor returns can decline as fund trading increases, it is important to understand all sources of income for a fund before committing capital to a new investment.

ABSOLUTE VERSES RELATIVE RETURNS

Most investors are familiar with relative-return strategies. Most mutual funds are managed in a way that promises to maximize relative returns. Relative-return funds have returns that are highly correlated to traditional investments. This makes sense, as equity mutual funds purchase stocks, and bond funds purchase fixed-income securities. These funds typically only purchase securities, so they are expected to lose money when that market falls. In a bear market, managers make no apologies for losing money; they simply claim that they provided the return of the asset class that you chose to invest in.

$$R_{\text{Portfolio}} = R_{\text{Risk-free}} + \beta[E(R_{\text{Market}} - R_{\text{Risk-free}})]$$

$$\text{Where beta} = \beta = \frac{COV_{R_{\text{Market}}, R_{\text{Portfolio}}}}{VAR_{R_{\text{Market}}}}$$

$$\text{Alpha} = \alpha = \text{return}_{\text{Portfolio}} - [R_f + \beta(\text{return}_{\text{Market}} - R_{\text{Risk-free}})]$$

In fact, many managers will claim superior performance when they lose 10 percent of your assets, if the market index falls by 20 percent. This is an excess return of 10 percent. However, it is not sufficient to simply compare the return of the fund to the return on the benchmark, as this simple comparison ignores the amount of risk taken by the fund manager. Jensen's alpha can be used to evaluate the relative return of managers, where the largest alpha, or risk-adjusted return, shows the manager with the greatest skill. Alpha is a measure of risk-adjusted return that requires the analyst to calculate the expected return on investments of similar risk. A low beta fund can have a positive alpha even when its returns are below the benchmark. Conversely, a high beta fund can have a negative alpha even when its returns exceed the benchmark.

In efficient markets, such as Treasury bonds or large-capitaliza-tion U.S. stocks, it is difficult for a manager to consistently provide a positive alpha to investors. In these cases, where managers struggle to provide excess returns, investors should consider investing in index funds. Index funds charge extremely low management fees and trade infrequently, thus minimizing taxes. In less efficient markets, such as international and small-capitalization securities, it is less difficult for a manager to generate positive alpha. In these cases, many investors may find that it is worth paying the extra fees to the active manager, as their in-depth research is more likely to produce market-beating returns.

As most mutual funds engage in a minimum of hedging and derivatives trading, the value of the fund rises in bull markets, and falls in bear markets. The sensitivity to market returns can be mea-sured by the beta of the fund relative to the benchmark. This lack of hedging can create a volatile return stream, where an equity investor has no place to hide during extreme bear markets, such as those experienced in the United States during 2000 to 2002.

Hedge funds and managed futures are designed to provide absolute returns. By minimizing the correlation to the returns to traditional markets, and having the ability to short securities and trade derivatives, absolute-return funds strive to produce consis-tent positive returns in all market environments. Absolute-return managers are not doomed to lose money when traditional invest-ment returns are negative, as their profits from the short side are designed to offset the losses from the purchased investments.

A good example is the 12 months ending September 2002. While the S&P 500 declined by 21.6 percent, eight of the nine com-ponents of the CSFB/Tremont Hedge Fund Index showed positive returns. The only hedge fund category that showed negative returns over this time period was long-short equity funds, which has the largest positive correlation to equity markets of any hedge fund strategy. If returns to traditional investments continue to be weak, hedge funds can expect to continue to attract increasing amount of assets. In short, as investors become disillusioned with relative returns in a bear market, more investors will choose to increase their asset allocation to absolute-return investments. In fact, from the inception of the CSFB/Tremont Hedge Fund Index in January 1994 to September 2002, hedge funds had an average annual return of 10.7 percent, while the S&P 500 returned only 6.59 percent. Not only did the hedge fund index produce higher returns, the volatility of hedge fund investments was much lower than equity market volatility over this time period.

Over the same time period, we see that an investor holding a diversified portfolio would have outperformed one investing only in stocks. By owning 60 percent stocks (40 percent U.S. large-cap, 10 percent U.S. small-cap, and 10 percent international stocks) and 40 percent bonds (20 percent U.S. corporate and 20 percent U.S. Treasury), an investor would have earned an average annual return of 11.5 percent, with an annual volatility of 11.8 percent. While hedge fund investors earn a slightly lower return, they do so at much lower levels of volatility.

Hedge fund investments can be categorized by the volatility of returns to their investment style. (See Fig. 1-8.) Low-volatility funds,

FIGURE 1–8

Morgan Stanley Capital International investment management process. *(Reprinted by permission of MSCI.)*

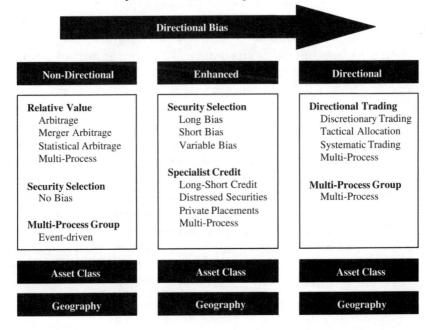

A granular classification system allows for a more sophisticated portfolio construction process.

or nondirectional funds, include the arbitrage, equity market–neutral, and event-driven strategies. As these funds typically experience annual volatility levels of 3 to 6 percent, many of these managers may use higher levels of leverage. These are broad categories, as arbitrage can apply to investments in convertible bonds, equities, fixed income, or currencies. This can increase their potential returns, while providing volatility closer to levels experienced in traditional asset classes. Investors can choose to add additional leverage to these low-volatility funds, increasing both the risk and the potential return of their investments.

Other hedge fund strategies have medium-volatility levels, using an enhanced directional bias. These funds typically mix long and short positions in unequal weights, so are typically less volatile than long-only funds. Long-short equity funds, long-short fixed-income arbitrage funds, and distressed-securities funds fit in this category.

Finally, many hedge fund strategies are fully directional, even more volatile than traditional investments. Short-selling and emerging-markets funds can experience volatilities of nearly 20 percent, while global macro funds and managed futures funds can take unhedged directional positions of significant size.

Figure 1-9 outlines the characteristics of the MSCI hedge fund classification standard. Perhaps the most attractive feature of the MSCI classification system is that it allows fund managers and investors to benchmark performance by a true group of similar funds. If an index separates thousands of hedge funds into just 10 categories, there can be a wide variety of fund styles within a category. For example, funds in the long-short equity category may trade stocks only in the United States, only in Europe, only in Japan; or they can be diversified worldwide. Funds in the long-only equity category are often focused on a specific sector, perhaps financial companies or technology stocks. In an index with a limited number of strategy categories, all funds within the larger strategy are grouped together, even though there can be a much more specific categorization. When different funds are grouped together, funds within a broad category can have a lower correlation to other funds in the category, making it more difficult for investors to earn the average return to the strategy.

FIGURE 1-9

Morgan Stanley Capital International Hedge Fund Classification Standard. *(Reprinted by permission of MSCI.)*

Every fund in the MSCI Database is classified according to its relevant characteristics. Examples:
- Relative Value - Arbitrage - Fixed Income - Developed Markets - North America - Mortgage Backed
- Security Selection - Long Bias - Equity - Global Markets - Europe - Information Technology

Primary Characteristics

Investment Process			Asset Class	Geography		
Process Group	Process			Area	Region	

Directional Trading — Process: Discretionary Trading, Tactical Allocation, Systematic Trading, Multi-Process

Relative Value — Arbitrage: Merger Arbitrage, Statistical Arbitrage, Multi-Process

Security Selection — Long Bias: No Bias, Short Bias, Long Bias

Specialist Credit: Long-Short Credit, Distressed Securities, Private Placements, Multi-Process

Multi-Process Group: Event-Driven, Multi-Process

Asset Class: Commodities, Convertibles, Currencies, Equity, Fixed Income, Diversified

Area: Developed Markets, Emerging Markets, Global Markets

Region (Developed Markets): Europe, Japan, North America, Pacific ex Japan, Diversified

Region (Emerging Markets): EMEA, Asia Pacific, Latin America, Diversified

Region (Global Markets): Europe, Asia ex Japan, Asia, Diversified

Secondary Characteristics

GICS Sector: Consumer Discretionary, Consumer Staples, Energy, Financials, Health Care, Industrials, Informational Technology, Materials, Telecom Services, Utilities, No Industry Focus

Fixed Income Focus: Asset-Backed, Government Sponsored, High Yield, Investment Grade, Mortgage-Backed, Sovereign, No Fixed Income Focus

Capitalization Size: Mid and Large Cap, Small Cap, Small and Mid Cap, No Size Focus

Through the use of both primary and secondary characteristics of a fund, MSCI calculates much more specific performance indices. Of course, the more specific the classification becomes, the smaller the number of funds in each category. For example, under the MSCI scheme, funds trading long-short equity strategies in Japan and the United States would be contained in different categories at the most granular level. Similarly long-only sector managers in technology would not be directly compared to long-only managers who focus on banking companies.

Investors in absolute-return funds may have different objectives. Those who are seeking returns that may be similar to, or larger than, the returns to equity securities would invest in funds that are return enhancers. While return-enhancing funds offer high returns, they also have higher return volatility and a stronger correlation to the returns of traditional stock market investments. Given their high correlation and volatility levels, these funds may often be measured by their relative returns.

Instead of seeking high returns, investors may focus on the fund strategies that are portfolio diversifiers. While the returns to these funds more closely approximate fixed-income return levels rather than equity return levels, investors find other benefits from owning diversifying funds. These diversifying funds typically have absolute-return objectives and lower volatilities and correlations to traditional investment returns. Given these characteristics, portfolio diversifying strategies offer investors the opportunity to earn positive returns when traditional investments are declining in value, which reduces portfolio volatility.

Figure 1-10 illustrates which funds qualify as return enhancers or portfolio diversifiers. Only three fund categories offer both features, including long-short equity, short sellers, and distressed securities. In Chapter 2, we will describe the correlation characteristics of each fund strategy and show how hedge funds can improve the investor's efficient frontier. By allocating assets to hedge funds, investors have the opportunity to reduce the volatility of their investment portfolio without significantly reducing their expected return.

Some of the most aggressive investors in alternative investments are public pension plans and college and university endowment funds. Because these investment pools are characterized by

FIGURE 1–10

Return enhancers and portfolio diversifiers. *(Undiscovered Managers, LLC.)*

	Return Enhancers	Portfolio Diversifiers
Absolute-Return		
Relative-Value		
Long/short equity	◆	◆
Equity-market neutral		◆
Convertible arbitrage		◆
Fixed-income arbitrage		◆
Opportunistic		
Global macro	◆	
Emerging markets	◆	
Short sellers	◆	◆
Long only	◆	
Event-Driven		
Risk arbitrage		◆
Distressed securities	◆	◆
Commodities		
Managed futures		◆
Private Equity		
Venture capital	◆	
Mezzanine	◆	
LBO	◆	
Real Estate		
Private real estate		◆
REITs		◆

very long holding periods, they have the opportunity to place a small portion of their assets in illiquid strategies. Figure 1-11 describes the results of the 1992 National Association of College and University Business Officers (NACUBO) survey of college and university endowment funds. At this date, funds had an average allocation of 54 percent in equities, 38 percent in fixed-income and cash products, and 11 percent in alternative investments. These alternatives included real estate, mortgages, venture capital, private equity, natural resources, and distressed investments.

Several changes can be noted in endowment investment allocations over the last 10 years. (See Fig. 1-12.) First, we notice that the portion of international investments has risen from 9 percent to

FIGURE 1—11

Asset allocation of U.S. college and university endowments.
(NACUBO endowment study, 1992.)

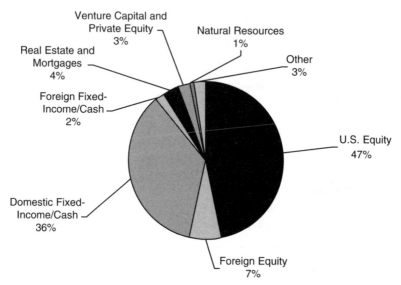

1992 Dollar-Weighted Mean Allocation

15 percent, showing a dramatic shift toward global investments.
The asset allocation is now much more diversified, with 50 percent
in equities, 25 percent in fixed income and cash, and a full 25 percent of the portfolio in alternative investments. While natural
resources and real estate allocations are relatively stable, we see
dramatic growth in venture capital/private equity and hedge fund
investments. While the allocation to venture capital/private equity
doubled, the allocation to hedge funds increased from less than 3
percent in 1992 to 11 percent in 2002.

Smaller endowment funds, which have less than $100 million
in assets, typically have less than 3.4 percent of their assets in
hedge funds, as they may need this limited amount of assets to
remain liquid to meet the current needs of the institution. As assets
rise, the endowment is more focused on the perpetual needs of the
institution and needs a much smaller fraction of the assets for current operations. These larger funds, then, take much larger stakes

Asset allocation of U.S. college and university endowments.
(NACUBO endowment study, 2002.)

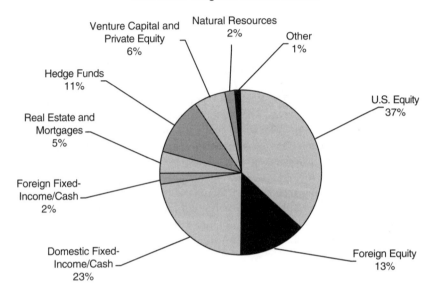

2002 Dollar Weighted Mean Allocation

in alternative investments, as the need for liquidity is much smaller.
Endowments with $100 million to $500 million in assets allocate up
to 7.4 percent of dollar-weighted assets to hedge funds, while those
with assets of $500 million to $1 billion have an 11.5 percent stake.
The largest endowments allocate nearly 30 percent of their assets to
alternative categories, including 14.7 percent of their assets in hedge
funds, as well as 9.3 percent in venture capital/private equity and
5.9 percent in real estate. The smallest endowments, by contrast, allocate far less than 10 percent of their endowments to these alternative
categories.[5]

Funds of funds are a popular investment with small and
medium-size endowments, typically attracting between 15 and 25
percent of the assets these funds allocate to hedge funds. The largest
endowments, which can afford to allocate over $100 million to hedge
funds, do not typically invest in funds of funds, but they will hire
their own manager to select investments in single-manager hedge

funds. Given their conservative nature, it is no surprise that endowments generally focus on absolute-return investments. Typically, these investors avoid the most volatile hedge fund categories, with almost no allocations to emerging markets, dedicated short selling, or global macro funds.

ENDNOTES

1. S. McCrary, *How to Create and Manage a Hedge Fund: A Professional's Guide.* New York: John Wiley & Sons, 2002, p. 195.
2. "Millionaire Has-Beens: The Ranks of High-Net-Worth Individuals in the United States Have Thinned, Thanks to You Know What." Viewed at http://money.cnn.com/2003/06/11/pf/millionaire/millionaires/.
3. R. Smith, "Commercial Buying Activity Slows at Some Public Real Estate Firms," *Wall Street Journal*, August 20, 2003.
4. "A Shakeup at Soros Funds: Two Top Managers Depart; Quantum Fund Reorganizes amid Big Tech Losses." Viewed at http://money.cnn.com/2000/04/28/mutualfunds/soros/index.htm.
5. National Association of College and University Business Officers, *2002 Endowment Study*. Washington DC: Author, 2003.

CHAPTER 2

Portfolio Effects of Hedge Fund Investments

So far we have learned that hedge funds typically have a slightly lower return and a significantly lower volatility than traditional investment funds. When the risk of an investment falls faster than the return, the investment can provide a higher return for each unit of risk incurred. This means that most hedge funds offer a risk/reward relationship that is significantly more attractive than most stock market investments.

Few investors have their entire portfolio invested in hedge funds. Given the limited capacity of hedge funds, it would be impossible for all investors to allocate half of their funds to this asset class. However, we have seen many aggressive pension and endowment funds dramatically increase their allocations to hedge funds in recent years. In the year 2000, educational institutions invested 7 percent of their endowment in hedge funds. This asset allocation has rapidly increased to 11 percent over the last two years. With the limited capacity and availability of hedge funds, most investors are unable or unwilling to increase their allocation of alternative investments to above 25 percent of their portfolio.

If traditional investments comprise 75 to 95 percent of most investor asset allocations, we must understand how a small allocation to alternative investments will change the characteristics of our portfolios. Diversification is the key reason investors are attracted to hedge funds. The lower the correlation between a hedge fund style and traditional investments, the more effectively that hedge fund class will diversify traditional portfolios. Consider the style correlations relative to the returns of the S&P 500, as presented in Figure 2-1. The most diversifying hedge fund strategies are convertible arbitrage with a correlation of 0.13 and fixed-income arbitrage with a correlation of 0.03. Notice that managers in these styles attempt to hedge away market risk, where the funds have as many short positions as long positions. These offsetting positions reduce the correlation to market movements. Managed futures funds, which have a −0.25 correlation to the S&P 500, are expected to offer the best risk reduction powers for investors with large equity market investments. While global macro funds have a low correlation of 0.24 to U.S. stocks, they are seen more as return enhancers than portfolio diversifiers due to their higher standard deviation of returns.

Most hedge fund strategies, as well as the CSFB/Tremont index, have correlations to stocks of between 40 percent and 58 percent. These medium correlation strategies include emerging markets, equity market–neutral, event-driven, and long-short equity strategies. Dedicated short sellers of stocks have a correlation of −78 percent to the S&P 500, which makes short funds more of a hedging technique than a diversification technique.

Figure 2-2 shows the correlations of hedge fund strategies to the returns to the MSCI World Sovereign Bond Index^{SM}. Generally we find that hedge fund strategies have much higher correlations to stock markets than to fixed-income investments. Most hedge fund strategies have a correlation between −0.18 and +0.10 to worldwide bond markets, meaning that hedge funds offer returns that are generally uncorrelated to this traditional investment category. We can understand why emerging markets funds have a −0.23 correlation to bond markets, as investors are likely to purchase the safe assets in sovereign bond markets during times of volatility and stress in the emerging markets. Similarly, we see that managed futures funds have a 0.36 correlation to bond markets. This is understandable, as many of the trades in this style are focused on the interest rate and currency markets.

Remember the efficient frontier? This is a graph of the risk-return characteristics of a portfolio, with the annualized return on the y axis and the annualized standard deviation of returns on the x axis. A portfolio is defined as efficient (or optimally diversified) if the portfolio has the maximum return attainable for a given level of

Correlations of hedge funds to S&P 500.

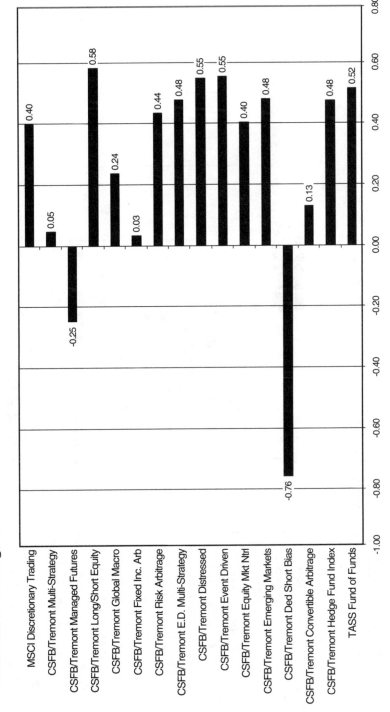

Correlations of hedge funds to MSCI World Sovereign Debt Index.

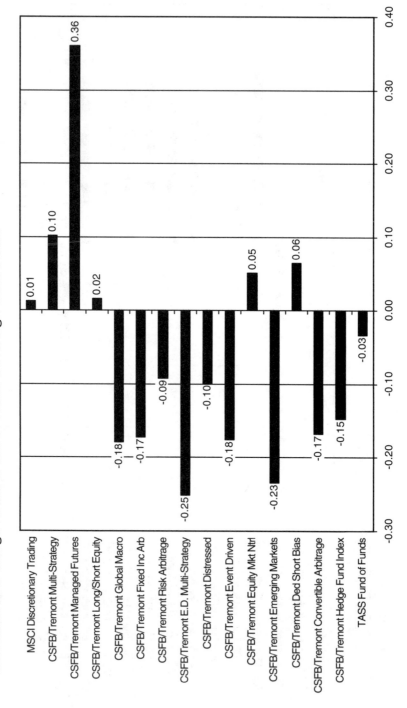

risk or the minimum risk for a given level of return. The low levels of correlation between hedge fund and traditional investment returns means that adding hedge funds to a traditional portfolio is extremely diversifying, which dramatically improves our efficient frontier.

Investors are always trying to move their portfolios to the northwest in risk-return space. This allows investors to improve returns without increasing risk or to reduce risk without sacrificing returns. The lower curve in Figure 2-3 shows all combinations of traditional stock and bond investments from 1994 to June 2003. Over this time period, investors who placed all of their funds in the S&P 500 earned an average annual return of 11.46 percent with a standard deviation of annual returns of 16.11 percent. The Sharpe ratio of the S&P 500, calculated as the excess return over the risk-free rate, divided by the standard deviation of returns, is 0.44. The least risky portfolio can be found by investing 25 percent of assets in the S&P 500 and 75 percent in the MSCI World Sovereign Fixed Income Index^SM. This conservative portfolio would have yielded a return of 7.75 percent with a risk of 6.14 percent and a Sharpe ratio of 0.55.

Investing in alternative investments is expected to improve the efficiency of our portfolio by offering higher returns or lower risk relative to portfolios only invested in traditional asset categories. We can see that by adding investments in the CSFB/Tremont Hedge Fund Index, our investments become more efficient. The top curve in Figure 2-3 shows the improvement in portfolio risk and return from adding an allocation to hedge fund investments. A portfolio 50 percent invested in the S&P 500 and 50 percent in the hedge fund index returned 11.41 percent, with a risk of 10.82 percent and a Sharpe ratio of 0.65. This portfolio offers similar returns to a portfolio entirely invested in stocks, but with nearly one-third less risk. Similarly, a portfolio invested 50 percent in the bond index and 50 percent in the hedge fund index offered returns of 8.92 percent, with a standard deviation of 4.99 percent and a Sharpe ratio of 0.91. Not only does this portfolio offer 1.17 percent greater annual return than our conservative traditional portfolio, it is also 20 percent less risky. We can clearly see, then, the potential that hedge fund investing offers, allowing investors to dramatically reduce portfolio risk without sacrificing returns.

By adding alternative investments to our traditional portfolio, we see that the Sharpe ratio increases and the largest and smallest monthly returns fall in magnitude. Not only is our new portfolio

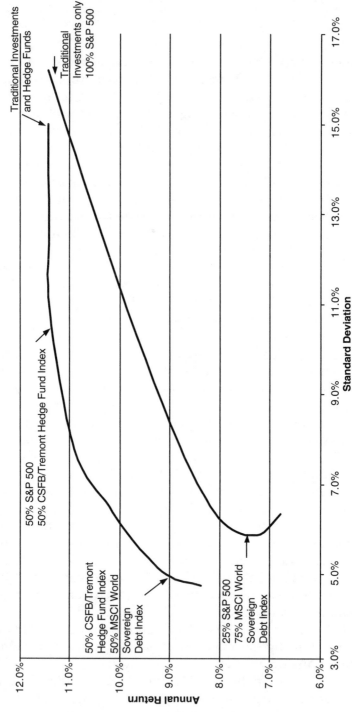

FIGURE 2-3

Improving efficient frontiers by allocating assets to hedge funds.

50% S&P 500
50% CSFB/Tremont Hedge Fund Index

Traditional Investments
and Hedge Funds

Traditional
Investments only
100% S&P 500

50% CSFB/Tremont
Hedge Fund Index
50% MSCI World
Sovereign
Debt Index

CSFB/Tremont Hedge Fund Index

25% S&P 500
75% MSCI World
Sovereign
Debt Index

Annual Return

Standard Deviation

12.0%
11.0%
10.0%
9.0%
8.0%
7.0%
6.0%

3.0%   5.0%   7.0%   9.0%   11.0%   13.0%   15.0%   17.0%

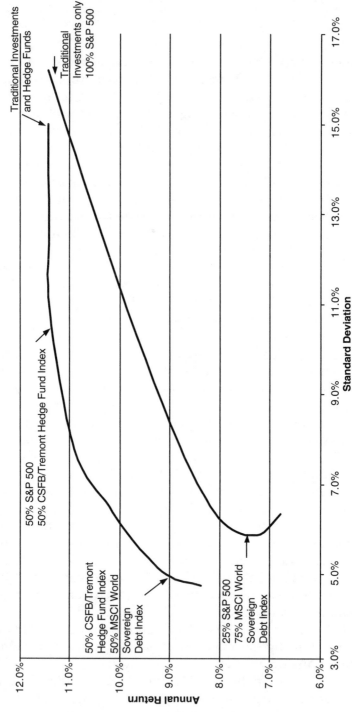

36

less volatile in standard deviation terms, but there is an improvement in our minimum monthly return. We would expect positive returns in our alternative portfolio that offsets losses in our traditional investments during periods of weak returns to traditional investments.

While we can estimate the improvement that alternative investment strategies can bring to a portfolio of traditional investments, we must also understand that historical risks, returns, and correlations are only estimates of the future characteristics of these investments. Should returns fall, and risks or correlations increase, alternative investments will not be nearly as successful in improving the Sharpe ratio of our portfolio as we had previously estimated. We must also realize that most investors will be unable to place 50 percent of their portfolio in hedge funds. While a realistic 10 percent allocation to hedge funds can reduce portfolio risk, the risk reduction will not be of the magnitude illustrated in our efficient frontier.

Traditional investors need diversification most when the stock market is experiencing a time of negative returns. Ideally, a portfolio would be fully invested in stocks during bull markets and fully invested in cash or investments of rising or stable values when stock prices are falling. While it is impossible to achieve consistent success in this type of market timing, we can see that investors will receive the largest benefit when hedge funds earn positive returns during times of weak stock prices.This leads us to search for alternative investment styles that have higher correlations to stocks during times of large positive equity market returns, and lower correlations to stocks when equity prices are weak. Figure 2-1 showed the absolute correlation, that is, the average return to hedge funds in all equity market conditions. Figure 2-4 shows the conditional correlations between hedge fund returns and returns to the S&P 500. This graph shows that conditional correlations are defined relative to the state of the stock market, separating hedge fund returns between times of rising and falling stock markets. Unfortunately, we see that most hedge fund strategies have higher correlations to stock prices when the equity market is falling than when stock prices are rising, which means that correlations can increase dramatically as stock prices fall. Rather than giving us protection from falling stock prices, most hedge fund strategies are likely to decline in value during times that stocks are under pressure. This means that hedge

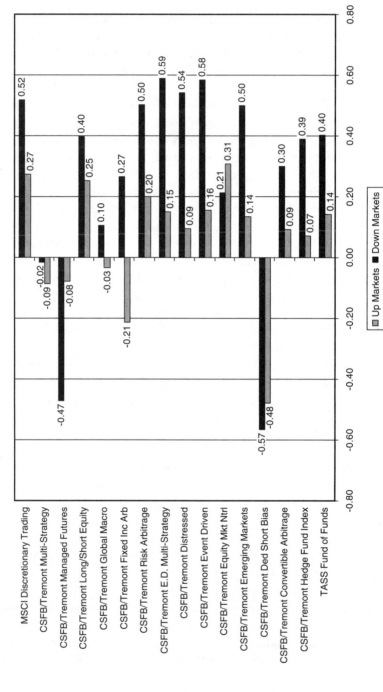

FIGURE 2-4

Up and down correlations to S&P 500.

funds are not as effective diversifiers as may be indicated by the average correlations. As hedge funds are most diversifying to a portfolio of traditional investments when they earn positive returns that offset the losses in our stock portfolio, many investors may choose to underweight these hedge fund styles in order to maximize the effectiveness of the diversification of their portfolio. However, a few styles offer true diversification, with higher correlations to stock prices in bull markets and lower correlations to stock prices in bear markets. In this case, managed futures and global macro funds seem to offer the best diversification potential of all alternative investment strategies. The CSFB/Tremont Managed Futures Index offers a return that is −0.08 correlated to stocks in up markets and −0.47 correlated to stocks in down markets. This large negative correlation in falling stock markets makes these investments an excellent hedging vehicle. Similarly, the CSFB/Tremont Global Macro Index is uncorrelated to stocks in all time periods, with conditional correlations of −0.03 during rising equity markets and 0.10 in falling stock markets. As you can see, the ability of managed futures funds to earn positive returns is independent of the return to equity markets.

Figure 2-5 explains that the conditional correlations of hedge funds to the MSCI World Sovereign Debt Index are much more favorable than the conditional correlations to stock prices. Most hedge fund styles have conditional correlations between −0.20 and +0.20, meaning that hedge funds are generally uncorrelated to fixed-income investments, whether interest rates are rising or falling. Once again, global macro funds and managed futures funds have attractive conditional correlation patterns. Relative to bond market investments, the CSFB/Tremont Equity Market–Neutral Index has an excellent conditional correlation structure. Equity market–neutral funds offer a 28 percent correlation to bond markets when interest rates are falling and a −0.10 correlation when interest rates are rising. These funds, then, offer profit opportunities in all interest rate scenarios.

Fung and Hsieh use principal components analysis (PCA) to separate funds into five separate risk classes.[1] Each class is relatively uncorrelated to each other class, meaning that each type of fund has different sources of returns. These five classes include distressed securities, long-only funds, global/macro style, trend-following

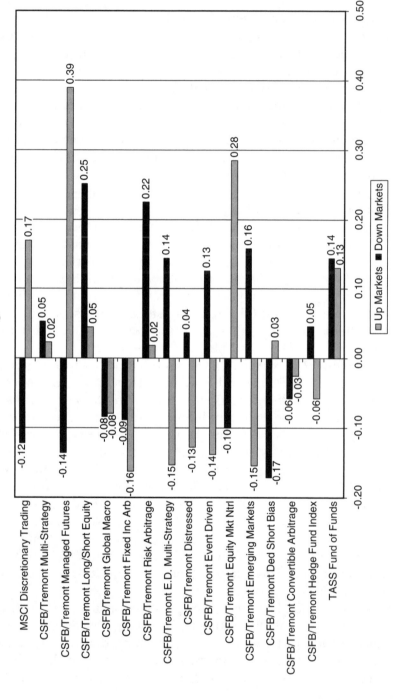

FIGURE 2–5

Up and down correlations to MSCI World Sovereign Bond Index.

in major currencies, and trend-following on diversified markets. Because these classes have little correlation to each other, a mixture of these fund styles will best diversify the portfolio of hedge funds, which will most effectively hedge a portfolio of traditional investments. Most market-neutral or hedged funds are unexplained by PCA, which implies that these funds do not have a consistent correlation to market indices or other hedge fund styles.

Fung and Hsieh also relate alternative investment categories to how their return pattern matches a mix of traditional and derivatives investments, presenting the returns to each style sorted by the return to the U.S. equity markets.

Figure 2-6 shows a figure similar to that produced by Fung and Hsieh, where in the worst 20 percent of months, the MSCI World Equity Index^{SM} falls by an average of –5.94 percent per month, while the MSCI Systematic Trading Index^{SM} rises by an average of 2.06 percent in months of rapidly declining stock prices. This figure shows the returns to managed futures funds when traditional investment index returns are sorted into quintiles. In this example, we see that the returns to the MSCI Systematic Trading

FIGURE 2-6

MSCI Systematic Trading Index versus MSCI World Equity Index. Monthly returns sorted by quintiles, January 1994 to June 2003.

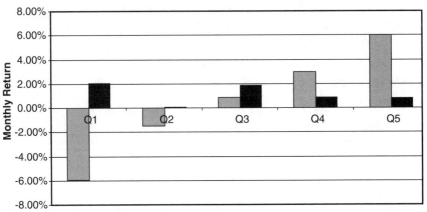

Return Quintiles

▣ MSCI World Equity Index ▪ MSCI Systematic Trading Index

Index are relatively uncorrelated to the returns of the MSCI World Equity Index. In fact, the highest returns to these managed futures funds come at times when equity markets worldwide are falling the most quickly.

Trend following CTAs have their highest returns in volatile markets, and weaker returns in more tranquil markets. This return pattern matches that of an investor who purchases straddles (both puts and calls) on U.S. stocks. CTAs, therefore, are good protection against falling stock markets and may substitute for the purchase of puts on equity indices.

Global macro funds underperform stocks in up markets and outperform stocks in down markets. These funds provide similar returns to the purchase of puts and sale of calls on a U.S. stock portfolio. This hedge fund style may replace tactical asset allocation funds, which seek to improve returns through market timing.

Fixed-income arbitrage funds have little correlation to stocks and have a stable return in most market conditions. However, these funds, such as those once managed by Long-Term Capital Management, can have large losses during times of market crisis. Obviously, it is difficult to measure this risk profile with standard statistics, where a fund may earn 1.5 percent a month for five years with minimal volatility, and then lose over 20 percent in a single month. This return profile matches that of a seller of put options on equity indices.

Similar graphs will be presented in each chapter on hedge fund styles, as a way to illustrate the behavior of hedge fund returns conditional on the sorted performance of traditional equity and fixed-income markets.

ENDNOTE

1. W. Fung and D. A. Hsieh, "A Primer on Hedge Funds," *Journal of Empirical Finance* 6 (1999): 309–331.

CHAPTER 3

Measuring Hedge Fund Performance

In order to determine which investment best fits our needs, we must analyze the historical return and risk of each fund style. There are many ways to compute both statistics, and the method of calculation can often change the conclusions. While we have over 100 years of history for the U.S. stock market, hedge fund databases may provide only ten years of historical data. We must be careful, then, when directly comparing the risk and return of traditional investments to alternative investments, as hedge fund returns have not been tracked during all types of market environments.

Most investors think in terms of annual returns, but hedge funds typically report monthly returns. Monthly returns are annualized using the following calculation:

$$[(1 + \text{monthly return}) \wedge 12] - 1$$

Similarly, quarterly returns are annualized by calculating

$$[(1 + \text{quarterly return}) \wedge 4] - 1$$

For example, a 1 percent monthly return converts to an annual return of 12.68 percent, while a 3 percent quarterly return annualizes to 12.55 percent. Notice the more frequently we compound the return, the higher the annual return.

It is considered inappropriate, however, to annualize returns that are earned in less than one year. To illustrate with an absurd example, assume that an options investor doubles his money in

one month, which frequently happens with a single option position. Annualizing this monthly return of 100 percent gives us an
annual return of 409,500 percent, which is 4095 times the original
investment. It is clearly not reasonable to expect any investor to
earn returns of this magnitude during the course of one year, as the
investor would need to double his entire capital, including profits,
each month over the course of the year.

The most proper way to calculate returns is by using geometric
averages. To find the geometric average over n periods, typically
years, we simply take the nth root of the terminal wealth. If a portfolio has increased by 198.6 percent over 6 years, the average annual
geometric return is

$$[(1 + 198.6 \text{ percent}) \wedge (1/6)] - 1$$

which is 20 percent. This is the same as dividing the final portfolio
value by the beginning portfolio value and then taking the nth root.
Assuming a final portfolio value of $298,598 and a beginning port-
folio value of $100,000 and a time of 6 years, we find that the average
annual geometric return is 20 percent.

To find the terminal wealth from a series of gains, simply multiply each year's ending wealth by the next year's return. With
annual returns of 15 percent, 12 percent, and 18 percent, the terminal
wealth calculated using the geometric technique is

$$1.15 \cdot 1.12 \cdot 1.18 = 1.51984,$$

which is a total return of 51.98 percent over the three-year period.
Using the geometric formula

$$[(1 + 51.984 \text{ percent}) \wedge (1/3)] - 1$$

we can find the average annual return of 14.97 percent.

Note that this geometric return differs from the arithmetic average of 15 percent. While the arithmetic average of returns, found by
summing each annual return and dividing by the number of periods,
is simple to calculate, it can also be misleading. Arithmetic average
returns consistently overestimate the total returns over long com-
pounding periods. The arithmetic return will increasingly diverge
from the geometric return as the annual returns become more volatile.
Geometric average returns can also be called time-weighted returns.

Throughout this book, we will present hedge fund performance
with a standardized set of figures. Figure 3-1 uses the example of

FIGURE 3–1

CSFB/Tremont Hedge Fund Index performance, 1994 to 2003. (MSCI, reprinted by permission; TASS, CSFB/Tremont, http://www.hedgeindex.com.)

The CSFB/Tremont Hedge Fund Index is calculated from the monthly returns to over 400 hedge funds carefully selected from 10 different trading styles. This index is asset-weighted, which gives the largest funds a more significant impact on index returns.

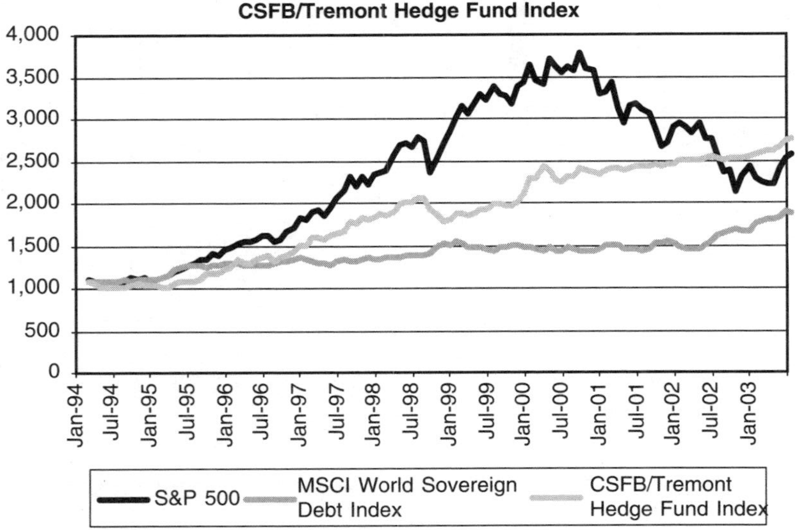

CSFB/Tremont Hedge Fund Index

	CSFB/Tremont Hedge Fund Index
1994	-4.35
1995	21.68
1996	22.22
1997	25.92
1998	-0.36
1999	23.43
2000	4.84
2001	4.41
2002	3.05
Annual Return	11.35
Annual Standard Deviation	8.69
Skewness	0.13
Kurtosis	1.71
Sharpe Ratio	0.80
Sortino Ratio	1.66
Alpha vs. S&P 500	8.01
Beta vs. S&P 500	0.26
Alpha vs. MSCI World Debt	12.09
Beta vs. MSCI World Debt	-0.20
Best Monthly Return	8.53
Worst Monthly Return	-7.55
Best Annual Return	25.92
Worst Annual Return	-4.35
% Winning Months	69.3%

Legend: S&P 500, MSCI World Sovereign Debt Index, CSFB/Tremont Hedge Fund Index

FIGURE 3–1

Continued. (MSCI, reprinted by permission; TASS, CSFB/Tremont, http://hedgeindex.com.)

Correlation to	CSFB/Tremont Hedge Fund Index
TASS Fund of Funds	0.91
CSFB/Tremont Hedge Fund Index	1.00
CSFB/Tremont Convertible Arbitrage	0.40
CSFB/Tremont Ded Short Bias	–0.48
CSFB/Tremont Emerging Markets	0.65
CSFB/Tremont Equity Mkt Ntrl	0.33
CSFB/Tremont Event Driven	0.66
CSFB/Tremont Distressed	0.57
CSFB/Tremont E.D. Multi-Strategy	0.68
CSFB/Tremont Risk Arbitrage	0.37
CSFB/Tremont Fixed Inc Arb	0.45
CSFB/Tremont Global Macro	0.86
CSFB/Tremont Long/Short Equity	0.78
CSFB/Tremont Managed Futures	0.09
CSFB/Tremont Multi-Strategy	0.14
MSCI Discretionary Trading	0.44
MSCI Systematic Trading	0.21
3 mo Tbills	0.12
S&P 500	0.48
MSCI World Sovereign Debt	–0.15
Average to Hedge Fund Strategies	0.42
Average to Traditional Investments	0.15
Conditional Correlations	
S&P 500 Up Markets (71 mo)	0.07
S&P 500 Down Markets (43 mo)	0.39
MSCI Bond Up Markets (65 mo)	–0.06
MSCI Bond Down Markets (49 mo)	0.05

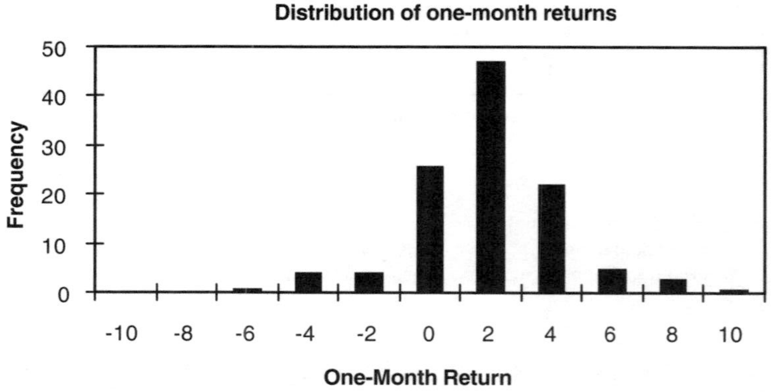

Distribution of one-month returns

the CSFB/Tremont Hedge Fund Index. These performance tables and graphs show annual performance from 1994 to 2003, while the monthly performance covers the time period from January 1994 to June 2003. This figure shows a number of important statistics that are described in this chapter, including correlations, skewness, kurtosis, Sharpe ratio, Sortino ratio, and the percent of winning months.

Figure 3-2 shows that the correlation between the hedge fund index and the S&P 500 averages 0.48 over this nine-year period. However, this correlation can be quite volatile, ranging from 82 percent in the period of the LTCM crisis to only 18 percent in summer 2000, when hedge funds were relatively uncorrelated to a crashing market of technology stocks. The correlation to the MSCI World Sovereign Debt Index averages −15 percent, but ranges from −60 percent to +38 percent. Interestingly, the correlation between hedge funds and bonds was negative for every period between 1994 and 2000, while generally moving to a positive correlation since the end of the year 2000.

Figure 3-3 illustrates hedge fund returns relative to returns of the S&P 500 using a scatter plot of monthly returns. This chart can

FIGURE 3-2

CSFB/Tremont Hedge Fund Index: 24-month rolling correlation to traditional investments.

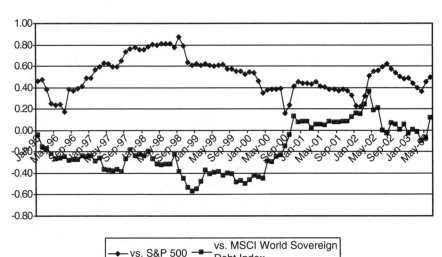

F I G U R E   3 – 3

CSFB/Tremont Hedge Fund Index versus S&P 500: monthly return pairs, January 1994 to June 2003.

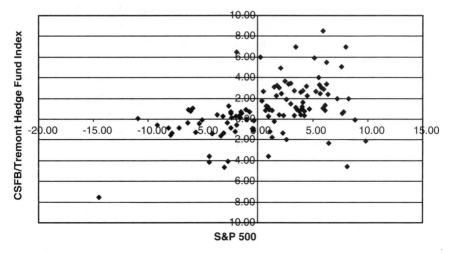

illustrate the percent of winning months for each investment, as well as offering a visual clue to the correlation between two strategies. Finally, we can see the returns to each strategy in extreme months, offering a clue to when the hedge fund strategies are likely to underperform.

Figures 3.4 and 3.5 are examples of returns sorted by the stock or bond market return environment. The first quintile, Q1, contains the 20 percent of months with the largest losses, while the fifth quintile, Q5, contains the 20 percent of months with the largest gains to the traditional investment strategy. For the months contained in each quintile, we then calculate the average returns to the hedge fund strategy. Figure 3-4 shows us that the CSFB/Tremont Hedge Fund Index has its highest returns when bond market performance is below average. This shows that hedge fund investments are diversifying, offering their largest gains in times when bond markets are falling.

Figure 3-5 shows that the correlations between the returns to hedge funds and equity market investments are much higher than the correlation to the returns on fixed-income investments. Hedge funds typically have negative returns when stock markets post their worst losses, showing that hedge funds are not offering diversification when it is most needed.

FIGURE 3-4

CSFB/Tremont Hedge Fund Index versus MSCI World
Sovereign Bond Index: monthly returns sorted by quintiles,
January 1994 to June 2003.

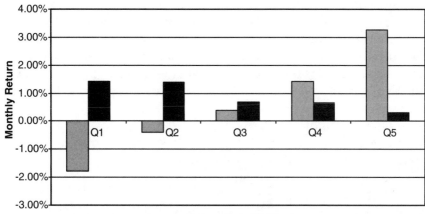

Return Quintiles

MSCI World Sovereign Debt Index   CSFB/Tremont Hedge Fund Index

FIGURE 3-5

CSFB/Tremont Hedge Fund Index versus S&P 500: monthly
returns sorted by quintiles, January 1994 to June 2003.

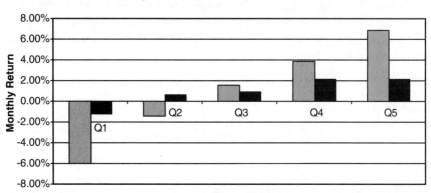

Return Quintiles

S&P 500   CSFB/Tremont Hedge Fund Index

For many alternative investments, especially venture capital, the total amount committed and the total amount invested may be very different. For example, assume that you have promised a venture capital fund manager a $10 million investment. Instead of having you send the entire amount to the fund at one time, the manager will ask for funds only when he needs capital to make a new investment. CFTC rules don't allow the total committed capital to be used in performance calculations. The correct way to calculate returns is based on the total amount invested to date, not the total amount of capital promised to the fund over the life of the investment.

Dollar-weighted returns are based on a series of cash flows, where you can calculate returns including inflows and outflows of new funds. To calculate dollar-weighted returns, you need to know the timing of the cash flows and set up a discounted cash flow equation to calculate the internal rate of return (IRR). Using a spreadsheet, you can find the IRR by modifying the discount rate until the net present value of the series of cash flows is equal to zero.

Leverage makes investment returns more volatile. The Association for Investment Management and Research (AIMR) publishes performance presentation standards (PPS). AIMR PPS require that returns be calculated on the total investment amount, including the use of borrowed funds. To calculate a one-period levered return, divide the ending portfolio value by the sum of the beginning portfolio value and the margin interest paid, and then subtract 1. This method of calculating returns assumes that all assets are fully paid.

To calculate the returns to a short sale, we simply multiply our formula for long returns by -1. The formula for calculating the return to a long investment is

$$(\text{Buy price} - \text{sell price}) / \text{buy price}$$

For short sales, we calculate the return as

$$(\text{Sell price} - \text{buy price}) / \text{sell price}$$

To calculate returns to open short positions, simply assume the recent closing price as the buy price.

It is difficult to calculate the return to swaps, options, and futures positions because they require little to no initial investment. These derivatives have minimal weight when calculating their initial value relative to the portfolio value, so it is inappropriate to find portfolio return by calculating the sum of the product of the return on each investment and the weight of each investment. To find returns to portfolios that contain derivatives, simply compare the ending value of the portfolio to the beginning value of the portfolio, without attempting to determine the percentage return for each investment in the portfolio.[1]

Investors in traditional investments typically use standard deviation as the primary risk measure. Standard deviation, often noted by the lowercase Greek letter sigma (σ), is the square root of the sum of the squared differences of each return relative to the mean return, divided by the number of observations minus 1. Standard deviation is the square root of the variance, and variance is the standard deviation squared.

Standard deviation works best as a risk measure for return distributions that closely approximate the normal distribution. Portfolios that contain derivative positions may not follow a normal distribution. The typical difference between portfolios with and without derivatives is that buyers of options have the ability to truncate the distribution of returns. For example, a portfolio that is long stocks and long equity index puts has an asymmetric distribution, where the size of potential gains is significantly larger than the potential losses, and the distribution is skewed to the right. Unfortunately, many hedge fund strategies are skewed to the left, where the fund earns small positive returns for many months, only to see one disastrous month of extremely large losses.

$$\text{Standard deviation} = \sigma = \frac{\sqrt{\sum_{t=1}^{n} (r_i - r_{mean})^2}}{n - 1}$$

Standard deviation assumes that all volatility in portfolio returns is risky. Many investors consider upside and downside deviations from the mean return to have very different qualities. Investors can earn large returns from upside volatility, so this "risk" is seen as very different from the downside volatility that causes investor losses. An investor would prefer an investment with a very high standard deviation if losses were limited. This brings us to the idea of downside semivariance, where only negative returns are included in the standard deviation calculation. There are two types of downside semivariance calculations: this measure can be calculated either relative to mean returns or to some fixed threshold return. If r^* is zero, this assumes that you are counting only returns that actually lose money and reduce the value of your investment. If r^* is a higher number, such as 5 percent, you are counting downside risk relative to the return target of 5 percent, counting any returns below your target as risky.

$$\text{Downside semivariance} = \frac{\sum_{i=1}^{n} \min(r_j - r^*, 0)^2}{n - 1}$$

$$\text{Downside deviation} = \sqrt{\text{downside semivariance}}$$

Our discussion during the first chapter showed that hedge funds typically have lower returns, but lower volatility, than traditional investments. Besides the low correlation between the returns to hedge funds and traditional investments that improves the risk-return of a portfolio of alternative and traditional investments, there is one other key advantage of hedge funds. Absolute-return strategies, including hedge funds, are able to offer higher levels of return for a given level of risk than is available from traditional investments. Obviously, an investor prefers to earn very high risk adjusted returns, which can either be earned from high returns or low risk.

There are three measures of reward-to-risk ratios that are popular with hedge fund analysts. The Sharpe, Sortino, and Treynor ratios all measure the returns earned for each unit of risk. The ratios differ by the type of risk that the investor chooses to measure.

$$\text{Sharpe ratio} = \frac{\text{return}_{\text{Actual}} - \text{return}_{\text{Risk-free}}}{\text{standard deviation}_{\text{Return}}}$$

By far the most popular measure of reward-to-risk is the Sharpe ratio. This ratio is computed by dividing the return to the fund in excess of the risk-free rate by the standard deviation of returns. The Sharpe ratio is derived from the capital asset pricing model, which is frequently used as a test of market efficiency. If the market is efficient, the CAPM predicts that each security will generally be fairly priced, and it will be difficult for active managers to outperform their benchmark or for market-neutral managers to have a positive Sharpe ratio. We can use the Sharpe ratio to test where a portfolio lies on the efficient frontier. As the portfolio moves to the northwest in risk-return space, the portfolio becomes more efficient and the Sharpe ratio increases. As we move to the north, returns increase. As we move to the west, risk declines. Either or both of these moves will increase the Sharpe ratio.

The Sharpe ratio for absolute-return strategies should be much higher and less volatile than the Sharpe ratio for relative-return and traditional investment strategies. A relative-return strategy often has high volatility, and may frequently underperform the risk-free rate or show negative returns, both of which produces a negative Sharpe ratio. Absolute-return strategies seek to beat the risk-free rate in each time period, implying that the Sharpe ratio will be positive in more periods.

As you can see from Figure 3-6, nearly all hedge fund strategies have higher Sharpe ratios than traditional stock and bond indices. For example, the Sharpe ratio of the CSFB/Tremont Hedge Fund Index is 0.80, far exceeding that of the S&P 500 (0.44) or the MSCI World Sovereign Bond Index (0.34). Funds that take large directional bets, such as emerging markets and short-selling funds, have Sharpe ratios below that of equity investments. The highest Sharpe ratios come from funds that carefully match the risks of their long and short positions to produce returns with extremely low volatility. These funds include convertible arbitrage and equity market–neutral funds.

The Sharpe ratio declines as the volatility of return increases, which assumes that the fund should be penalized for all standard deviation in returns, whether this deviation is positive or negative. The Sortino ratio, calculated as the returns in excess of the risk-free rate divided by the downside deviation of returns, only penalizes for losses and downside risks. The Sortino ratio will have higher values than the Sharpe ratio, as only a portion of the total risk is included in the calculation of the Sortino ratio. Funds with large upside volatilities can be more easily found through the use of the Sortino ratio than by the Sharpe ratio, so investors searching for funds with higher levels of "good volatility" would choose funds based on the Sortino ratio.

$$\text{Sortino ratio} = \frac{\text{return}_{\text{Actual}} - \text{return}_{\text{Risk-free}}}{\text{downside deviation}_{\text{Return}}}$$

As you can see from Figure 3-7, the rankings of hedge fund strategies by the Sortino ratio are very similar to the rankings by

FIGURE 3-6

Table of Sharpe ratios by strategy. (MSCI, reprinted by permission; TASS, CSFB/Tremont, http://www.hedgeindex.com.)

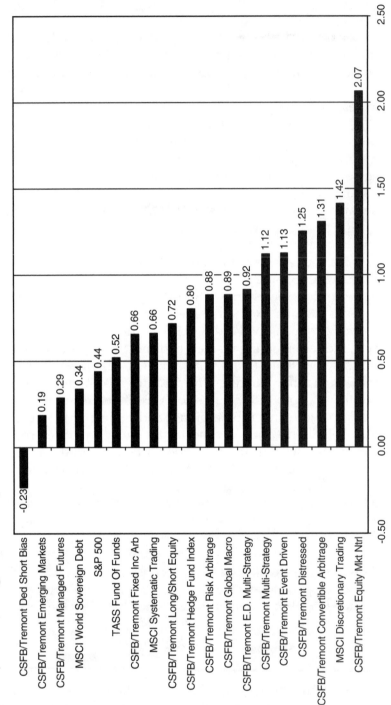

Table of Sortino ratios by strategy. (MSCI, reprinted by permission; TASS, CSFB/Tremont, http://www.hedgeindex.com.)

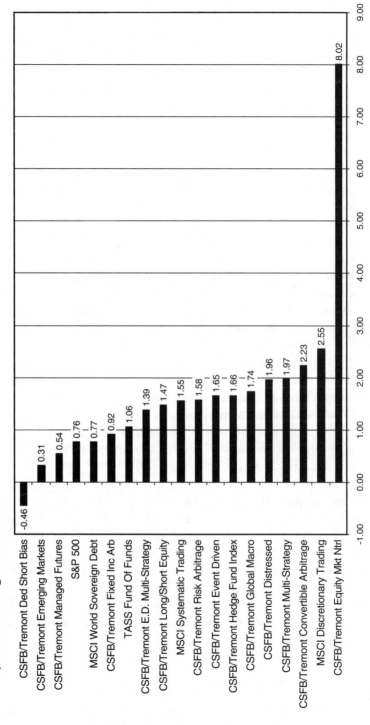

Sharpe ratio. Once again, short selling and emerging markets funds are not attractively ranked by the Sortino ratio. Similarly, convertible arbitrage and equity market–neutral funds are among the best strategies when ranked by the Sortino ratio. The MSCI Discretionary Trading Index also scores well on both measures.

$$\text{Treynor ratio} = T = \frac{\text{return}_{\text{Actual}} - \text{return}_{\text{Risk-free}}}{\text{Beta}}$$

The Treynor ratio, calculated by dividing the return in excess of the risk-free rate by the beta of the fund, makes a number of important assumptions that may limit the applicability of this ratio to the analysis of absolute-return strategies. Remember that beta is calculated through a regression between the returns of the fund and returns on the benchmark. In many cases, absolute-return strategies will not have a benchmark, or the returns to these strategies are uncorrelated to traditional benchmarks, meaning that their beta is close to zero by design. The use of beta assumes that systematic risk is the dominant risk in the portfolio and that beta explains a large portion of the risk of the fund. If the fund focuses on stock-specific risk, credit risk, or futures markets, and hedges away the systematic risk, a measure that computes the risk of the fund using only beta will be inappropriate. However, the Treynor ratio may be a very appropriate statistic for a mutual fund or a long-only hedge fund that is benchmarked to a traditional investment index.

Because many financial market returns, especially those used in hedge fund trading strategies, are not normally distributed, the analyst should closely measure how the returns to their investment deviate from the assumption of a normal distribution. The Sharpe ratio measures the mean and variance of returns, which are the first and second moments of the return distribution. If returns are not normally distributed, then ranking funds by the Sharpe or Sortino ratio may be misleading. The third moment of the distribution is measured by skewness, while the fourth moment is called kurtosis. The normal distribution has a skewness and kurtosis of zero.

$$\text{Skewness} = \frac{n}{(n - 1)(n - 2)} \sum \left(\frac{r_i - \bar{r}}{\sigma} \right)^3$$

FIGURE 3-8

Illustration of skewness.

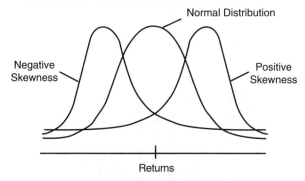

An illustration of skewness can be seen in Figure 3-8. Investors desire positive skewness, where the probability of positive returns is higher than if the distribution were truly normal. Positive skewness can often come from the purchase of call or put options, or from a fund manager that has market-timing skill. Investors may wish to avoid funds with negative skewness, where the probability of negative returns is higher than those implied by the normal distribution. Negative skewness can arise from funds that are sellers of options or those that assume significant event risk.

As Figure 3-9 illustrates, the S&P 500 has negative skewness of -0.60, while the CSFB/Tremont Hedge Fund Index offers a nearly normal skewness of 0.13, and the MSCI World Sovereign Fixed Income Index offers positive skewness of 0.40. This positive skewness can be seen during a flight-to-quality market, as investors buy government debt during times of uncertain equity markets.

$$\text{Kurtosis} = \left\{ \frac{n(n + 1)}{(n - 1)(n - 2)(n - 3)} \sum \left(\frac{r_i - \bar{r}}{\sigma} \right)^4 \right\} - \frac{3(n - 1)^2}{(n - 2)(n - 3)}$$

Kurtosis is defined as the fourth moment of the normal distribution. As can be seen in Figure 3-10, a distribution with positive kurtosis has a much higher than normal probability of extremely large or small returns. Financial markets often have leptokurtic distributions, characterized by "fat tails," where the probability of crashes is much larger than implied by the normal distribution. A normal distribution with zero kurtosis assumes that moves of 5 standard deviations are

FIGURE 3-9

Table of skewness by strategy. (MSCI, reprinted by permission; TASS, CSFB/Tremont, http://www.hedgeindex.com.)

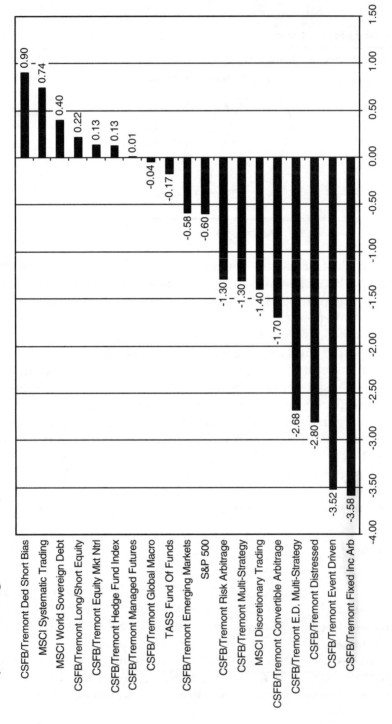

FIGURE 3-10

Illustration of kurtosis.

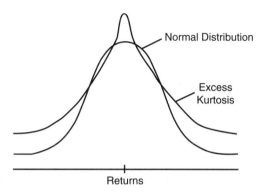

Returns

nearly zero. Therefore, a stock market crash such as the one we experienced in 1987, a 34 standard deviation move, is nearly impossible in a normally distributed market without kurtosis.[2] In financial markets, it seems like a 100-year flood occurs every five years. Dramatic evidence of fat tails occurs with regularity in financial markets, demonstrated by negative earnings surprises, corporate takeover announcements, stock market crashes, and currency devaluations.

Unfortunately, the hedge fund strategies with the largest Sharpe ratios often have negative skewness and large kurtosis. If these values are large, the benefits of investing in hedge funds may be largely offset by the risk of extreme losses that result from investing in funds with negative skewness and the fat tails measured by kurtosis. Indeed, many hedge fund strategies are based on accepting the event and liquidity risks that other investors choose to sell. If hedge funds regularly accept event, liquidity, and fat tail risks, their past history of risk and return may overstate the portfolio benefits of investing in these strategies.

Brooks and Kat say that investors picking funds based on a high Sharpe ratio are not getting as good a deal as they think. Investments seem more profitable, or less risky, when the odd-numbered moments, mean and skewness, are positive and large. Similarly, investors desire that the even-numbered moments, variance and kurtosis, are small. Funds with the highest Sharpe ratios often have the least desirable skewness and kurtosis properties.[3] For example, Figure 3-11 shows that convertible arbitrage funds have a Sharpe ratio of 1.31, a skewness of −1.70, and a kurtosis of

FIGURE 3-11

Table of kurtosis by strategy. (MSCI, reprinted by permission; TASS, CSFB/Tremont, http://www.hedgeindex.com.)

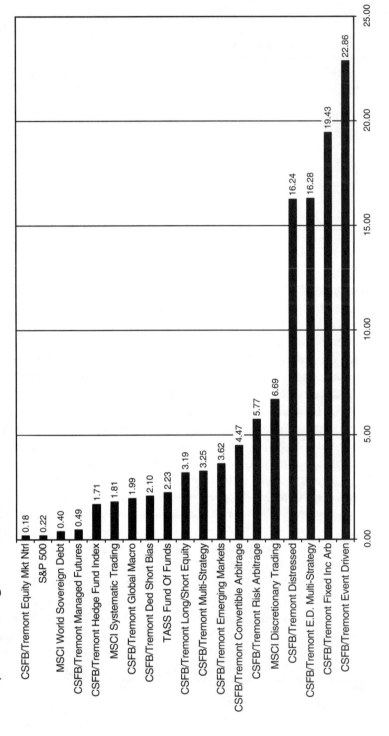

4.47. Event-driven funds have a Sharpe ratio of 1.13, with a skewness of –3.52 and a kurtosis of 22.86. Fixed-income arbitrage funds have a Sharpe ratio of 0.66, with negative skewness of −3.58 and a large kurtosis of 19.43. Investors who include estimates of skewness and kurtosis in their asset allocation optimizers will pick much lower hedge fund allocations than investors who simply rely on mean-variance analysis and ignore the unattractive higher moments of hedge fund investments. Investors who consider all four moments in the normal distribution may no longer find hedge funds to be attractive investment opportunities, even though the Sharpe ratios can be much higher than those offered by traditional investments.

A drawdown is defined as the maximum percentage loss from the high-water mark. Hedge fund investors often request the fund to disclose the size of their largest drawdown, as they may feel that the mean and standard deviation of returns are not sufficient to fully understand the risk of the fund. To find the largest drawdown, we calculate the difference between the high-water mark, which is the highest monthly closing NAV, and the subsequent lowest monthly closing NAV. Typically, month-end values are used in this calculation, so larger drawdowns will not be disclosed if they occur at a time other than at month end. A related statistic is the time, measured in months, that it takes to move from the point of the largest drawdown to regain the losses and set a new high-water mark.

$$\text{Drawdown} = \frac{\text{recent high-water mark} - \text{lowest subsequent monthly close}}{\text{recent high-water mark}}$$

A statistic that is exclusive to absolute-return strategies is the percentage of months that a fund posts gains. The percent winning months statistic is calculated by dividing the number of months that the fund posted positive returns by the number of months the fund has been invested.

$$\text{Percent winning months} = \frac{\text{number of months with positive returns}}{\text{total number of months invested}}$$

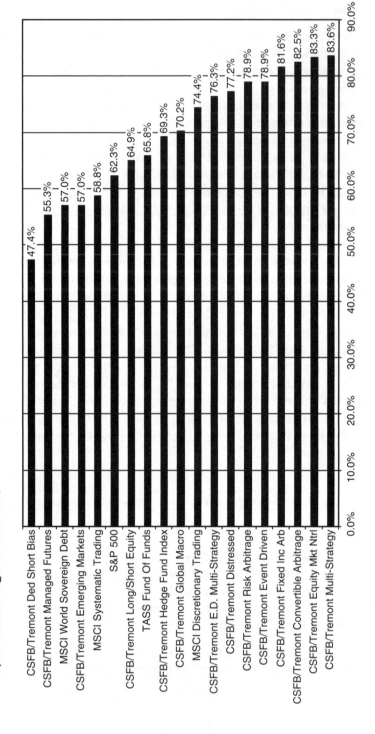

FIGURE 3–12

Table of % winning months by strategy. (MSCI, reprinted by permission; TASS, CSFB/Tremont, http://www.hedgeindex.com.)

Low-volatility funds, especially market-neutral funds, are more likely to have a higher percentage of winning months, while higher-volatility strategies, especially those that are correlated to equity markets, are likely to have a lower percentage of winning months, especially when stocks enter a bear market. Figure 3-12 shows that carefully hedged low-volatility funds, such as fixed-income arbitrage, convertible-bond arbitrage and equity market–neutral funds, can post positive returns in over 80 percent of all months. By contrast, relative-return investments, such as short-selling or investing in traditional stock or bond indices, show profits in only 47.4 percent to 62.3 percent of all months.

Other investors may prefer to focus on the largest monthly gain and loss posted by a fund. A fund could post very consistent returns with low volatility, with just one bad month. In this case, the fund could have a low standard deviation, with a large monthly loss. For funds with this risk profile, you can see why it is valuable to have the fund disclose the magnitude of its best and worst months.

ENDNOTES

1. This chapter benefits from the discussion in Chapter 9 of Stuart McCrary's *How to Create and Manage a Hedge Fund.*
2. S. Da Silva, R. Matsushita, and I. Gleria, "International Finance from Macroeconomics to Econophysics," University of Brasilia, unpublished working paper, 2003.
3. C. Brooks and H. M. Kat, "The Statistical Properties of Hedge Fund Index Returns and Their Implications for Investors," *Journal of Alternative Investments* (Fall 2002) 5: 26–44.

CHAPTER 4

Hedge Fund Risk Management and Due Diligence

Many investors perceive hedge funds to be extremely risky invest-ments. While the vast majority of the 7000 plus hedge funds are care-fully managed, it seems that the infrequent hedge fund disasters grab the headlines and cloud the reputation of the industry. Many market participants can relate stories of a hedge fund that failed after taking on too much leverage, or a fund whose founder spent the investors' money on houses and personal travel, or the black-box fund that dramatically changed its style to invest in the startup businesses of the manager's friends and family. In each case, the investors lost money, often leading to scandal within the investor's organization.

It is difficult for investors to measure the risk of investing in a given hedge fund. Many funds don't want to disclose their strate-gies, while many investors don't know which factors to consider when performing due diligence on a new fund manager.

Most fund companies truly want to earn high returns at low risk to their investors. Obviously, the long-term success of any hedge fund manager relies on keeping the investors happy. Not only do investors care about risk and return, but they also care about the fund's trading style, customer service, and where their assets are held in custody. The funds that make it easier for investors to truly understand their operations are the most likely to dramatically increase their assets over time, given an acceptable performance record. But this is easier said than done. Even the funds with the smartest traders and the most ethical of intentions can face many roadblocks if they haven't considered all of the sources of risk that can arise in the hedge fund business.

In the next two chapters, we will take a comprehensive look at evaluating and managing the risk of hedge funds. How can investors be sure that their new fund manager has the infrastructure and knowledge of risk to make their investments as safe as possible? How should the fund company structure its operations to make investors as comfortable as possible? By answering these questions, it is hoped that both investors and fund managers can improve their probability of success in what can often be a risky, illiquid, or misunderstood world of investing.

LIQUIDITY RISK

The first risk that we will consider is liquidity risk. Liquidity is defined as the ability to quickly close positions at a price close to the current market price. Liquidity is the greatest in high-volume, exchange-traded stocks, options, and futures. Liquidity can change with market conditions and can be especially volatile for complex bonds and over-the-counter derivatives positions. Some hedge funds invest in securities that have nearly no liquidity at any price, such as private placements or venture capital investments. When the positions of a fund become increasingly illiquid, the probability that a fund will fail significantly increases.

How can you tell if a fund has an exposure to liquidity risk? There are a number of statistics that can indicate the liquidity of a fund's positions. The first consideration is whether the fund has diversified or concentrated positions. If a concentrated fund has only 20 positions, and the top 5 holdings comprise 60 percent of assets, the change in the price or volume of any one security can have a large impact on the fund. We can assume that a diversified fund that has 50 to 100 positions, with only 25 percent of their assets in the top 10 positions, will have less exposure to liquidity risk than the concentrated fund.

The second way to gauge the liquidity risk of a fund is to consider the size of the fund's positions relative to the average trading volume in those securities. If a diversified $100 million fund trades only S&P 500 stocks and liquid futures contracts, the liquidity risk is low. If a $1 billion fund is concentrated in 20 small-cap stocks that trade in low volumes, the liquidity risk is much higher. Liquidity risk can be demonstrated by a large bank that purchased a small mutual fund company. The company's best fund was a small-cap growth fund that had dramatically beat its benchmarks over the trailing three years. The fund manager from the bank was afraid to manage or rebalance the fund when he realized that the fund held positions that were larger than the total trading volumes over the last 20 trading days. In order to liquidate a position, the new manager would have to trade half of the daily volume in each stock over the next two trading months. Clearly this fund was taking significant liquidity risk. We had to wonder whether the excellent track record of the fund was derived from superior stock selection or if the prices of the stocks increased simply because of the buying pressure from the fund manager. It is difficult to accumulate positions of this size without having an impact on the market price of the securities you are purchasing.

You may also want to determine how the liquidity of a fund's securities may change during stressful market events. Consider the impact of the Long-Term Capital Management crisis of 1998 on the worldwide liquidity of risky fixed-income securities. During this time of high worldwide systemic risk, markets experienced a flight to quality, where investors were selling risky fixed-income securities and purchasing safe government bonds. As investors worldwide simultaneously attempted to sell complex securities and risky government and corporate debt, the bids disappeared. If you own securities that may fail to attract buyers at any price during a time of market stress, your fund has significant liquidity risk. To measure this risk, it can be helpful to gather data from stressful markets, such as October 1987 or the fall of 1998. An analysis of the changes in volume, bid-ask spreads, trading costs, and correlations for the types of securities you trade can help the fund estimate the likely impact on the value of the fund, given a market crisis and a decline in liquidity of your holdings.

When determining the costs of liquidating positions, you may want to consider the 75/20 question: How long will it take to liquidate 75 percent of the portfolio with minimal price impact? How long will it take to liquidate your portfolio without trading more than 20 percent of the daily volume?Liquidity risk is one reason that funds choose not to disclose their positions. If other traders know that a particular fund has a large position in an illiquid security, they may change their trading prices to make it more expensive for the fund to exit that position. Before you enter a trade, you must understand what it will cost you to get out of the trade. If you have an understanding of the behavior of securities during adverse market conditions, you may be able to know how and when to start closing positions. Traders who can anticipate a liquidity crisis and exit positions before the rest of the market can dramatically reduce the probability of large losses or the failure of their fund.

The fund should be especially sensitive to liquidity issues when it is highly leveraged or short-selling securities. When all of your positions are fully paid, you may be able to wait out the liquidity crisis and choose not to close any positions when your securities are trading at distressed prices. When you are trading on margin, or short-selling securities, your broker or another market participant may cause you to close out some positions. When you have no control over the timing of your trades, your exposure to a liquidity crisis can be extremely large.

As you can see in Figure 4-1, the leverage employed by hedge funds varies widely. As a general rule, leverage should be related to liquidity. We can see this relationship, as distressed securities and emerging markets funds use the lowest degree of leverage. The highest levels of leverage are typically found in global macro funds or market-neutral funds, especially in fixed-income arbitrage. Ineichen estimates that equity long-short, distressed securities, emerging markets and short-selling funds typically have less than 2 times their equity in total assets, a low level of leverage. Hedge fund styles that carefully balance their long and short positions to minimize fund volatility are able to carry higher levels of leverage. Equity market–neutral and risk arbitrage funds can lever up to 5 times their equity, while convertible arbitrage leverage can reach 10 times equity. Even after the demise of Long-Term Capital Management, fixed-income arbitrage funds typically control 20 to 30 times their equity capital in total assets.[1]

The liquidation policies of a fund and the types of investors a fund attracts can also create liquidity risk. If your fund has only four investors and one investor decides to exit the fund, this can mean the withdrawal of 25 percent to 50 percent of your assets. If

FIGURE 4-1

Global hedge funds: use of leverage as of December 2002.
(Van Hedge Fund Advisors International, 2003.)

Hedge Fund Style	Don't Use Leverage	Use Leverage		
		Low (<2.0:1)	High (= >2.0:1)	Total
Aggressive Growth	24.5%	59.3%	16.2%	75.5%
Distressed Securities	48.2%	45.6%	6.1%	51.8%
Emerging Markets	36.3%	46.8%	16.9%	63.7%
Fund of Funds	31.9%	51.0%	17.1%	68.1%
Income	43.2%	29.7%	27.0%	56.8%
Macro	11.3%	37.1%	51.6%	88.7%
Market Neutral - Arbitrage	18.3%	22.8%	58.8%	81.7%
Market Neutral - Securities Hedging	25.4%	29.5%	45.1%	74.6%
Market Timing	38.2%	22.9%	38.9%	61.8%
Opportunistic	20.8%	44.5%	34.7%	79.2%
Several Strategies	30.2%	38.8%	31.0%	69.8%
Short Selling	32.6%	44.2%	23.3%	67.4%
Special Situations	20.7%	60.1%	19.2%	79.3%
Value	26.3%	56.3%	17.4%	73.7%
Total Sample	27.0%	45.1%	27.9%	73.0%

you are trading illiquid securities, or if you promise investors that you will return their investment with one week's notice, the loss of a large investor can cause significant losses to your remaining investors. Make sure that your policy for investor withdrawals is consistent with the liquidity of your trading positions. It doesn't make much sense to allow investors to reduce positions with 30 days' notice if the majority of your positions are venture capital investments with one-year lockup periods. There are a number of common factors that can lead to the underperformance and eventual liquidation of a hedge fund. Anything that a hedge fund manager can do to avoid these issues, or address them before they get to crisis proportions, will make the fund more attractive to investors.

The beginning of the end of a hedge fund is often a liquidity crisis, which can arise when the fund has significant withdrawals or the prime broker refuses to offer additional credit. If investors desire to suddenly withdraw a significant portion of the assets of the fund, the fund may be unable to close its positions quickly at fair prices. For this reason, it is important to match the withdrawal policy of the fund to the liquidity of the fund's securities. For funds with significant investments in less liquid securities, it may be necessary to ask investors for a three-month notice before withdrawing funds or have investors agree that their investments can be returned in securities rather than in cash. A fund that allows investor withdrawals more quickly than it anticipates the orderly liquidation of securities in a distressed market will very likely experience a liquidity crisis at some point. Funds may also wish to have a large variety of investors, as the risk of investor defections increases dramatically when a few investors control the majority of the assets of the fund. A liquidity crisis may also arise when the fund has reached its credit limit with its prime brokers or when the brokers increase margin requirements during times of market stress. A contributing factor to the liquidation of Long-Term Capital Management was that most brokers raised the margin requirements for fixed-income arbitrage traders in the summer of 1998. To avoid this risk, funds should have backup lines of credit and be careful not to increase leverage to levels above what can comfortably be managed when market conditions worsen.[2]

The next steps in the liquidity crisis arise when the fund begins closing positions to meet requests for investor withdrawals or to fund margin deficits. Unfortunately, the fund will usually experience these liquidity events when the market is undergoing a time of stress and the fund has been posting negative returns. If the fund is trading illiquid securities, or if the vast majority of assets in a market segment are controlled by hedge funds trading similar strategies, the fund may find it difficult to close its positions. If all of the players in a specific market niche attempt to close their positions at the same time, the prices realized from these trades will be much different than previously anticipated, increasing the losses of the fund and the time that it takes to liquidate the fund's positions.

Finally, as the price of assets continues to move in unfavorable directions, the demand for cash by investors and brokers increases, causing increased liquidations into an unfavorable and unforgiving market. For highly levered funds, this often causes investors to conclude that the value of their assets is worth less than the amount of their loan. This may lead to the forced liquidation of the fund; the remaining investors may find that their investments are worth nothing, while the prime broker or the principals of the fund may be responsible for the losses, depending on the legal structure of the fund and broker relationships.

Smart funds will attempt to avoid a liquidity crisis. The probability or the magnitude of a liquidity crisis can be reduced by thoroughly understanding the nature of your investors and your trading strategies. Carefully choosing investors, withdrawal policies, and investments with sufficient liquidity and limiting the amount of leverage can be important goals that may one day make the difference between a fund that is no longer a survivor and a fund that lives on to take advantage of the casualties of its competitors. Those funds that are buyers when everyone else is selling can often make significant gains if they have the assets and credit lines to survive the immediate crisis.

MODEL RISK AND PRICING RISK

There is a close link between liquidity risk and other risks, such as pricing and model risk. There is little question about the valuation of exchange-traded instruments, as each exchange posts a daily settlement price for all listed securities. It is easy to calculate a daily net asset value for a fund that only holds exchange-traded securities. In fact, many market data systems providers can link to an Excel sheet, where you can compute up-to-the-minute pricing on your worldwide portfolio of stocks, futures, and options.

However, hedge funds can and do invest in many securities that are not exchange-traded. While it may be easy to report a fair daily value for liquid government bonds, not all over-the-counter (OTC) traded securities are priced or traded each day. Consider three classes of investments that can be difficult to value: complex and illiquid fixed-income securities, over-the-counter derivatives, and venture capital investments.

Convertible bonds, mortgage-backed securities, and high-yield bonds can often be illiquid and difficult to value. Owing to their small size and high demand, some of these issues may trade very infrequently, if at all. Insurance companies are especially interested in convertible bonds and have been known to buy these bonds at issuance and hold them until maturity. If it has been one week, or even one month, since your bond has last traded, you may want to price it relative to a comparable bond or by your proprietary pricing model. Of course, the prices produced by your model are especially sensitive to some important assumptions, such as credit spreads, stock price volatility, or the level of future mortgage pre-payments. If the fund's values of these variables do not match the assumptions of other market participants, these complex and illiquid bonds may not be able to be sold at the price reported to investors at the month-end NAV.

Over-the-counter derivatives are the agreement between the fund and a bank or broker to exchange a series of cash flows based on a custom formula. These derivatives can be as simple as a plain vanilla call or put on a stock that does not have exchange-listed options. Some OTC derivatives can become extremely complicated, such as an option on a five-year swap between two callable dual-currency bonds. As the definition of the derivative becomes more complex, the pricing model to revalue those derivatives also becomes increasingly complex. In many cases, the derivatives may depend on the price of two or three assets, as well as assumptions of volatility and correlations.

Usually, an OTC derivative can only be closed with the same counterparty that opened the trade. This creates a special risk for the fund that wishes to close a trade before maturity, as the counter-party knows your position and may not want to let you exit the position before maturity at an advantageous price.

Since only the fund and the counterparty usually care about the price of a particular OTC transaction, there may be no inde-pendent source to value these positions. Because the fund must report a monthly NAV to its investors, it must estimate a value of the OTC derivatives on a regular basis. These values are subject to model risk. If the pricing model is incorrect, or if the fund estimates the values of correlation or volatility incorrectly, the value of these derivatives reported to investors may be materially different from the price these positions would bring if closed immediately with the counterparty. Funds may be tempted to report stale prices for these positions or change estimates of volatility or correlation to make the NAV of the fund more favorable than realistic.

Venture capital investments can be extremely difficult to value and nearly impossible to sell. Imagine that a fund places a portion of its assets in a $1 million investment in a startup biotechnology firm. By definition, this $1 million should be used to fund the operations of the firm, including salaries, office space, legal fees, and research supplies. This is meant to be a long-term investment that can earn substantial returns over a five-year period, especially when the firm creates a drug that earns FDA approval and successfully floats an initial public offering. The company is supposed to spend your money to improve and develop its operations, so it will be unable to return any cash to you before a portion of the company is sold. How can you value this investment? You may want to benchmark the valuation to publicly traded biotechnology companies and take a large discount from this valuation, given the illiquidity of your investment in the private company. The best way to value the firm is based on the valuation awarded in subsequent rounds of venture capital funding. Unfortunately, it may be months or years between new investments in the firm. A popular way to value venture capital investments is the lower of cost or market. Positions are carried at cost until there is a compelling reason for the fund to reduce the valuation, such as a decline in the value of all public stocks in the sector or a failure to successfully execute important parts of the business plan. Many funds may be tempted to delay the write-down of the value of their companies, as each revaluation of the firm can reduce the NAV of the fund. Once a portion of the firm is sold, either to another venture capital firm or in the public markets, revaluing these positions becomes much easier and more reliable.

COUNTERPARTY RISK

As was emphasized in the bailout of Long-Term Capital Management or in the demise of Enron, numerous banks and trading firms may have exposure to a single failing company or fund. Each time you trade a derivative, borrow or lend funds, or execute a trade, counterparty risk is created.

The first type of counterparty risk is created when a trade is executed. Any time you agree to buy or sell a security, there must be another party that agrees to take the other side of that position. There is always a risk that the other trader in the transaction will settle the trade using the previously agreed terms.

Funds should be especially careful of OTC trades, as these trades are only backed by the credit of your counterparty, and not the credit of a clearing firm. The risk that the trade will not settle increases as your gains in the trade grow, and as the credit rating of your counterparty declines. This risk is minimized for trades executed on an exchange, especially if a strong clearing corporation that demands trade settlement in one to three business days backs that exchange. Settlement risk can be extremely high in some emerging markets, especially those that settle all trades at month end, giving some trades nearly 30 days to post large gains or losses before they are settled. Generally, counterparty risk is minimized by shortening the time between the trade date and the settlement date, as well as trading only on exchanges backed by strong clearing firms or by executing trades with counterparties with strong credit ratings.

Many investors will only trade derivatives on exchanges backed by strong clearing corporations. The risks of OTC derivatives trading can be very large, as many trades involve long dated options and swaps with the potential to create large exposures. Consider a fund that purchases an option from a derivatives dealer and pays the premium in full. The dealer has no risk after the premium is paid, but the fund has accepted counterparty risk from the dealer. As the fund's profit in the position grows, the dealer owes the fund larger amounts of cash. The larger the amount owed from one party to another, the larger the amount of counterparty risk.

Exchanges minimize counterparty risk through the daily mark-to-market treatment of gains and losses. At the end of each trading day, the clearing corporation will settle all gains and losses, causing the day's losers to fund the gains of the day's winners. In this structure, we would expect counterparty risk to be less than one day's price volatility. If a trade is made in the OTC derivatives market without a mark-to-market treatment, we can see how the counterparty risk can grow over time. While daily market moves are typically less than 5 percent, the total amount due under a multiyear OTC swaps contract without regular settlements can easily exceed 50 percent of the notional value of the trade. Option buyers can face even larger counterparty risk, as the premium is typically a small portion of the underlying value of the asset.

Funds and dealers can manage this counterparty risk in a number of ways. Perhaps the easiest way is to only execute trades with counterparties with top credit ratings, with the option to close the trades when their credit is downgraded. Many market participants will sign the International Swap Dealers Association (ISDA) agreement, which standardizes the credit and settlement terms of OTC swaps and options trades. These agreements specify the procedures to be followed when a deal is collateralized or liquidated or when one counterparty files for bankruptcy protection. If you are worried about the exposure to a specific firm, you may ask for collateral before the trade is executed, or you may request a credit limit, whereby the firm must compensate its counterparty each time a specific dollar loss limit is reached.

One of the most important parts of the ISDA agreement is the procedure for netting positions. Many traders may have dozens of positions with a given counterparty; some will show profits, while others will show losses. A bankrupt firm may be tempted to demand payment for all of its profitable positions while refusing to pay for its losing trades. Under a netting agreement, all of the positions are combined, and the total cash that can be claimed by one party is the sum of all gains and losses.

Counterparty risk is created with each repurchase agreement and financing transaction. Under a repo agreement, one firm sends securities to another, which agrees to lend the borrower money against that collateral. As long as the loan and the collateral are of equal values, the counterparty risk is minimized. However, once the value of the collateral falls below the value of the loan, the lender of the cash has credit exposure to the lender of the securities. Conversely, when the value of the collateral rises above the value of the loan, the lender of the securities has credit exposure to the lender of the cash. These problems can be magnified if the collateral is difficult to borrow, especially if the owner of the collateral purchased it from a short seller. If the short seller cannot deliver the collateral, or if the repo dealer lends the collateral to someone who cannot return it, the costs of failing to deliver these securities can be quite substantial.

A firm may wish to quantify its counterparty risk. It is straightforward to calculate the potential loss, which is the difference between the current price and the trade price, or the difference between the value of the collateral and the value of the loan. It is much more difficult to estimate the probability of default. Many firms are interconnected, so the risk of your counterparty failing can be related to failures by other firms and market events, and not simply to the creditworthiness of your counterparty. A fund may want to perform due diligence before accepting funds from new investors. The best types of investors are those who understand the risks and rewards of your strategies and will remain invested through periods of expected volatility. Ideally, investors will stay in your fund for many years and give you months of notice before withdrawals. Hot money investors, those who are not committed to investing for the long term and will move their money at the first sight of volatility, can have a large impact on the fund. Withdrawals on short notice can cause the rapid liquidation of positions, often in market environments where this type of trading is expensive. While the potential fee income from these short-term investors can seem attractive, be sure to consider the potential impact on fund liquidity if these investors decide to leave your fund as quickly as they arrived.

The choice of a prime broker is another very important decision for a new fund. The prime broker with the best ability to borrow securities, highest credit limits, lowest margin rates, and highest short stock rebate can dramatically improve the returns of a fund. Prime brokers must be careful about the clients they accept and the documentation that is needed to open new accounts. Prime brokers settle trades and arrange financing for hedge funds, and thereby accept the credit risk, market risk, and legal risk of dealing with these clients. If a fund trades on margin and the value of collateral falls below the value of the loan, the broker may eventually be responsible for those losses. Therefore the credit rating and asset levels of the fund are vital to the decision of the broker to accept the fund as a client, and to the level of margin available to and collateral required of the fund.

The prime broker will be responsible for settling and clearing all of the trades of the fund. The broker has a real time record of each fund's positions, so the information available to determine credit and margin decisions is readily available. Unfortunately, the fund may be trading with several prime brokers, so each broker may not be able to see the full positions and assets of the firm. It is within the prime broker's authority to set margin requirements that vary by fund or type of trade. It is even possible for the broker to raise the required collateral for trading when he or she senses a decline in the creditworthiness of the fund.

Prime brokers may want to diversify their clients relative to their trading style. If your clients manage a number of funds with different risk exposures, it is unlikely that they will all experience simultaneous losses. You can see how it could be difficult to be known as the best prime broker for fixed-income arbitrageurs if those funds become the majority of your clientele. An environment such as 1998, when most fixed-income funds suffered losses in the wake of the Russian bond default and the demise of LTCM, could spell disaster for a prime broker. The more diverse your client base, the smaller the impact of a failure of a single fund or type of trading strategy.

LEGAL RISK

The prime broker's main legal risk is in how he or she closes positions in response to losses in margin accounts. It is important to carefully document the legal rights of the broker to liquidate collateral when the fund is losing money on levered positions. Ideally, the prime broker would like to have netting agreements in place, as well as letters of credit that guarantee the fund's losses, even if the fund will liquidate or declare bankruptcy. The prime broker would like to retain the right to change margin requirements when necessary, and should also control the liquidation of collateral when the firm is unable to fund its margin calls. The broker would like to quickly close the positions with the highest liquidity, while the fund would like to take its time to liquidate positions at the best price. The broker that lets the fund control the liquidation of securities to meet margin calls may be increasing his or her counterparty risk, especially if the fund refuses to close positions in a timely manner.

Prime brokers have become increasingly sophisticated in recent years. Hedge funds can generate large trading commissions, as well as large interest income from cash and securities lending. As such, many brokerage firms have set the goal to attract more hedge fund clients. They can do this through the offer of preferred commissions or financing rates, or through the provision of new technology services. Brokers that produce real-time risk numbers or worldwide trade executions through a single system may have a competitive advantage that allows them to attract or retain the most profitable hedge fund clients. If the prime broker is a department of a larger bank or investment firm, the relationship with a hedge fund can be even more profitable if the organization can sell derivatives or insurance products to the fund or its investors.

While I am not an expert on the legal status and regulation of hedge funds, I do understand one thing: it is imperative to retain an experienced attorney to properly document the operations of your fund and to comply with all necessary regulations. A failure to have proper legal documentation of your fund can cause legal liabilities for the principals of the fund or unwanted and unnecessary taxes for fund investors. Many investors, especially institutions, are savvy enough to understand when the fund has not been properly structured, so a fund without the proper legal status may struggle to attract new investors to the fund.

The private placement memorandum is the most important legal document of the fund. This carefully written memo will outline the goals and risks of the fund, which are stated in explicit detail. Most funds err on the side of caution, including even risk factors with very remote probabilities. Their goal is to include every possible risk of the fund, so that investors cannot later sue if the fund underperforms or fails because of a previously undisclosed risk factor.

The fund should keep a close watch to ensure that its traders and portfolio managers stay within the risk and margin limits. Some of these limits will be set in the private placement memorandum, while others will be defined by the prime broker or internal policy. An important control is to separate the trading function from the clearing and risk management functions. Traders can be tempted to overtrade, hide losses, or trade inappropriate securities if an independent observer is not closely watching them.

It is also imperative that funds know their investors. If a fund accepts investments from nonaccredited investors or places onshore (U.S.) investors in offshore funds, it can jeopardize the unregulated status of the fund or cause legal problems for its investors. The USA PATRIOT Act of 2001 adds another regulatory burden to funds, as funds must guarantee that all investors earned their wealth through legitimate means and that their investors have no relationships with drug dealers or terrorist organizations.

Legal risk is not limited to the fund manager. Prime brokers must be careful how they document their relationship with each fund, as this documentation governs the rights of brokers to protect themselves from the losses that a fund may incur. Brokers should explicitly dictate terms of the margin agreement, including the right to set and change margin requirements at any time and the right to liquidate the securities of the fund if the fund does not meet the terms of the margin agreement. A failure to carefully design these agreements could jeopardize the collateralized status of the broker's loans to the fund, and subject the broker to lengthy delays and possible losses from the liquidation of the fund's assets.

MANAGER RISK AND DUE DILIGENCE

Investors should always be careful about investing in hedge funds, but performing due diligence is most important with new funds, as this is where manager risk can be the greatest. Thousands of new funds have been started in recent years, each by traders with different experiences, goals, and sophistication. Some funds may be very cooperative in providing information about their operations, while other funds, especially those with offshore operations, may be much less forthcoming with this vital information.

Zurich Capital Markets offers a due diligence survey. If a fund manager completes the survey of information about its firm, Zurich will offer this information to investors. This process could save the firm the time of answering the same list of questions from each potential investor, while new investors may feel more comfortable investing with firms that have chosen to disclose information about their funds. There are hundreds of questions that investors could ask, but they fall into several general categories.

Investors should consider the background of the principals of the firm. Do they have significant experience trading a related strategy for a major fund or brokerage firm? Have they invested a significant amount of their personal assets in the fund? Do they have the proper licenses and a clean compliance or criminal record? Do they answer your questions in a quick and knowledgeable way that shows that they understand the business and have respect for their clients?

These background checks can now be outsourced to private investigators such as Backtrack Reports. Investors certainly want to check the resume, trading experience, educational credentials, and compliance background of their fund managers. Beyond this experience, however, there may be many other areas that can present red flags to investors. First, investors would want to make sure that the manager's full attention is devoted to fund management. One fund manager may be undergoing a messy and distracting divorce, while another may have a full-time job or own a company that doesn't focus on investments. Next, investors may also wish to know details of the manager's personal life. Most investors would prefer a manager with a good reputation to one that has been convicted of drunk driving. Finally, some fund managers have previously been sued for investment losses. This disclosure could have saved investors from losses involving Victor Kozeny or Conrad Seghers, as they had been the targets of litigation years before investors allocated assets to their most recent funds.[3]

Once you are satisfied that the background of the fund managers meets your high standards, you must turn your attention to their investment process. Are the investment decisions made by a single person, an investment committee, or a computer system? Is their system qualitative or quantitative in nature? Can someone else make the trading decisions, or will the departure of a key manager necessitate the liquidation of the fund? Has this decision-making process been in place for a long time, or has the fund recently started trading a new strategy? Will the fund provide transparency and disclose its holdings and trading strategies, or is the fund run like a black box, where investors get little or no information?

Investors finally turn their attention to the risk management systems of the firm. Do you feel that the firm understands how its returns are generated and what risks it needs to take to earn those returns? Does the firm have a defined risk management system, employing stops to minimize losses during turbulent markets? Have the managers carefully considered the liquidity of their positions in unstable or volatile markets? Does the firm have an idea of the capacity of its strategy, and is it willing to close the fund to new investments when assets have grown close to this limit? Does the portfolio manager price all positions, or does a different department or an independent firm handle that?

Before an investor places assets with a new hedge fund, there are a large number of concerns to address. William Miller II of Commonfund provides some checklists that can assist investors in their due diligence process, with 12 general risks on one list, and 26 specific risks on another list. We have already addressed many of these risks, but it is easier to investigate all of the risks when they are listed in one place. Investors should only commit assets to the fund after they are satisfied that the fund passes these tests.[4]

The three general areas of concern are the legal arrangements and asset custody issues, manager reputation and performance reporting, and the risk management systems in place at the fund. First, the investor should be satisfied that the fund has the appropriate legal structure, that the fund is acceptable under its internal guidelines, and that its assets will be placed in the custody of a reputable third-party custodian. If the investor is not satisfied with these issues, an allocation to the fund is not recommended, regardless of the promised return of the fund.

The areas with perhaps the largest number of concerns are the manager reputation and performance-reporting categories. In this area we can focus on the experience of the manager, the track record of the fund, the way returns are calculated and reported, and whether the fund trades with a specific, predictable style that is benchmarked to an appropriate index. We can also add here the "smell test"—the general feeling you get when speaking to the fund manager. Do you get the feeling that the manager cares about you as a client and will look out for your best interests, or does the manager act as if he or she has something to hide?

The most quantitative area is that of risk management. There are many questions that we need to answer before investing in a fund. What types of risk is the manager taking, and where does the fund expect returns to come from? Does the fund carefully monitor risk and reduce positions before the losses exceed some precalculated loss limit? Is the fund trading illiquid securities or consistently selling options? Does the firm diversify its positions over a large number of securities, or does it operate a more concentrated fund?

Many of these issues cannot be explored through databases or quantitative analysis, but only through personal conversations with representatives from the fund company. Rather than committing to invest with a fund quickly, careful investors may perform these tasks of due diligence over a period of weeks or months, only investing when they are completely satisfied that this particular fund is going to be careful with their assets and make their best efforts to generate high returns at truly lower levels of risk.

QUANTITATIVE AND QUALITATIVE RISK MANAGEMENT

After investors are satisfied with the qualitative nature of the fund manager, their attention will turn to quantitative risk management. Value-at-risk (VAR) methodology attempts to quantify market or event risk to estimate the potential losses of a fund. Assuming a normal distribution of returns, we can forecast the potential losses given estimates of mean returns, standard deviations, correlations, and the total assets of the fund. VAR methodology does not provide any new information; it simply transforms the mean and variance of the fund into estimates of potential dollar losses. For example, an investor may want to know how much money he or she could lose in a month with a 5 percent probability. To compute the VAR, we simply perform a one-tailed statistical test using the properties of the normal distribution. We use a one-tailed test because we are only considering potential losses, rather than both losses and gains from both tails of the distribution.

Assume that we need to compute the monthly VAR for a $1 million position in a fund with 12 percent annual returns, 8 percent annual risk, at a 5 percent probability. A one-tailed test with a 5 percent probability using a normal distribution will use a z score of 1.65, which can be found in the tables describing the normal distribution. Most fund numbers are stated in annual terms, so we need to convert all of these inputs to monthly observations.[5]

Monthly $ VAR = [average monthly return − (monthly standard deviation × z score)] × $ size of positions.

Monthly $ VAR = (12% annual / 12 − (8% annual / √12 × 1.65)] × $1 million

Monthly $ VAR = (1% − 3.81%) × $1 million
= −2.81% × $1 million = $28,105

To interpret this VAR estimate, the investor could expect to lose an amount greater than $28,105 in about one month each two years. This VAR estimate does not specify the maximum expected loss, only that a loss exceeding this estimate will occur approximately once during each 20-month period.

Many analysts worry that VAR is not a sufficient statistic to determine potential losses. There are many drawbacks to VAR, and these drawbacks are magnified with the types of trades managed by hedge funds. VAR assumes that returns are symmetric and normally distributed. Many studies show that financial market returns have fat tails, where large gains and large losses are much more likely than estimated by a normal distribution. Hedge funds with negative skewness and high kurtosis have returns that aren't normally distributed, so it is important to model the potential losses using a more sophisticated model than VAR.

Financial markets are prone to bubbles and crashes, where 5 percent daily moves in stock indices, or 50 percent moves in individual stocks, happen on a frequent basis. Using a normal distribution, these moves may be between 5 and 20 standard deviations. Statistics assume that these events are extremely rare, but every trader knows that these events are regular fixtures of our markets.

Perhaps the largest drawback of VAR analysis comes when hedge funds trade options. VAR assumes that returns are normally distributed and symmetric, while options give funds the ability to truncate or skew the distribution of returns. If a fund is long put options, VAR is likely to overestimate potential losses without counting on the insurance features of put options during market declines. If a fund is short put options, VAR will dramatically underestimate potential losses, as the fund may post steady gains at low volatility, until the fund suddenly fails during a market crash. Funds that sell options 2.5 standard deviations out-of-the-money will profit 99 percent of the time, producing a fund with high returns, low risk, and a high Sharpe ratio. The 1 percent of the time that options sellers will lose money can incur very large losses, however, and these losses occur during times of market stress—exactly when hedge funds are expected to offset the losses in traditional investments.

Given the limitations of using VAR analysis for hedge funds, many analysts will supplement VAR with scenario analysis. Starting with a complete list of the fund positions, scenario analysis can estimate fund gains and losses given changes in market activity. With an understanding of the nonlinear characteristics of many positions, we can change assumptions of market returns, volatility, and correlations in many different ways. After computing fund returns under hundreds of potential scenarios, the fund and its investors have a better sense of the potential losses and the scenarios that produce those losses. A fund may want to determine the scenarios that produce the largest losses, then consider if it can reduce the down-side risks of the fund without incurring excess costs or reducing the expected return of the fund.

If you are building a portfolio of funds for your own investment purposes, or to sell a fund-of-funds product, you must understand the sources of risk and return for each new investment. Ideally, you would want to diversify the sources of market risk in your portfolio, so the failure of any one fund in your portfolio is unlikely to be accompanied by losses from your other hedge fund investments. A fund manager should move beyond a beta or duration-neutral portfolio to consider many other sources of market risk that can arise in a portfolio.

The most obvious source of market risk is the direction of exposure of the fund. In the U.S. equity bear market of 2002, we saw that funds with long equity positions earned returns significantly below the funds with net short positions. Funds with an opportunistic exposure have market-timing models, meaning that investors may be unable to predict whether the fund will be net long or net short during a given month. Funds that are duration neutral or beta neutral attempt to minimize their exposure to market movements, and are unlikely to have a high correlation to funds with net long or short market exposure.

You may remember the relationship between the type of trading strategy and the risks and returns by market environment. Investors desire to build a fund portfolio where some funds gain in volatile or choppy markets, while other funds gain in nonvolatile or trending markets. Trend-following CTAs have their highest returns in volatile markets, and weaker returns in more tranquil markets. This return pattern matches that of an investor who purchases straddles. Global macro funds underperform stocks in up markets and outperform stocks in down markets. These funds provide similar returns to the purchase of puts and sale of calls on a U.S. stock portfolio. Fixed-income arbitrage funds have little correlation to stocks and have a stable return in most market conditions. However, these funds can have large losses during times of market crisis. This return profile matches that of a seller of put options on equity indices. If all of your funds show losses in one particular type of market condition, your portfolio is more risky than desired, even if the current levels of correlation make the funds seem unrelated.[6]

Just because a fund is very careful to remain beta or duration-neutral doesn't mean that the returns of the fund are uncorrelated to market conditions. Market risk can arise when funds have large spread positions, even though they have neutralized the risk to major market movements. Equity and fixed-income managers have very specific, yet very different, forms of spread risk.

Consider the U.S. equity markets of 1997 to 2001. A manager could be beta-neutral but lose significant amounts by betting on value versus growth stocks. Managers who were long value stocks and short growth stocks in 1997 to 1999 could have lost 20 percent each year on the value-growth spread, even when they were beta-neutral. Conversely, the same managers who were long growth stocks and short value stocks could have lost 20 percent each year in 2000 to 2001. Other spread exposures can include mismatches between the market capitalization or industry composition of long and short positions.

Fixed-income managers may be duration-neutral, which hedges their exposure to small parallel shifts in the yield curve. However, a duration-neutral portfolio often maintains risks relative to the shape of the yield curve, credit spreads, liquidity, and flight-to-quality. The LTCM example is very instructive about the cost of being long less liquid and more risky securities during a time where investors flocked to liquid and high-quality government securities. A manager could be duration-neutral while buying lower-quality credits and shorting higher-quality credits. If the economy does not recover as anticipated, and credit spreads widen further, this portfolio can be quite risky, even though the fund has little interest rate risk, as measured by duration.

Perhaps the largest change in the hedge fund world in recent years is a transfer of power from individual to institutional investors. In the early days of hedge funds, high-net-worth individuals contributed the vast majority of assets. In recent years, however, many institutions are dramatically increasing their allocations to hedge fund investments. The most aggressive investors are state pension funds and university endowments, some of which have placed more than 20 percent of their assets into alternative investment categories in recent years. These changes are likely to have a large impact on the way that hedge funds are managed and will cause a shift in the types of funds that are able to attract new investments.

Many individual investors did not seem to mind a lack of transparency by funds. As long as the fund was delivering the promised returns, individuals did not press for full disclosure of fund positions and trading strategies. These investors almost gave funds the ability to trade whatever and however they chose, as long as the fund was able to generate consistent trading profits. It was in the fund's best interest to disclose as little as possible about its proprietary trading models and the resulting positions, as competition in the same strategy or securities from other market participants could reduce the returns or increase the risks of the fund.

While individual investors may not have cared much about the transparency of funds, institutional investors demand transparency and style purity. Funds that refuse to disclose positions and trading strategies, or cannot stick to a well-defined trading strategy in one market, are unlikely to be able to attract significant new assets from institutional investors.

Most institutional assets today are being invested with the largest funds. Not only do the largest funds have the longest track records and the largest amount of assets, they also have the financial ability to install reporting systems that meet the strict standards of their new investors. In fact, many institutional investors are requiring transparency and documentation of trading procedures that far exceed the hedge fund regulations imposed by the Securities and Exchange Commission. It seems that institutional investors are not pleased with the lack of regulations governing hedge funds, so they are writing their own rules. Funds unwilling to jump through all of these hoops to please the institutions will be unable to participate in this growing part of the business.

Institutional investors are unlikely to commit assets to newly created funds for a number of reasons. First, institutions would like to see a track record of at least three years. This minimal amount of time allows them to start the analysis of the risks and returns offered by the fund. A second reason that institutions may not invest in a new fund is that they require significant reporting capabilities, and most new funds are unable or unwilling to make these investments in computing capabilities. Finally, institutions often need to invest large sums and need to know that managers can handle the increased amount of assets. If a manager has ten $1 million accounts, he or she is unlikely to earn a $20 million investment from an institution. A manager would need at least five to ten $10 million clients to attract an investment of this size, as an institution wants to be a small part of a large fund, and not commit to an investment that will be more than half of a fund's assets.

Some investors may have very different feelings about new funds. They may believe that small funds offer the highest probability of new strategies and large gains. If they wait for the fund to establish a three-year track record, the fund's best years may have already passed, or the fund may have attracted significant assets from other investors and closed the fund, leaving those investors who waited to invest without an opportunity to participate in the gains of the new fund.

We have already discussed both qualitative and quantitative analyses of hedge fund risks. It is important to analyze funds from both perspectives, as a sole reliance on one over the other could lead to some important oversights that could change your decisions on whether to invest in a fund.

Quantitative measures can be forward-looking or backward-looking and often focus on the risk-reward relationship of the fund. In some cases, such as liquidity or leverage analysis, quantitative tools can be used to enhance your qualitative understanding of the fund's operations. It is important to run quantitative models frequently, as it is imperative to understand if and when the backward-looking view is not a good representation of the future prospects of the fund. Many analysts feel that you need to change your investment strategies quickly when the skill of the manager seems to be declining or the market is becoming increasingly more efficient.

Qualitative measures often focus on the fund managers and their control over their operations. It is important to understand the experience of the managers and their level of attention to the risk management and careful custody of client assets. Once the analyst understands the trading strategy of the fund, it is imperative to understand how and when market forces may conspire to make the trading strategy less lucrative or obsolete. Inevitably, when we talk about quantitative risk management, the discussion will turn towards "the Greeks." There are many ways to measure the risks of investing, and a number of these risks can be referred to by a shorthand method, where each risk is mapped to a separate Greek letter. Greeks measure the change in one attribute when the values of another attribute changes. Risk managers and derivatives traders should instinctively know the type of risk denoted by each term whenever they enter a risk management discussion. While many of these statistics are frequently calculated for an individual security, they are most useful when computed at the portfolio level.

Once fund managers measure and understand each specific risk in their portfolio, they are able to better hedge their exposures or concentrate their bets in the areas they best understand.

Many of the Greeks only apply to options, as options (or securities with embedded options) are the only securities that are priced using volatility. Vega is the change in the price of an option given a change in implied volatility. Derivatives of Vega include nu, which is the change in Vega given a change in the price of the option, while epsilon is the change in Vega given a change in the implied volatility of an option.

Most options dealers attempt to keep a book with as little delta risk and as little rho risk as possible, seeking to neutralize the value of their options portfolio relative to changes in the price of the underlying security and interest rates or dividends, respectively. However, many options dealers take large active positions in Vega, as they feel that they have a good understanding of volatility. When volatility is expected to increase, dealers will attempt to be net buyers of options, which is long Vega, so their portfolio value will increase as volatility rises. When volatility is likely to fall, dealers often are net sellers of options, so they can have a short Vega exposure, attempting to profit as volatility declines.

When the fund trades bonds, foreign securities, or exotic derivatives, many other risks come into play. Chi measures the change in the price of an asset given a change in currency rates. As the dollar declines in value relative to foreign currencies, securities denominated in foreign currencies increase in value. Omicron is defined as the change in the asset price given a change in credit risk. This is an important statistic to traders of bonds and credit derivatives, where the value of bonds declines with a downgrade in the credit quality of the firm. Finally, cross gamma estimates the change in asset prices with a change in correlation. Exotic derivatives, such as options on the spread in prices between two securities, increase in value as the correlation between the two securities falls.

RISK MANAGEMENT AND MONITORING SYSTEMS

A keen understanding of the exposures of your portfolio is one of the first and most important steps in quantitative portfolio risk management. These exposures should be frequently and comprehensively measured, as risks change over time and the neglect of just one type of risk could be sufficient to cause the failure of a fund. Scenario analysis is greatly enhanced when the analyst has ready access to these statistics, as it becomes much easier to estimate changes in the value of a portfolio when you understand how sensitive the portfolio is to each of these important risk factors.

There is an important new trend that is leading funds to monitor enterprise risk management in addition to their traditional risk management focus on each fund or portfolio manager. Ideally, a fund management company will control the risks of each fund in addition to the risk of all the funds offered by the firm. It is in the firm's best interest to have its risks diversified by fund. For example, a firm that offers a market-neutral equity fund should avoid taking credit risk in that fund if its fixed-income arbitrage funds have high exposures to credit risk.

Ideally, if one fund or fund style underperforms or loses assets, the other funds offered by the firm should be uncorrelated and still able to attract new assets. Let us take an example from the mutual fund world—two fund management companies, Janus and Fidelity. Janus was able to gather significant assets in its growth funds when growth was outperforming the market in 1997 to 1999. However, as growth underperformed the market in 2000 to 2002, Janus lost assets as investors moved their money to value, index, or bond funds offered by other firms. Janus lost these assets to other firms as this firm concentrated on growth funds without developing a wide variety of competitive funds in other style categories. Fidelity offers a much more diversified group of funds that places the fund company at much less risk when a change in style returns impacts the market. If investors become disappointed with the growth market or Fidelity's growth funds, they may simply move their assets to a value, index, or bond fund within the Fidelity family, leaving the assets of the firm unchanged.

While it may be daunting to start a project to quantify the risks of all operations of a fund company, there are certainly benefits to calculating this information, even if you begin on a small scale. While it may take significant efforts to verify every trading algorithm and recreate the trading desk analytics, these expensive and complex tasks are not necessary to the functioning of a basic firmwide risk management system. A simple system only needs to understand the exposures of each fund and have a way of combining those exposures. Simply adding the exposures of each fund to arrive at a firm-wide risk management measurement will overstate the risks, as this simple sum of risk exposures does not take into account that some funds may have positions that reduce the risks of other funds. While this may seem like an appropriately conservative measure, an overestimation of firm-wide risk may cause some of the firm's funds to overlook profitable trading opportunities when they know that the firm is near its limit for that specific type of risk.

Funds with a functional risk management system may find that they have a competitive advantage in attracting new investor assets. If they can report risk numbers in a frequent and sophisticated way, they may be able to impress investors with their risk management system, even if the fund is unwilling to provide complete transparency of its positions.

A firm-wide risk management system should include estimates of market risk, credit risk, and operational risks. We have previously discussed how market risk can be estimated using a combination of value-at-risk and scenario analysis. The modeling of the credit risk of counterparties and bond holdings can be more complex, as credit defaults are discrete and infrequent events that can be difficult to model, given the limited availability of data on defaults. Once you have the inputs to a credit risk model, you would want to supplement VAR analysis with scenarios, as VAR may understate credit risk after a time of high credit quality in the economy. Operational risk is more qualitative in nature, so it may be difficult to build quantitative risk models in this area. Building careful controls into your custody and trader supervision process can be effective in reducing the operational risk of your fund company.

Investors are especially interested in fund risk information as they seek to build efficient portfolios of hedge funds. As investors have better information on the risk profile of each fund, they are better able to build a portfolio of funds that is diversified not only relative to their risks and returns but also to the sources of fund risk. We can assume that market risk and credit risk are correlated, but operational risk may be independent of these other risk measures.

LIMITATIONS OF QUANTITATIVE RISK MANAGEMENT

A large part of the demand for hedge funds comes from the academic research showing that fund returns have low correlations to the returns of traditional investments, which reduces the risk of portfolios that have allocated assets to hedge fund investments. If everyone believes that hedge funds are high-return, low-risk, low-correlation investments, the assets allocated to these funds will continue to grow.

Unfortunately, there are many reasons to worry that our optimal asset allocation may not be as efficient as we assumed. Any decline in returns or increase in risks or correlations will make hedge funds much less effective in improving the diversification of the investor's portfolio. The first caveat that we want to explore is the modeling issues that arise from the way that the hedge fund databases have been built. Many studies on the diversifying power of hedge funds were released in the late 1990s, using data over less than a 10-year period, with a large reliance on returns generated during the equity bull market. If these studies include the Long-Term Capital Management debacle of 1998 or the equity bear market of 2000 to 2002, the optimal portfolio may include a lower allocation to hedge funds, as they may be more risky than previously believed.

Other issues surrounding the modeling of hedge fund returns and risks include survivor bias and selection bias. Survivor bias occurs when a database is populated with funds available today and includes only the past returns of funds still in existence. This reduces our estimate of hedge fund risk and overestimates returns, as funds that were liquidated in the past, presumably with higher risk and lower returns, are not included in the database. Because many hedge fund databases rely on fund managers to report their returns, selection bias may be included in the databases. If fund managers report the returns of their best funds while burying the track records of their less successful funds, the database will once again overstate the benefits of hedge fund investing. Mark Anson of the California Public Employees Retirement System estimates that the total impact of these biases can overestimate the returns of hedge funds by up to 4.5 percent annually. This can create unrealistic expectations about the future return to hedge funds that could lead to unsatisfied investors and anemic asset growth in the future.[7]

Once you have a trustworthy system for reporting hedge fund returns, you must answer the question of how to calculate hedge fund risk. Databases are likely to provide the monthly return of each fund, categorized by fund style. These databases may allow you to calculate reliable value-at-risk numbers, but they usually do not contain the information necessary to perform scenario analysis or lead you to an understanding of the nonlinear characteristics of the fund. While knowing the style of the fund may assist you in making these risk measurement decisions, different trading strategies of funds may lead to dramatically different risk profiles, even between funds within a given style category.

Given the limitations of database analysis for building portfolios of hedge funds, funds of funds do not rely simply on databases. Fund-of-funds managers spend significant time visiting each manager, attempting to become comfortable with the risks of the funds that cannot be seen through a simple analysis of the historical returns of each fund.

Perhaps the most prevalent measure for ranking the performance of hedge funds is the Sharpe ratio, defined as the performance of the fund in excess of the risk-free rate, divided by the standard deviation of the returns of the fund. Unfortunately, many popular hedge fund strategies, such as options trading, can produce misleading Sharpe ratios. Therefore, you must carefully analyze the trading strategies of the fund to understand if its Sharpe ratio is an appropriate measure of its risk-adjusted return.

The best way to build a fund with a high Sharpe ratio is to be a seller of options. If you write options that expire worthless, this will look like a high-return, low-risk strategy during most market environments. For example, if a fund sells options 2.5 standard deviations out of the money, the fund will profit 99 percent of the time. Depending on the path of the market, a manager can compile up to an eight-year track record of high-return, low-risk investing. Such a track record may attract significant assets from investors who are unaware of the perils of a short option strategy.

However, times of market turbulence are inevitable, and the most volatile 1 percent of markets can cause significant losses. Making matters even worse, funds with large option-selling operations will experience their largest losses at times when your traditional investments are losing money, ruining your portfolio diversification strategy and causing losses when you can least afford them. Mark Anson simulates a fund with 9 percent returns for seven years, with a catastrophic loss in the eighth year. During the first seven years, the fund has a Sharpe ratio of 10, far above the average hedge fund Sharpe ratio of 0.4. During the eighth year when the short options strategy implodes, the firm has a Sharpe ratio of -11, leaving the fund with a return below Treasury bills since inception. After the fund has a significant decline, this risk will be presented by a negative skewness and a high kurtosis of the fund's returns.[8]

Before you invest in a fund with a short track record and a high Sharpe ratio, it pays to investigate the fund's trading strategy. If there is a large allocation to short options, this strategy may be much more risky and much less lucrative than previously assumed. However, if the manager does not earn his or her gains from nonlinear or very illiquid investments, then you may have found a hedge fund worthy of your investment.

ENDNOTES

1. A. M. Ineichen, *Absolute Returns: The Risk and Opportunities of Hedge Fund Investing*. Hoboken, NJ: John Wiley & Sons, 2003.
2. V. R. Parker, ed., "Sound Practices for Hedge Fund Managers," *Managing Hedge Fund Risk*. London: Risk Waters Group, 2000.
3. A. B. Colter, "Digging for Dirt among the Hedges," *Wall Street Journal*, July 30, 2003.
4. W. P. Miller, "Fund of Funds: Risk Management Issues for Endowments and Foundations" in V. R. Parker, op. cit.
5. S. McCrary, *How to Create and Manage a Hedge Fund: A Professional's Guide*. Hoboken, NJ: John Wiley & Sons, 2002.
6. V. R. Parker, ed., "Sound Practices for Hedge Fund Managers," *Managing Hedge Fund Risk*. London: Risk Waters Group, 2000.
7. M. Anson, "Hedge Fund Risk Management for Institutions" in V. R. Parker, op. cit.
8. Ibid.

CHAPTER 5

Cases in Risk Management

Chapter 4 listed a variety of risks incurred by hedge funds as well as a number of ways to monitor and mitigate those risks. While having risk management and due diligence checklists may be helpful to some investors and fund managers, others may prefer case studies of actual funds that were forced to liquidate after large investment losses. As you read about Long-Term Capital Management and Richard Dennis, make sure that these types of risks are not present in your funds.

LONG-TERM CAPITAL MANAGEMENT

Long-Term Capital Management (LTCM) was started as a hedge fund in 1993 when a group of highly successful fixed-income arbitrage traders left Salomon Brothers under less than ideal circumstances. Given their reputation for earning phenomenal profits and having some of the best minds in the business, including future Nobel Prize winners Myron Scholes and Robert Merton, they had no problem raising over $1.25 billion in capital from investors. Many investors, however, chose not to allocate assets to the fund, as LTCM documentation disclosed that the fund was expected to be extremely volatile and highly leveraged. Other investors declined to invest, as they seemed uncomfortable that the lead partner, John Meriwether, was reluctant to reveal the details of LTCM's anticipated trading strategies.

LTCM computers searched the world for opportunities for fixed-income spread trading. During the first four years of the fund, LTCM delivered phenomenal returns, earning approximately 20 percent in 1994, 40 percent in 1995, 40 percent in 1996, and 17 percent in 1997, net of fees. This performance satisfied investors who had paid higher than normal fees of 2 percent of assets plus an incentive fee of 25 percent of profits. By 1998, the fund had increased in size to $7 billion, including investment gains and additional capital contributions. The partners generally reinvested their profits in the fund, eventually controlling nearly $2 billion in fund assets.

Given the large size of the fund and the stellar pedigrees of the partners, many banks were anxious to do business with LTCM. Not only did the banks expect to earn significant commission and financing revenues, they also hoped to share in the trading ideas of the firm. LTCM used the banks' eagerness to their advantage, negotiating fees and margin requirements down to levels that were risky and unprofitable for the banks. In many cases, LTCM was allowed to place trades in the repurchase market with zero haircut. Because LTCM was able to execute many trades without being required to post any margin, the fund was able to reach astounding levels of leverage. LTCM typically executed each side of a spread trade with different counterparties, which prevented their brokers from understanding their trades and attempting to profit on their insights.

At a time when LTCM had $5 billion in investor's equity, the assets on their balance sheet totaled $125 billion. This 25-to-1 balance sheet leverage was in addition to their off-balance sheet positions. These swaps, options, and derivatives had a notional value of $1.25 trillion. Of course, many of these trades were meant as spreads, which tend to be less risky than outright positions.[1]

Problems for LTCM did not begin to emerge until 1997, even though this astounding level of leverage had sowed the seeds of disaster from the day of its founding. During 1997, the fund earned only a 17 percent return to equity capital, far below the 33 percent compounded annual return in its first three years. During a safe and quiet economic environment, LTCM had profited handsomely from tightening credit spreads. The yields on risky bonds had reached very low levels in relation to safe government bonds, showing that the market had faith that the worldwide economic situation would continue to remain strong. Unfortunately, the future profit opportunities in credit spread trading had also fallen, as corporate, mortgage, and emerging markets bonds are never expected to trade at lower yields than safer government bonds. In other words, credit spreads should never trade below zero. Selling mortgage-backed securities at 30 basis points over Treasuries offers a much lower profit opportunity than when the trader is able to sell this spread at over 100 basis points. Of course, markets often seem the most calm immediately before a storm of risk. Once credit spreads reach a low point, they are almost destined to dramatically widen the next time the market hits a crisis of confidence. Experienced traders reduce positions when the risk-reward relationship becomes skewed against them. As the profit opportunities decline and risks increase, rational traders reduce the size of their positions. LTCM, however, did exactly the opposite.

In the fall of 1997, LTCM returned $2.7 billion to investors. Many investors were disappointed in the fund's decision to liquidate their highly profitable investment, but the fund insisted. LTCM felt that because the size of the fund had grown too large and spreads had fallen so much the fund would be unable to earn 30 percent returns without further increasing leverage. Of course, the partners and their favored investors were able to keep $4.7 billion in the fund. Even though the fund returned assets to their investors, they chose not to reduce the size of their positions. Just as the trading opportunities were becoming less lucrative and more risky, the fund chose to dramatically increase its leverage.[2]

LTCM's experience and history showed significant skill in fixed-income arbitrage. The fund purchased risky and illiquid bonds around the world, including mortgage-backed securities, corporate bonds, and the government bonds in emerging markets nations, while short-selling the bonds of well-regarded government issuers. Many of these trades, such as spreads between U.S. Treasury bonds of very similar maturities or bets on new nations being added to the Eurocurrency, were relatively low risk and nearly guaranteed convergence. After a successful beginning, the traders felt that their models were transferable to other investment strategies based on converging spreads.

Once LTCM started selling equity options or trading spreads between equity securities of two companies expected to merge operations, they were trading in a relatively unknown area. In quiet markets, fixed-income spread trading may have symmetric risk-reward properties. If this were the case, then a trade expected to earn 50 basis points would have an expected risk of only 50 basis points. If the fund is able to earn profits on 60 percent of its trades and the risk-reward is symmetric, profitability is nearly guaranteed in the long run. LTCM didn't seem to understand that merger arbitrage has a much different risk-reward relationship. Traders in this market know that the returns to a successful merger may be $1 per share, while losses from failed mergers can be $10 per share or more. In order to profit in merger arbitrage, a trader needs to be correct more than 90 percent of the time.

The key assumption to LTCM's strategy of 25-to-1 leverage is that fixed-income spread trading had only one-twenty-fifth of the risk of outright long-bond positions. This can be the case in quiet markets, when the correlation of long and short positions can be over 97 percent. The fund relied on value-at-risk (VAR) analysis to justify its levels of leverage and anticipate possible trading losses. VAR assumes that the correlation and volatility patterns of the past will be repeated in the future, and that the positions of the firm do not influence market prices. Philippe Jorion, an expert on VAR, analyzed these assumptions as follows.[3] If the correlation between the fund's long and short positions was assumed to be 0.965, then the monthly volatility was expected to be 8.1 percent. If the correlation fell to 0.80, the monthly volatility of these spread trades explodes to 19.2 percent. The implications of this change in volatility are significant. For a given level of capital, the high-correlation strategy would be expected to post catastrophic losses once in a 900-year period, while the lower-correlation assumption would blow up once each 26 years.

LTCM's models assumed that the relatively quiet market environment of the last five years would continue, meaning that correlations and volatilities would be stable. Even though there is a plethora of examples of crisis markets where these assumptions would be violated, such as the 1987 stock market crash where credit spreads widened over 200 basis points in a week, there is no evidence that LTCM modeled such extreme scenarios.

LTCM determined the level of its leverage by targeting a daily volatility of returns of $45 million. Jorion questions why LTCM didn't reduce its leverage when the daily volatility of the fund reached over $200 million on several occasions in 1995, 1996, and 1997. If the fund's returns were more than four times as volatile as expected, then a rational trader would be reducing the amount of leverage employed. At the height of the crisis in 1998, LTCM was losing hundreds of millions of dollars on consecutive days, clearly exceeding the volatility assumptions. Like Enron, LTCM had increased leverage to attempt to maintain a constant or growing return on equity (ROE) in the face of a declining return on assets (ROA). Neither firm stopped to think that reducing exposure to the business was a logical choice in times of declining profitability.

LTCM was widely diversified, owning bond positions in nearly 30 countries. In each case, it assumed that the spreads within a market or region were highly correlated to each other. It also assumed that trades in the Russian bond market were uncorrelated to trades in the U.S. mortgage market. Unfortunately, LTCM discounted the maxim "In a crisis situation, correlations tend to go to one." When investors are not concerned about risk, it is usually safe to assume that these disparate markets have little relationship to each other. However, when the market perception of risk rises rapidly during a crisis, investors tend to sell risky assets and buy safer assets, wherever they are located in the world.

LTCM had the idea that its positions in fixed-income securities worldwide were uncorrelated, and its models convinced the traders that the spread between risky and safe securities would converge. Unfortunately, Russia defaulted on its debt in August 1998 and started a worldwide flight to quality. When the IMF refused to come to the aid of emerging-markets investors during this default, investors worldwide became much more risk-averse.

What LTCM assumed were uncorrelated positions became highly correlated during this flight to quality. LTCM typically held long positions in illiquid, complex, and risky securities worldwide and short positions in U.S. Treasury securities. When everyone was afraid of credit risk, investors all around the world simultaneously chose to buy Treasuries and sell all risky and illiquid securities, making LTCM a loser on both sides of the spread. At the same time, LTCM was short swap spreads and equity market volatility, where prices can increase quickly during times of market stress. Short-option, short-liquidity strategies can post significant profits in times when volatility is falling and spreads are decreasing. However, these strategies tend to post significant losses during times of market stress, when volatility rises and spreads widen much faster than they converge in safer times.

Fixed-income arbitrage funds had been extremely successful in the mid-1990s, when many other hedge funds and investment banks were trading positions similar to LTCM. When it came time to liquidate these positions in a market crisis, LTCM found that most market players were unwilling to take LTCM's position at fair prices, as the other banks and funds were facing losses on similar positions. The assumption that LTCM was a price taker was violated, as its trades were so large, leveraged, and well known that the managers found that no one would buy their risky securities at any price, which increased their losses. Bond dealers and other funds knew that LTCM had to sell, and the sheer size of these sales scared buyers away. Because of this rapid decline in liquidity, LTCM seemed paralyzed, unable to reduce its positions. The fund had 30-to-1 leverage at the beginning of 1998, with $120 billion in assets on $4 billion in equity capital. In the fall of 1998, in the wake of the Russian crisis, LTCM was losing $500 million per week and was unable to liquidate its positions. As the losses compounded, its leverage also increased. If the fund had $100 billion in assets with $1 billion in capital, its balance sheet leverage was 100-to-1, in addition to the off-balance-sheet derivatives exposure. At this point, a decline in asset prices of only 1 percent would have wiped out its equity capital.

In fact, there were worries that the size of LTCM's position could have created a risk to the worldwide financial system if it were forced to quickly liquidate. The assets of this hedge fund were similar to those controlled by Merrill Lynch, Salomon Brothers, or Lehman Brothers. LTCM was much more risky, however, with higher leverage, more concentrated bets, and a lack of income from commissions and underwriting. The Federal Reserve Bank was concerned that certain bond markets would cease to trade if LTCM were forced to immediately sell. The stock prices of many investment banks had declined 40 to 50 percent in a matter of weeks, as the market estimated each bank's losses in similar trades in addition to its exposure to LTCM.

The Federal Reserve Bank stepped in to coordinate liquidity of the fund, including easing the federal funds rate and encouraging bankers to lend more to LTCM to prevent panic selling of bonds. A consortium of 14 banks recapitalized LTCM with $3.65 billion. In actuality, some of these firms had already contributed to the leverage of LTCM; so many banks were simply trying to save their own loans to the fund. Other banks, while they had no direct relationships with LTCM, had significant risks to their own positions if LTCM were caused to liquidate. Ultimately, the crisis blew over and a risk to the financial system in the United States was averted. The banks recouped their investments, but LTCM was eventually liquidated in 2000. The partners lost nearly all of the $2 billion in fees they reinvested in the fund, and many LTCM employees had borrowed to increase their stake in the fund. Surprisingly, LTCM partners were blessed with investor capital a second time, provided that their leverage was lower and their risk management was stronger.

What did LTCM do wrong and how can future fund managers prevent such a crisis? The four major mistakes were the excessive use of leverage, the underestimation of tail risk, large positions in strategies where it did not have trading expertise, and overestimating the liquidity in markets such as five-year equity options, which was dominated by only five major sellers. When a fund is trading with 30 to 300 times its equity capital, it only takes a small event to wipe out the original investments. After LTCM, it is unlikely that banks and brokers would allow another hedge fund to reach these levels of leverage.

LTCM also assumed that fat tails didn't exist and that correlations don't change. This experience, as well as the numerous "100-year floods" that seem to come every five years, should show us that we need a healthy respect for risk; we need to understand that correlations can change and that 10 standard deviation moves happen much more frequently than many in the investment community typically assume. Leverage and risk assumptions should include catastrophic scenarios, such as those experienced in the 1987 stock market crash, the 1994 Mexican peso crisis, or the 1998 Asian devaluations.

Traders should also be careful when they attempt to transfer their experience, skills, and models to trading a different strategy. LTCM demonstrates that fixed-income arbitrage and merger arbitrage have very different risks. Just because a trader has been successful in one market doesn't guarantee that he will not have disastrous results when trading a different strategy. Lowenstein calculated that LTCM lost $1.3 billion on its short-variability positions in equity options, larger than the $1.1 billion in losses from its core business of fixed-income arbitrage. He concluded that LTCM would not have failed if it stuck to its core strategy and didn't place massive trades in illiquid markets such as equity volatility and swap spreads.[4]

Finally, fund managers need to understand that market liquidity and leverage exposures need to have a negative correlation. If a fund chooses to have high levels of leverage, it must focus its trading on the most liquid markets, which guarantee a rapid exit at a reasonable price during times of stress. Futures markets often maintain, or even enhance, their liquidity during volatile markets. If a fund chooses to trade less liquid investments, such as risky bonds or private placements, the traders should realize that these positions may not be able to be sold during a crisis market, even at dramatically reduced prices. The more liquidity risk a fund assumes, the less leverage should be applied to those positions. Investors who have the liquidity to purchase investments during a crash or a time of rapidly widening spreads have an opportunity for spectacular gains. Those who are forced to sell at that time make headlines with their spectacular losses. It should be no surprise, then, that Warren Buffet nearly purchased the assets of Long-Term Capital Management after risky bonds fell to their cheapest prices in years.

RICHARD DENNIS

Richard Dennis started his career on the Mid America Exchange in 1970. He started trading on this miniversion of the Chicago Board of Trade (CBOT) with less than $2000 in capital. Only 20 years later, his net worth was estimated at $200 million. His first large gains were in 1973 soybean futures markets traded at the CBOT. In 1978, he moved from being a floor trader to an upstairs trader, which allowed him to trade a wider variety of markets. We can learn many lessons from Dennis's career about floor trading, upstairs trading, managed futures, and systematic trading. His well-documented rules about trend following and risk management are especially important.

Jack Schwager, in his *Market Wizards* book series, interviews a number of famous traders, hoping to pass along some of the systems and psychology that made them fantastically wealthy.[5]

The first lesson Schwager relates from Dennis concerns the significant trends in the 1973 soybean market. Dennis believes that 95 percent of a trend follower's profits will come from 5 percent of his trades. If more than 60 percent of your trades will be unprofitable, you must make sure that the gains from the infrequent winning trades are more than large enough to offset the more frequent losses. The biggest trading mistake, then, in Dennis's view, is to not take full advantage of the largest profit opportunities. In order to maximize the profits from the large winning trades, it is important not to place limits on the markets. He questions the wisdom of traders selling soybeans at a limit up price, as the price is likely to trade higher on the next day, because the exchange limited the price movement in the current trading day. Dennis will hold a trade until it is obvious that the trend has turned. While this allows him to make sure that he does not close out a trade too early, it can also mean that the trade stays open long after the trend has reversed. This strategy can lead to giving back a significant portion of the profits on a trade.

In 1978, Dennis retired from the floor to focus on trading upstairs. This can be a difficult transition. A floor trader generally focuses on short-term profits, often in time frames shorter than 10 minutes. Because of the order flow that is sent to futures exchanges, floor traders often have the ability to buy at the bid price and sell at the offer price. It makes sense, then, that floor traders would trade very frequently, as each trade offers the expectation of profit from earning the bid-ask spread. When traders move upstairs, they lose the information advantage of the floor and are more likely to pay the bid-ask spread. Because trading costs and the time to execute trades rise significantly, the upstairs trader will generally trade much less frequently than a floor trader. After a stressful time adapting to the upstairs trading style, Dennis was able to earn significant profits in a much wider variety of futures markets than were available to him on the CBOT floor.

After Dennis's successes in both floor and upstairs trading, he started an innovative and famous experiment. He made a bet with William Eckhardt, a famous trader in his own right who is profiled in Schwager's *New Market Wizards*.[6] While Dennis thought that traders could be taught to earn profits in the markets, Eckhardt was more prone to believe that only certain types of people could make excellent traders. In order to test this hypothesis, the pair hired 13 trainees in 1984. These trainees were called "the Turtles," as Dennis thought that good traders could be bred as easily as turtles grow in a Singapore turtle farm.

At the core of the training program was a set of trading rules that Dennis had developed. While the rules were very simple, they could be difficult to strictly follow during times that trading profits were hard to come by. The Turtles experiment allowed some traders to be enormously successful. Those who were unable to complete the program often failed for psychological reasons, as they were unable to open and close trades as required by the system.

Dennis and the Turtles followed a systematic, trend-following system. They purchased contracts of financial and commodity futures that were expected to experience a trend of rising prices, while selling short those futures that they thought would enter a sustained decline in prices. Rather than considering the fundamental developments in each market, their system relied on purely technical rules. These rules are assumed to earn the most profits when trading is fully computerized. Trader intervention is likely to reduce the profits of the system, as the rules were designed to take advantage of flaws in human decision making. If a system developer finds a reason to second-guess his trading, he is encouraged to test the rule. If the rule is successful over long periods of time, then the trader should add the rule to the system. If the rule has not been consistently successful, then this intervention is not necessary.

While the rules remained secret for years, several Turtles recently decided to publish them on the Web in order to thwart unethical traders, some of them failed Turtles, who were selling inaccurate or incomplete versions of the Turtle system.[7] Because much of the success comes from following the system, they feel that a failed trader is unable to support new traders following the rules, as they had previously failed the market's psychology test.

If you are able to purchase a trading system for a few hundred dollars, it is not likely to offer profitable trading rules. If the system were truly valuable, then it would not be for sale at a discount price. Many of the systems offered for sale are tested in one market for a limited time frame. While the system performs well over the development period, the parameters were likely optimized over that time period, and markets are unlikely to repeat exactly the same behavior in the next year.

A number of the original Turtles had extremely successful careers as CTAs, and many have reached the top of the managed futures performance charts in recent years. Of course, these rules were developed in the early 1980s, and most systematic CTAs are trading more sophisticated systems today. The three main rules for the system showed the formulas for position sizes, entry prices, and exit prices.

Position sizes were determined by the dollars at risk per trade. The system will recommend positions based on units, where each unit risks 1 percent of account equity. Every unit has an equal dollar risk, which standardized position sizes by the size of the futures contract and recent price volatility. Larger and more volatile futures contracts will have smaller position sizes per unit, while smaller and less volatile contracts would have larger position sizes. Strict risk management rules covered the number of units allowed in single markets, correlated markets, or a given long or short direction. Each trader was only allowed to risk 2 percent of capital in a given position, and stop losses are mandatory. If the trade causes a 2 percent loss, you close out the position immediately and without question. The best way to multiply losses is to ignore a stop-loss signal from the system.

The prices at which the Turtles were instructed to enter the trades were based on a remarkably simple breakout system. With a 20-day system, you would assume an up trend and buy when the current price exceeded the highest price over the last 20 trading days. Under the 55-day system, you would assume a down trend and sell short when the current price fell below the lowest price traded over the last 55 days. Of course, the rules were symmetric, so you would short commodities on 20-day lows and buy contracts on 55-day highs. Turtles would typically scale into trades, opening one unit at the breakout price and opening up to three additional units as the trend became larger and more defined. More volatile markets had wider stops and reentry points, while the stops and reentry points were much tighter for less volatile markets.

A Turtle would only exit a profitable trade if he or she was sure that the trend had turned, or not materialized. For example, if you bought futures on a 20-day high, you could only close the position when those same futures hit a 10-day low. Conversely, if you were short futures on a 55-day breakout, you could only cover your short on a 20-day high. These systems were designed to ensure that the trader would always have a position in the direction of a spectacular trend, ensuring large profits from the most memorable moves in the markets. However, this system can be very slow to close out trades, allowing traders to give back a large portion of the gains from following the trend.

Of course, these systems can be extremely unprofitable when markets are volatile and trend less. Constantly trading in search of a trend can be very expensive, as the manager gets whipsawed. Whipsaw trading can generate large losses, as the trader buys in search of an up trend, only to sell at a lower price when the up trend doesn't happen. To combat this downfall of trend-following systems, many managed futures funds will develop countertrend systems that can profit in the times when trend following systems are posting losses.

Over the years, these rules have been refined in a number of ways. Instead of simply having the price penetrate a previous high or low, some traders will wait until the price crosses a moving average. While this system may capture a smaller portion of profits, it can benefit from a reduced number of whipsaws. Others may have tighter stops on markets that have provided significant profits, or they will protect their gains with options. Finally, some will supplement the technicals with fundamentals, seeking to systematically predict commodity prices using supply, demand, and inventory estimates or understand the currency markets using interest rates and inflation forecasts.

Over time, Dennis delivered over a 25 percent compound return to his investors, showing the return potential to managed futures trading. Unfortunately, his funds were extremely volatile. His funds were liquidated three times, shelling investors with drawdowns of between 35 percent and 49 percent from the high-water mark.[8] He found that managing public money could be lucrative, as you can profit from the investments of others. However, there is a high emotional toll when you lose nearly half of your investors' assets, and impatient investors cause the fund to liquidate months before similar funds post large profits. At the end of the *Market Wizards* interview, he wondered if the management and incentive fees were worth the emotional pain caused by his investors' suffering.

Despite the Turtles' insistence that the system's recommended trades be religiously followed, it seems that Dennis himself would habitually override the system. When he opened his third public fund in 1996, after having liquidated his first two funds after large drawdowns, his investors insisted on an interesting restriction. In order to ensure that Dennis was trading solely by the system, and not using his personal discretion to override the system, a separate firm was hired to monitor the trades recommended by the system.[9] If Dennis broke these rules by placing trades other than those recommended by the system, the auditing firm would notify the investors, who would then have the option of withdrawing their funds.

What lessons can we learn from Richard Dennis and the Turtles? First, hedge fund managers must realize the enormous responsibility of managing other people's money. While there is a tremendous opportunity to profit from incentive fees, large drawdowns can be emotionally difficult to endure. Second, it is vitally important to have a strong risk management system. Stop losses and reasonable position sizes can reduce the probability of losing your equity over a short time period. Third, psychology is extremely important in investing. If you are not strong enough to trade when you need to, and not trade when you shouldn't, perhaps money management is not a good fit for your personality. Finally, if you are trading using a system, you shouldn't second-guess the system. Buy when it says buy, sell when it says sell, and close a trade when you are instructed to. If you realize that a specific situation is leading to consistent losses, test to see if this suggests that a new rule can be profitably added to your system. Build the system yourself, as any system offered for sale was likely built in a manner that ignores the caveats of modeling, including restrictions on overfitting, in-sample modeling and testing, and look-ahead bias.

ENDNOTES

1. P. Jorion, "Risk Management Lessons from Long-Term Capital Management," *European Financial Management* 6(2000): 277–300.
2. R. Lowenstein, *When Genius Failed: The Rise and Fall of Long-Term Capital Management.* New York: Random House, 2000.
3. P. Jorion, "Risk Management Lessons from Long-Term Capital Management," op. cit.
4. R. Lowenstein, *When Genius Failed,* op cit.

5. J. D. Schwager, *Market Wizards: Interviews with Top Traders,* New York: Harper & Row, 1989.

6. J. D. Schwager, *The New Market Wizards: Conversations with America's Top Traders.* New York: HarperCollins, 1992.

7. "The Original Turtle Trading Rules." Viewed at http://www.originalturtles.org/docs/turtlerules.pdf.

8. M. Allison, "Dennis Trading Group Crashes for Investors," *Chicago Tribune,* October 3, 2000.

9. G. Burns, "High Roller Richard Dennis Is Back at the Table. This Time, Computers Decide on His Trades," *Chicago Tribune,* August 1, 1997.

CHAPTER 6

Starting and Managing a Hedge Fund

Most hedge fund managers start a new fund to either manage their personal fortune or to increase their personal fortune by sharing in the profits of their investors. Many managers may focus too much on the investing and trading aspects of the fund while overlooking many important considerations of running the management company. It is important to realize that each new fund is an entrepreneurial venture, which can have all of the challenges of starting and running a new company. Successful entrepreneurs will structure their business in a way to maximize the value of their company even if one of their products should prove unsuccessful. In order to maximize the wealth of the hedge fund manager, the fund company should be structured in a way that it can survive the failure of a single fund or the departure of a star manager. In order to ensure that the management firm survives, the fund should be a separate entity from the management company, and the firm should manage funds with several distinct styles.

The hedge fund is designed as an investment partnership that controls cash, investments, and debt. Each fund can hire a management company, which is designed as a consulting firm that designs and implements investment decisions. Each management company can run numerous hedge funds, ideally isolated from the risks of a specific hedge fund. Unfortunately, the average hedge fund only lives three years, and few funds survive longer than seven years. A hedge fund may close for many reasons: poor performance, an out-of-favor investment style, the departure of a star money manager, or large withdrawals of client funds.[1]

A smart management company will design its operations to minimize the probability or impact of each of these events. A management company with just one fund will be held captive to the returns of a single investment style. For example, a company that ran a single fixed-income arbitrage fund may have closed its fund, and therefore its management company, in the aftermath of the Long-Term Capital Management crisis of 1998. However, that same firm may have survived if it managed several funds, especially a global macro fund that had the opportunity to profit from the turbulent bond markets. A company that offers several funds may also be able to maintain the funds of its investors even if they decide to reallocate assets to different types of funds.

It may be easier to achieve these goals if you focus on funds that have lower risks and lower correlations to traditional investments. It is easy to see how a short-selling fund could face investor withdrawals during an equity bull market, and how an emerging-markets fund could lose assets during a time of flight to quality and market contagion. Perhaps most important is the type of client you attract and how you form and manage the expectations of your investors. If you emphasize short-term performance, you may be attracting "hot money" investors, who will pull their assets at the first sign of diminished performance. If you market your fund as low-risk, you may attract patient investors who will stay for a while. If the risk of your fund increases, however, these investors will be tempted to withdraw from your fund. If you have taken significant efforts to educate your clients and understand their needs and objectives, and have carefully cultivated the relationship, you may have a higher probability of retaining their assets, even in tough times. If your clients trust you and appreciate your advice, they are likely to stay with you longer than will clients that have a more distant relationship.

A management company may build few assets and little equity, and can be unlikely to survive after its funds close. This can result from a hesitance to build retained earnings, which can result in dividing each year's profits between the partners without reinvesting profits in the firm.

It would be nice to be able to sell your management company, even after the closing of one fund. Very few single-fund companies have any value that can be transferred to a new owner. The majority of management companies that are sold are fund-of-fund managers, where the closing of one hedge fund will have only a minimal impact on the assets managed by the firm. In many ways, running a hedge fund is similar to running any other type of business. Those familiar with the entrepreneurial process know that the majority of new companies fail within the first three years, and hedge funds are no exception. However, smart managers will know the obstacles before they begin their new fund. If you are careful to avoid some common mistakes, you should be able to increase the probability of success of your new fund company.

New hedge fund managers may have one of two personality traits, both of which can make it difficult to manage a fund. Unfortunately, these traits are opposites—either too much or too little focus—and both extremes can get a manager into trouble. It is possible for a manager to be too focused on the management of the assets of the fund. This could lead to a long track record of excellent performance, but other areas of fund management may be ignored. It will do little good for a fund to post top performance numbers if it neglects to raise capital for the fund, follow regulatory requirements, or present investors with performance and educational information. However, many of these tasks can be delegated to others. It is perfectly fine for fund managers to spend all of their time running money, as long as they hire competent professionals to oversee other administrative areas of critical importance.

Perhaps a more difficult mistake to overcome is a lack of focus. As institutional investors increase in importance in the hedge fund world, style purity is now more important than ever. If a hedge fund manager has "too many good ideas," he or she may be tempted to design trades in an eclectic manner, switching between styles on a regular basis. This is fine if your fund is presented as one that mixes styles within the relative value universe. However, if your fund is marketed as one that sticks to a specific style, these diversions can lead to client defections and even legal liabilities.

You must also remember that you are running a business. As a business, you must manage revenues, costs, personnel, long-term strategy, marketing, and strategic partnerships. In order to be successful, you must understand and manage all of the risks and opportunities that each of these areas can create.

The first goal to understand is that the fund exists to maximize profits. Maximizing profits can be a very different goal than maximizing assets under management or maximizing revenues. How can maximizing assets under management hurt profits? This depends on the liquidity of your strategy and the size of the market inefficiency you are exploiting. If you have a scalable strategy in a liquid market, it may make sense to attract as much capital as possible. However, if your strategy invests in illiquid markets where inefficiencies can disappear quickly, it can make sense to close the fund to new investment in order to protect the returns to your initial capital. Consider a $1 billion fund with a 5 percent hurdle rate that is only able to return 5 percent a year because it has raised too much capital. The 1 percent management fee of this fund is only $10 million, and the fund earns no incentive fee because it is unable to earn excess returns above the hurdle rate. Contrast this to a $300 million fund that can earn a 20 percent annual return, with the same 5 percent hurdle rate. This fund earns a management fee of $3 million and an incentive fee of 20 percent of the 15 percent gains above the hurdle rate, which is $9 million. The smaller fund can earn annual fees of $12 million, which exceeds the total fees of a less successful fund with more than three times the amount of assets under management.

Maximizing revenue can be inconsistent with maximizing profits when the cost structure of the firm is extremely high. Perhaps you hire a star manager with a $2 million annual guaranteed salary, or offer marketers a 5 percent commission on all funds they raise. If the fund does not earn the returns you hoped for, and you have high expenses, you will not be able to reap large, or any, profits from your management company. A more sensible cost structure would be one with low fixed expenses that offers large bonus potential to your traders and marketers. Offering star managers or marketers 10 percent of the annual revenue of the firm, or 20 percent of the fees on the assets they generate, can be a much less risky deal for the management company, as these participants share in both the gains and the risk of running the fund. In low-return years, the profits of the fund company can fall, but so does the compensation of the employees. In good years, all participants earn compensation far above what they had previously anticipated. Be careful, however, of designing your fund or asset-gathering process around a single star manager. If this manager does well, she may ask for increasing levels of compensation, because she knows how important she is to the firm. If the manager decides to leave your fund, many of your investors may move their assets to her new firm. Ideally, you would create a fund and a management company that can survive a move by a star manager to another firm.

Fund managers should realize the importance of marketing and understand the value of strategic partnerships, especially if the fund manager is more focused on managing money than on managing the firm. It may be a profitable strategy to outsource your fundraising efforts or back-office operations, as there are many firms that specialize in these tasks. If the deal is structured correctly, it can be extremely cost-effective to pay a large portion of the first-year fees to someone who is talented enough to attract investor assets. If these investors understand your fund strategy and patiently remain with your fund, third-party marketers can be very important to increasing the assets and the profitability of the fund. A fund-of-funds manager may be able to place significant assets with your fund. If you have been unsuccessful at raising assets on your own, it could be worth giving this manager an equity stake in your fund company when she attracts given levels of new money to your fund.

Investing can be a very risky business, and this risk can be magnified when derivatives and leverage are used to increase the notional value of investments above the capital invested in the fund. When a fund fails, the managers of the fund need to know that their liability is limited, even if their investments create more losses than the remaining capital in the fund. The owners of the fund and the management company would also like to segregate their business assets from their personal assets, so they can protect their personal assets if the fund is sued by an investor, broker, or counterparty. There are many choices of business models, and each has different ramifications for taxation and liability of the owners of the fund.

A C corporation is the traditional structure for large U.S. firms. Corporations exist in a distinct way from their owners, and corporations may survive far longer than any person. Corporations offer limited liability, which is great for stockholders who desire to ensure that their losses will not exceed their investment in the firm. There is no stated limit on the number of shareholders in a corporation, so large firms like Microsoft or General Motors may be able to attract millions of shareholders. There is a downside to the corporate structure, as corporate income is taxed once at the corporate level and a second time when the profits of the firm are distributed to the shareholders.

Partnerships have "pass-through" tax treatment, where each owner pays taxes on firm income relative to their percentage of ownership. Profits are taxed only once to the owners, and are not taxed at the firm level. Unfortunately, partnerships do not offer limited liability, so owners may lose more than their original investment if the firm's liabilities exceed its assets at liquidation.

The most prevalent business structure for hedge funds is a limited partnership, where a general partner assumes liability for the operation. This structure allows the same pass-through tax treatment, where all income is taxed once to the owners and never taxed at the firm level. All limited partners have limited liability, where their losses are limited to the amount invested in the firm. The general partner retains all liability, however, and can be liable for losses in excess of his or her investment in the firm.

In the future, we may see most hedge funds adopting either an S corporation or limited liability company (LLC) structure. An S corporation combines the limited liability features of a corporation with the pass-through tax benefits of a partnership. This is similar to a limited partnership, but one where no general partner is required. While many hedge funds are organized as S corporations, this may limit their options, as this structure allows a maximum of 35 investors and requires that all investors are individuals. If you want to have 50 investors, many of which are institutions, than the S corporation structure is not the proper one for your fund. The LLC is similar to an S corporation in most respects, but the LLC has no limit on the number of investors, which can make this structure more attractive to fund companies.

Many funds and management companies will combine a number of these entities in their structure. In many funds, an S corporation will be designed to be the management company and the general partner of a specific fund. This corporation will earn all revenue, pay all expenses, and employ all of the fund's employees. Each fund will be structured as a separate limited partnership, where all investors of the fund will be limited partners of the specific fund. If a management company runs a number of funds, it may separate the general partner function of each fund from the management firm. In this way, one management company can run a number of separate funds. This structure provides limited liability and pass-through tax treatment to the management company and all fund investors. All of the liability is focused in the general partnership, remote from any of the funds or the management company. Ideally, the failure of a single fund will not affect the operations of the management company or the fate of other hedge funds. Obviously, these structures are very important and quite complex. These decisions on the best way to structure fund and management companies are best left to attorneys with significant experience in the field and knowledge of current regulations. Regulations change over time, so it is imperative to work with someone well aware of the current regulatory environment.

Obviously, it is much easier to run a C corporation than any type of partnership. With a corporation, there is no need to find general partners to accept all liability, and there is no need to recalculate partnership agreements each time an individual invests or withdraws from the company. Partnerships are usually designed for one reason: to avoid the double taxation of firm profits that is present in the corporate structure.

For these reasons, many funds would like to be structured as a corporation, especially if they can minimize or eliminate the taxation of profits at the corporate level. This has led many funds and management companies to incorporate "offshore" in a country with different laws on corporate structure and taxation. Funds often incorporate in tax havens, countries that charge little or no tax on corporate profits. Because offshore funds are specifically designed to avoid paying taxes to the U.S. government, U.S. investors are not allowed to invest in funds managed offshore. If U.S. investors were participating in offshore funds, they could be subject to criminal liability for tax evasion.

Many funds will adopt a mirrored structure, with different entities accepting investments from American and foreign investors. All U.S. investors will invest in a limited partnership structured in the United States, while all foreign investors invest in the offshore corporation. You must be careful, however, if you have two distinct types of investors in the same fund. Many funds will make all trades in one account and move positions between the two entities on a regular basis, making trades at the closing NAV, to ensure that the returns to each investor are exactly the same. If you are trading futures or options, you must understand the rules for moving positions between entities. This mirrored-fund structure may not work well if the exchange requires that you pay a bid-ask spread each time you need to move positions within your firm.

ENDNOTE

1. This chapter benefits from the discussion in S. McCrary, *How to Create and Manage a Hedge Fund: A Professional's Guide.*

CHAPTER 7

Understanding U.S. Hedge Fund Regulations

Once you have located and hired an experienced attorney, you will ask her to compile three documents for your fund: the risk disclosure document, the partnership agreement, and the subscription agreement. Ironically, the most experienced attorneys may charge the lowest prices to prepare these documents, as they are familiar with the work and know how to quickly customize their previous work for your specific firm and fund.

The *risk disclosure document* is similar to the prospectus that is required for SEC-registered investments. Each fund will have a unique document that states the risks that may occur that can reduce the returns to investors in the fund. This document is designed to protect the fund manager from legal liability to investors, so every possible risk is disclosed here, even those that managers don't think are likely. Investors may find it difficult to sue a fund if they knew which risks existed before they invested, so fund managers will try to disclose every type of risk in order to legally protect the sponsors of the fund. While there are numerous risks present in hedge fund strategies, special attention is usually taken to disclose the risks of illiquid investment strategies.[1]

The *partnership agreement* defines the rights and obligations of each partner, whether they are managers or investors in the fund. This agreement will delineate performance and fee calculations, as well as the regulations regarding deposit to and withdrawal of

117

assets from the fund. Included in this document will also be the definition and identification of the general and limited partners, as well as the ability of partners to transfer or collateralize their interest in the fund.

Finally, the *subscription agreement* is necessary whenever a new investor places assets with the fund. Every investor has to disclose his or her assets and prove that he or she is a qualified or accredited investor who is eligible to invest in hedge fund vehicles. All investors also sign a statement that they have read and understand the risk disclosure document and that they agree that the risks of this fund are appropriate risks for them to take. Finally, all investors must also comply with the USA PATRIOT Act of 2001, disclosing their affiliations and business activities to prove that their assets have been earned in a legitimate way, and that there are no relationships with terrorists, drug dealers, or money launderers.

Before starting a fund or a management company, you must estimate the revenue and expenses of your operations. Be sure to include your opportunity costs. If you are currently employed in the securities industry, you will likely need to resign your employment to start the fund, given the strict conflict-of-interest rules in the industry. If the fund fails to attract significant assets, it is possible that your earnings can fall after you quit your job and commit full-time to the new hedge fund.

It can be difficult to start a fund if you don't have access to money to fund the start-up costs. Legal and accounting start-up costs can begin at $5000 and easily exceed $50,000 before any investor funds can be accepted. You need to estimate the cost of office expenses and salaries, which can be up to $300,000 in the first year. If it will cost you $350,000 to run the fund in the first year, and you assume that you only earn a 1 percent management fee, then you will need to raise $35 million in assets to fund your first-year expenses. If you think that you can earn 10 percent returns on your investments, you can include a 20 percent incentive fee in your calculations and break even with as little as $12 million in assets, assuming that investors won't demand a hurdle rate of return before paying incentive fees. If you are confident that you can raise $12 to $35 million in assets in your first year, and earn returns of at least 10 percent on this level of assets, then it may be worth a shot to open your own hedge fund.

Once you start raising money, it may be tempting to fantasize about the profits you can make as a hedge fund manager. If you raise $600 million and earn 30 percent annual returns, then your total fee income can exceed $40 million each year if investors do not demand a hurdle rate. However, you may want to contain your enthusiasm before bidding on a new yacht. It is important to realize that the average fund has less than $100 million in assets, that funds average 10 percent returns over time, and that investors may sometimes demand the use of a hurdle rate, which reduces your potential incentive fees. This could leave you with as little as $2 million each year in revenue, before you pay salaries and office expenses. Assuming that salary expenses may be 75 percent of gross revenue, you will have an annual income of only $500,000, plus your own salary if it is counted in this figure. Tempering this enthusiasm even further is the realization that most funds close in their first two to seven years of operations. Yes, there are hedge fund superstars who can earn $40 million a year or more. Just be realistic before you start your fund, as the vast majority of the 7000 hedge funds available today manage less than $100 million in assets. You may be able to provide a comfortable income for yourself and a couple of colleagues, but your income may likely differ little from what you could earn in a successful mutual fund or investment banking position.

Many hedge fund strategies are not scalable and only work with small amounts of assets under management. As hedge funds become extremely large, perhaps at more than $1 billion, returns tend to decline. In order to maximize the revenue of your firm, you need to find the optimal amount of assets for your strategy, which can often mean turning away assets in an effort to avoid diluting returns. To determine the maximum level of assets you can manage, you should consider the total amount of assets available to the strategy, as well as those already managed by hedge funds. You can manage larger amounts of assets as the size of your investment universe expands and as your holding period lengthens. If you hold positions for only one week on average, you are demanding higher levels of liquidity, so you must hold smaller positions or trade in a larger market. Many funds are reaching into new markets to enhance the capacity of their strategies, but you must be careful using this strategy. Do you really want to run a market-neutral fund of Chinese stocks, or are there some pitfalls to this strategy that you will only encounter once you begin trading?

Most hedge funds have chosen to remain unregistered. This decision has both costs and benefits. While unregistered funds may only accept funds from institutional and accredited investors, they may be able to run an opaque fund that does not disclose their positions on a regular basis.

Many institutional investors have been demanding increased levels of disclosure from their hedge fund managers. As funds calculate and disclose this information, as well as comply with National Futures Association (NFA) and Commodity Futures Trading Commission (CFTC) regulations, they may find that registering their funds with the SEC may not require significant additional disclosures. When the fund decides to succumb to SEC regulations, it must write a prospectus and distribute this document to all investors.

The line between mutual fund and hedge fund management companies is becoming increasingly blurred. Many hedge fund strategies are very low risk, low-correlation strategies that can be attractive to and appropriate for retail investors. After the U.S. equity bear market of 2000 to 2002, retail investors were especially interested in market-neutral funds. Their curiosity was rewarded with the release of several market-neutral funds managed by traditional mutual fund management companies. While choosing to submit your fund to additional regulation may not be an easy or pleasant process, it opens your fund to accept investments from unaccredited investors. These investors may only invest $10,000 in your fund, but the sheer size of this market may present opportunities that offset the costs of additional regulation and fund disclosures. Choosing to be a regulated fund also releases funds from the ban on advertising, which can be especially advantageous if your firm has compiled an impressive track record.

Registering as an investment adviser may give you an additional level of credibility with investors. If investors contact securities regulators and finds that you have a clean compliance record, they may feel more comfortable placing assets with your firm. If they find that you are not registered, they may have the temptation to think that you may be hiding something, or that you are not taking the money management business seriously. While the forms to register as an investment adviser may seem cumbersome, many firms sell software that carefully and automatically fills out these voluminous forms after the manager simply completes a series of interview questions. Registered investment advisers must regularly file Form ADV, which discloses their fees, details of their investment strategies, and their clients. This filing also requires an audited balance sheet. Late in 2003, the SEC issued a proposal that would require all hedge fund managers to register as investment advisers.

All investment managers must be cognizant of the regulations that govern the behavior of securities professionals and their firms. Hedge funds rely on a series of exemptions to these regulations in order to maintain their unregulated status.

The Securities Act of 1933 established the Securities and Exchange Commission. The SEC requires that all securities, other than those specifically exempted, must be registered with the SEC and provide a prospectus to all investors. Rule 506, regulation D, states that nonregistered investments must be sold as private placements. The most typical private placements are unregistered stock and bond investments as well as investments in hedge fund partnerships. In order to be exempt from the registration requirements, you must not advertise the security; also, it can be sold only to institutions and accredited investors. The presence of just one unaccredited investor may subject the security offering to the full disclosure and registration requirements of the SEC.

The Investment Company Act of 1940 outlines the rules that must be followed by investment companies. Mutual funds typically must follow the regulations of this act, which limits the types of trading and leverage funds can employ and requires that fund activities be disclosed to investors in a prospectus before their investment can be accepted. Hedge funds rely on a section 3(c)1 exemption to avoid these regulations. Funds exempt from the Investment Company Act must be sold to 99 or fewer investors, and these investments may not be offered for sale to the general public. If you receive a risk disclosure document or a private placement memorandum from a hedge fund, you will notice that each copy has a unique number, which identifies the investor to whom it was issued. Keeping close track on fund documentation assists the fund in limiting the distribution of fund materials, supporting the claim that they do not advertise to the public.

The Investment Advisors Act of 1940 was created to oversee the activities of money managers, especially those who were not governed by the Investment Company Act. This act includes regulations on record keeping, reporting, advertising, registration, and administration of adviser activities. It is imperative that investor funds be segregated from manager funds, ideally in a custody arrangement that prevents the managers and their creditors from accessing the funds. The act also requires managers to disclose performance to investors on a regular basis. The performance presentation standards of the Association for Investment Management and Research (AIMR) are appropriate methods for calculating and disclosing the performance of investment funds.

This act specifically bans the front-running of client orders, where managers buy or sell securities with the intent of profiting from knowledge of their client's orders. This ensures that a manager cannot purchase a stock for his own account, and then immediately execute a large client order to buy the same stock that increases the value of his personal account.

Soft dollars are also discussed in these regulations. A brokerage firm may rebate a portion of commissions paid, especially if the firm does not offer research to its clients. Soft dollars are perfectly acceptable when used to purchase third-party research that is of clear benefit to investors. There are many unethical uses of soft dollars, such as using these payments to sponsor travel by the manager that is unrelated to the management of client assets.

Section 203(b)(3) of the Investment Advisors Act provides exemption from registration for managers with fewer than 15 clients. Many hedge fund managers work for only one client, the hedge fund management company, and are therefore exempt from registration under the act. Exemption from the act requires that you don't advertise your services as an investment manager but leaves you free to discuss your services with accredited investors who contact your office.

The National Securities Market Improvement Act of 1996 increases the number of investors that can purchase private placements, but redefines the notion of eligible investors. Under section 3(c)7 of the act, a private placement can be purchased by up to 500 investors, but each of these investors must be a "qualified purchaser," a stronger requirement than accredited investor. Each qualified purchaser is an individual or family with over $5 million in assets or an investment adviser, trust, or institution with at least $25 million raised from accredited investors. The reason many hedge funds require large minimum investments is that the Investment Company Act limited each fund to 99 investors. Under the NSMI Act of 1996, the increase to 500 investors can allow hedge funds to dramatically reduce their minimum required investment. This reduction in minimum investment size can allow individuals to better diversify their assets between hedge funds.

The Employee Retirement Income Security Act of 1974 is meant to protect participants in employee pension plans from unsuitable securities, unscrupulous plan sponsors, and undiversified portfolios. ERISA holds managers to an even higher standard of care and diversification than is required under the Investment Company Act and prohibits certain types of transactions and fee structures. Funds are required to follow ERISA regulations when greater than 25 percent of their assets come from plans governed by ERISA. Many hedge funds will accept some money from ERISA funds, but will be very careful not to exceed 25 percent of assets. Some funds will actually refuse funds from pension plans if those new assets would cause them to exceed this threshold. One of the largest and fastest-growing sources of new hedge fund assets is from state pension plans, such as CALPERS, so managers should examine their operations to see what changes they would need to make to move their funds into compliance with ERISA. An ability to increase the amount of assets gathered from ERISA plans could make it much easier for funds to raise capital.

The Commodities Exchange Act of 1936 was amended in 1974. The NFA was created to regulate traders in the futures market. The NFA works closely with the CFTC, which oversees the work of futures exchanges. Nearly all hedge funds will be required to register as commodity pool operators if they trade futures, commodities, or options on futures. This act requires disclosures on the performance of futures funds and annual audits of futures trading firms.

ENDNOTE

1. This chapter benefits from the discussion in S. McCrary, *How to Create and Manage a Hedge Fund: A Professional's Guide.*

CHAPTER 8

Offshore Hedge Funds and Structured Products

U.S. VERSUS OFFSHORE FUND REGULATIONS

The regulations discussed in Chapter 7 focuses on funds domiciled in the United States and targeted to American investors. However, half of the world's wealth resides outside of the United States, so hedge fund managers must understand how to legally manage money for residents in a number of countries.

In order to comply with the U.S. taxing authority, the Internal Revenue Service (IRS) requires that all taxable U.S. investors may only invest in U.S.-based funds. Taxable U.S. investors should not invest in offshore funds, as the IRS might assume that these investors are doing so with the intent to evade taxation on their investment gains. Similarly, foreign investors should not invest in U.S. funds, as the gains in these funds might be subject to U.S. taxation. The simple rule is that U.S. investors should invest in U.S.-based funds, while foreign investors should invest in offshore funds.

Many developed countries are placing pressure on countries that are viewed as tax havens. These countries generally charge little or no income tax and offer secrecy laws that prohibit cooperation with taxing authorities in developed countries. Companies domiciled in these nations may be designed strictly for the purpose of earning tax benefits and lack infrastructure and operating activity. As these countries are assumed to be facilitating money laundering and tax evasion, the United States and the United Kingdom may sanction these countries and attempt to target their firms and investors for prosecution.

In order to avoid the appearance of operating a tax haven that appeals to the lack of transparency, Bermuda recently announced that it intends to more closely regulate hedge fund operations in that country. If the government requires funds to be listed on an exchange, funds with fraudulent intents or questionable practices will be less likely to operate in that country. By discouraging less ethical or more secret funds from operating in a jurisdiction, the reputation of funds domiciled in that country should improve. Countries with the best reputations will be able to attract institutional investors. Caribbean countries are trying to bolster their financial services industry given the recent downturn in tourism. TASS reports that 8 percent of global hedge funds are currently domiciled in Bermuda, 35 percent in the Cayman Islands, 26 percent in the United States, 17 percent in the British Virgin Islands, 3 percent in Ireland, and the balance of the funds are scattered worldwide.[1]

Increasingly, hedge funds are being listed on exchanges; 12 percent of funds of funds are now listed, usually in London, Zurich, or Ireland.[2] Of course, the geographic distribution of hedge fund assets will not mirror the distribution of domiciles. Figure 8-1 shows that nearly half of all hedge fund assets are invested exclusively in the United States, which is consistent with the world market capitalization weight of marketable securities. Funds that focus exclusively on European securities claim 13 percent of hedge fund assets, while Japan and Asia hold 5 percent. The remaining one-third of assets is diversified across the world, where a single hedge fund manager may control assets in several markets around the globe.

As institutional investors become more involved in hedge funds, transparency and disclosure should increase, which could reduce the use of secret operations in small countries. In order to attract or retain hedge fund business, countries must ensure that their regulations support investor demands for disclosure. Indeed, offshore funds are growing faster than U.S. funds, as high-net-worth U.S. investors are becoming a smaller portion of hedge fund investors. As U.S. tax-exempt institutions and investors from Asia and Europe increase their allocations to hedge funds, offshore

FIGURE 8 – 1

Geographical distribution of hedge fund assets. *(MSCI, reprinted by permission.)*

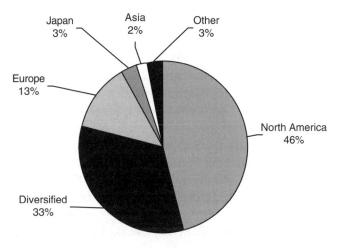

funds in reputable jurisdictions are expected earn a large portion of those assets.

If a U.S. manager runs an offshore fund, the IRS will be very strict and mandate a specific structure to ensure that the operations of the fund truly take place offshore. In order to satisfy the IRS that you are properly running an offshore fund, the fund company must pass 10 tests. There are companies in each tax haven specifically designed to provide these services to U.S. companies and ensure compliance with U.S. regulations. Many successful hedge fund companies house most of their operations in the Caribbean, living in an island paradise while obviously meeting the requirements of U.S. law. In order to qualify as an offshore fund, all 10 of these activities must take place outside the United States.[3]

1. Investor statements and reports
2. Public communications
3. Soliciting investments
4. Accepting and processing investments
5. Maintain accounting and corporate records
6. Fund audits

7. Publishing the fund's NAV
8. Board and shareholder meetings
9. All dividends and fund expenses, including salaries, are paid
10. Fund investments are redeemed

Notice that the IRS does not specify the location where trade decisions are made or where trades are executed. Obviously there are numerous funds where the investment manager lives and works in the United States, and an offshore company is hired or designed to solicit and administer investor funds. Many hedge fund managers will run funds in a variety of domiciles. By designing a mirrored-fund structure, one manager can operate both a U.S. and an offshore fund using the same trading strategies. Ideally, the manager will be able to allocate trades between the two funds to create the same return and risk opportunities for both types of investors.

The Taxpayer Relief Act of 1997 makes it easier for managers to run an offshore fund. The "Ten Commandments" for offshore funds were repealed with this act, but funds must still be very cautious about which activities are performed in which country.

Many governments around the world have specific regulations regarding hedge fund investments. In most cases, hedge funds are not publicly marketed, and many types of funds may only be purchased by high-net-worth individuals. In some countries, specific types of investments can be widely distributed, while others have a much more restricted clientele. As you would expect, fund management companies will engineer products that are available to the largest number of investors. Fund regulations have created a demand for new products, as funds of funds, guaranteed principal products, exchange-listed funds, or products sold by insurance companies are exempt from regulations in some jurisdictions where investments in single manager hedge funds are not generally allowed.

Hong Kong seems to have even stricter regulations than the United States. For Hong Kong investors to purchase a hedge fund, the fund must have $100 million in assets, while the manager has five years' experience, including two years' experience in the specific strategy. Investors must be able to invest a minimum of US$50,000, and be offered clear disclosures of diversification, leverage, and risk. Funds must be held by a registered and regulated prime broker to avoid placing assets in a risky custody situation. Finally, hedge funds are required to offer at least quarterly liquidity and can only charge incentive fees on an annual basis with a mandatory high-water-mark provision.[4] There does not seem to be an accredited investor provision, as the government has mandated significant disclosures and regulations. This may be the model for worldwide hedge fund regulation. Funds of all types may be offered to retail investors, but the government must maintain sufficient standards to make sure these investors are adequately protected.

However, Hong Kong regulations are much less strict when allowing investors access to fund of funds or guaranteed products. Funds of funds investments are available with a US$10,000 minimum investment, provided that all fees are fully disclosed and the fund has diversified its asset allocation between at least five single manager hedge funds, with relatively equal weights.

European mutual funds are regulated by the Undertakings for Collective Investments in Transferable Securities (UCITS) standards. Mutual funds that abide by these standards have one set of regulations in all European Union countries. UCITS funds are not allowed to sell short or have more than 10 percent leverage. These funds can trade derivatives, but must ensure that total derivatives exposure does not exceed the NAV of the fund. UCITS standards are typically not followed by hedge funds, which means that hedge funds follow a different set of regulations in each European country.

In the United Kingdom, hedge funds are not marketed to the public, yet UK investors are allowed to purchase offshore funds that have been approved by the Financial Services Authority. Typically, hedge funds can't be established in the UK, but UK firms may run a closed-end fund from an offshore location. Retail investors in the UK can purchase these funds when they are listed on the London Stock Exchange. Life insurance companies are attracting a growing share of hedge fund business by offering hedge fund investments in their life insurance products.

In Ireland, non-UCITS funds are only sold to professional or qualifying investors. Professional investors must place at least 125,000 euros in each fund, while qualifying investors have investment minimums of 250,000 euros per fund with a minimum net worth of 1.25 million euros. Funds of funds must disclose and limit fees and ensure adequate diversification across single-fund investments. Offshore funds are frequently listed on the Irish Stock Exchange and insurance company products are quite popular.

Luxembourg is a popular domicile of funds of funds, as the regulations make funds easy to set up. Non-UCITS funds in this domicile can sell short, trade derivatives, and lever positions up to three times their total capital.

INSURANCE PRODUCTS

Some consumers will purchase inexpensive term life insurance, seeking to provide a continuing income for their heirs should they die while their family still depends on their earned income. The reason that term insurance is inexpensive, however, is that this product only offers a death benefit for the term of the premium, usually one year. After that one-year period expires, there is no residual value or investment value, and a new premium must be paid the next year to ensure continuous coverage.

Other types of life insurance, such as variable life or whole life, have more expensive premiums but offer a different set of benefits. A portion of each annual premium is placed into an investment account, where the cash value grows over time. These types of insurance, then, offer some residual value to their owners, even before they pass away. Ideally, the investment gains will be large and can eventually be used to pay future premium payments. Variable life insurance gives policyholders the opportunity to select the asset allocation for this growing cash value. Many investors are discovering that hedge funds can be a desirable investment, so they are pressuring insurance companies to offer alternative investment vehicles.[5]

In some cases, investors may find life insurance products more attractive for their tax-sheltering features than for their insurance aspects. In the United States, death benefits are paid to heirs free of income tax liability. Hedge funds can be tax-inefficient, given the nature of their investments and the frequency of their trading. Investors have a significant incentive to seek tax deferral for the gains from their hedge fund investments, as they are typically taxed at the higher tax rates for short-term holding periods.

Private Placement Life Insurance (PPLI) allows U.S.-accredited investors to invest in life insurance, where the underlying assets are invested in hedge funds. Of course, the IRS is interested in any products that offer significant opportunities to shelter tax liability. Any products offered to investors must pass the IRS tests to ensure that they are truly designed as life insurance and not just a tax shelter. In order to qualify as life insurance, products must offer a significant death benefit, the assets must be diversified across at least five asset classes, and the investor is not allowed to directly control the investments. Investors must investigate the financial status of their insurance company, as these investments subject the policyholder to the insurer's credit rating. Insurance products can be a significant source of capital to hedge fund managers, but hedge funds must have flexible policies, especially when the investor dies before the lockup period has expired.

In some countries, regulators make it easier to invest in hedge funds by buying life insurance than through the direct purchase of single hedge fund investments. In Italy, the only way that retail investors can gain access to hedge fund investments is through insurance company offerings. Unaccredited German investors can purchase index certificates from insurance companies, where their investment performance is linked to a hedge fund index. Finally, in Switzerland, tax shelters are needed for the returns from fixed-income investments, while equity gains are untaxed, and therefore no sheltered products are needed for stock market investments.

GUARANTEED PRINCIPAL PRODUCTS

To counter the perception by some investors or regulators that hedge fund investments are risky, a portion of the industry has started to offer guaranteed principal products. Most popular in Europe, these products allow investors to allocate assets to hedge fund strategies without risking any of their capital. These funds promise that the value of the investment will equal at least the initial capital contribution at the stated maturity date, guaranteeing that the investor will not lose money, even if the hedge fund investments are unprofitable. For example, an investor who purchases a $1 million investment in a guaranteed product will be guaranteed to have investments valued at a minimum of $1 million at the maturity of the investment five years later. However, this fund may not easily allow withdrawals before the maturity date, and the investment guarantee is not valid before the maturity date. If the investor requests a redemption of his or her shares in the third year, there is some probability that the fund will have posted a negative return and the investor will realize losses at this early withdrawal date. Some countries will waive accredited investor requirements for guaranteed products, allowing retail investors to purchase these funds because of their significantly reduced risk profile.

How can funds guarantee that investors will not lose money? First, we must find a fund-of-funds manager that expects to offer a well-diversified pool of hedge fund investments that will produce steady returns with relatively low volatility. The plain vanilla structure will purchase zero coupon bonds with a significant portion of the investor's capital, while investing the balance with the fund-of-funds manager.[6] The future value of the zero coupon bond must equal the guarantee value at the maturity date. Therefore, the cheaper the zero coupon bonds, the larger the portion of investor funds are invested in the hedge fund product.

Interest Rate	Bond Price (5-Year Maturity)	Bond Price (10-Year Maturity)
5 percent	$783	$614
7 percent	$713	$508
9 percent	$650	$422

The two main determinants of zero coupon bond prices are time and interest rates, where the bond has the lowest price when interest rates are high and the maturity is long. An investor who purchases a $1000 guaranteed fund with a five-year maturity when interest rates are near 5 percent would purchase a bond for a price of $783, while the remaining balance of $217 would be invested in the hedge fund product. The investor has a much larger exposure to risky assets with a 10-year maturity investment when interest rates are near 9 percent, where the purchase of a $422 bond would be accompanied by a $578 investment in hedge funds. At the maturity date of this investment, the zero coupon bond is worth $1000, while it is hoped that the hedge fund investment is valued at more than the $578 purchase price. Investors should be careful to understand the credit risk of the fixed-income investment portion of a guaranteed product. The credit risk of a pool backed by high-quality government bonds is much less than if the bonds are the debt obligations of the fund sponsor, typically a bank, insurance company, or brokerage firm.

A more sophisticated version of this cash and funds investment would be a cash and calls strategy. While the investor still places the majority of his or her capital in zero coupon bonds, the balance of the funds is now used to purchase call options on a fund-of-funds investment. While this strategy may offer a higher level of participation in the gains to the hedge fund strategy, there is always the probability that the call options will expire worthless if the fund-of-funds investment declines in value over the life of the strategy. The investor will have a higher participation rate in the fund-of-funds gains when bond prices and options prices are low, generally when interest rates are high and the implied volatility price of options is low. Options dealers are generally not willing to sell fund-of-funds options priced at their 4.83 percent historical volatility, so investors may consider these options to be expensive when priced at significantly higher levels of implied volatility.

If the investor decides that the purchase of call options on fund-of-funds returns is too expensive, he or she may wish to replicate the options payoff by implementing a strategy of constant proportion portfolio insurance. CPPI is a contingent immunization strategy, where the zero coupon bonds are not purchased unless the fund-of-funds investments shows a significant loss. The manager will constantly track the cost of the zero coupon bonds needed to guarantee the investment against loss. The cost of the bonds will rise over time, as there is less time to earn interest on the bonds until the approaching maturity date. The fund manager will constantly track the threshold, or the difference between the current value of the account and the funds needed to purchase a zero coupon bond to guarantee the investment. When the cushion of gains or time is large, the manager can allocate a large investment to hedge funds, perhaps even using leverage. As the value of the investment falls closer to the threshold, hedge fund assets are sold to reduce the risk of the portfolio. If, at any time, the value of the fund falls to the threshold value, the fund-of-funds assets are sold and the bonds are purchased. This shows that CPPI is a path-dependent strategy, as the fund is fully invested in bonds for the remaining life of the fund once the threshold value is hit. Once the stop loss is touched, all hedge fund investments are sold and the strategy reverts to a 100 percent bond allocation to ensure against future losses.

A much less complex, and less trading-intensive, version of this strategy simply allocates 100 percent of the fund's capital to fund-of-funds investments. The fund remains fully invested until the asset level hits the stop loss, where the value of the assets is equal to the cost of purchasing bonds to guarantee the principal value of the investment. Once the stop loss is hit, the fund is 100 percent invested in bonds until maturity. Again, this is a path-dependent strategy, as the fund will revert to bonds when hitting the stop loss. The fund could later post significant gains that investors will not receive, as they had sold their investments before the fund recovered to post more respectable performance. This all-or-nothing strategy has a higher probability of hitting the stop loss than the CPPI strategy, as this version is 100 percent invested in funds of funds until the stop loss is hit. CPPI is less likely to hit the stop loss, as the manager will significantly reduce hedge fund investments as losses are realized. It makes sense then, that the manager with a 50 percent allocation to hedge funds will have a smaller probability of hitting a dollar stop-loss level than a manager with a 100 percent allocation to the same fund.

Fund-of-funds managers may find guaranteed principal structures as an attractive source of new investment capital. These products can attract a different clientele than their traditional funds, as guaranteed products are attractive to investors who may perceive hedge fund investments to be risky. In some countries, retail investors are allowed to purchase guaranteed funds, even though they are not legally allowed to purchase the fund of funds embedded in these structured products.

COLLATERALIZED FUND OBLIGATIONS (CFOS)

For years, banks have sold asset-backed securities (ABS). These debt securities are backed by the principal and interest cash flows from their lending activities. By far, the largest market is for debt backed by mortgages on residential and commercial real estate. Other types of loans sold in these structured products have included mobile homes, automobiles, and credit cards. Lenders who sell mortgage-backed securities (MBS) and ABS are able to raise funds from investors, which can be used to increase the capital these lenders have available to attract new borrowers. For example, government agencies, such as Fannie Mae, have more debt out-standing than the U.S. Treasury. This sale of MBS has added trillions of dollars of lending capacity to the U.S. mortgage industry. The availability of investor capital in the MBS market has been widely credited in assisting with record levels of homeownership and the decline in mortgage interest rates.

ABS and MBS can have very complicated structures, which are designed to isolate most investors from the credit risks of the underlying borrowers. A common structure is overcollateralization, where the pool of loans is sold to different investors at different credit ratings. A $100 million pool of credit card loans may sell $70 million of debt that is rated AAA. This debt is sold at a very low interest rate and is generally regarded as free of default risk, as this pool of loans would have to lose $30 million to defaults before subjecting the owners of these high-grade bonds to losses from the underlying borrowers. A second tranche may be rated BBB, still investment grade, and carry a higher coupon rate. We can see why the $20 million of BBB has a significantly lower credit rating, as these bondholders are exposed to credit risk after only $10 million in defaults on the underlying loans. The final tranche will be an unrated equity tranche. This tranche will typically offer a much higher interest rate, as these buyers are assuming all of the credit risk in the $100 million pool of underlying loans. If the original lender does not retain the equity tranche, it will be sold to investors with a high ability to accept credit risk. Many hedge funds will purchase the high-risk, high-reward equity tranche, where they are paid to insure against the credit risk of all loans in the pool. MBS sold by government agencies may not have the same overcollateralization structure, as the credit losses may be insured by private mortgage insurers or by an implied guarantee of the U.S. government.

Traditional ABS and MBS can be called cash flow–backed obligations, as they are repaid from the principal and interest cash flows on the underlying loans. Market value collateralized obligations are the newest structure in the ABS market, which are backed by the value of underlying investments rather than by cash flows generated by a loan portfolio. The first collateralized fund obligation (CFO) was offered in May 2002 by Man Group, the world's largest fund-of-funds operator.

Mark Anson details the terms of the second-ever CFO issue, which was sold by the Diversified Strategies Fund.[7] This CFO raised $250 million, which was invested in the firm's fund-of-funds product. Standard and Poor rated $125 million, AAA; $32.5 million, A; and $26.2 million, BBB. The remaining $66.3 million was placed in an unrated equity tranche. Coupon payments on the rated tranches ranged from LIBOR + 60 to LIBOR + 250.

The 26.5 percent placed in the equity tranche is a much larger degree of overcollateralization than is typically seen in the traditional ABS market. This equity tranche is required to absorb all losses from the fund-of-funds investment, as well as to insure that sufficient coupon income is available to the rated tranches. In addition to the large size of the equity tranche, S&P also put several restrictions on the investments of the underlying funds. The rating agency wanted to ensure that the funds underlying this investment would be well diversified and relatively liquid, with a focus tilted toward lower-risk hedge fund strategies. First, S&P required that 20 percent of the funds be placed in separate accounts, where assets have their highest liquidity and are not subject to lock-up periods or waiting periods for redemption requests. Next, it required that the underlying fund of funds be invested in at least 25 different funds, following at least four different strategies. Lower-volatility, absolute-value hedge fund strategies were allowed a higher allocation, while higher-volatility, relative-value strategies were allowed at lower weights. Finally, once the equity tranche had lost all of its value, the hedge fund investments would be liquidated, with proceeds used to repay the owners of the rated tranches and liquidate the CFO.

Fund-of-funds operators can find CFOs to be a very attractive structure for a number of reasons. The most important, perhaps, is that once the CFOs are sold, the manager is able to retain those assets until the maturity of the structure, as long as the underlying hedge fund investments are profitable. This is a source of sticky assets, as investors will sell their CFOs to other investors rather than requesting a withdrawal from the fund manager. Once issuers have sold the CFO, they often continue to manage the fund of funds, and even some of the underlying hedge funds, which gives them the opportunity to earn management fees and incentive fees. Issuers may also keep a significant portion of the equity tranche, where they can retain a significant levered investment in the underlying funds. If the hedge fund investments earn a larger return than is owed to the owners of the rated tranches, then the owners of the equity tranche can earn significant returns.

As with many other structures, regulations can also add to the attractiveness of the CFO structure. CFOs are classified as bonds, not hedge funds, for regulatory reasons, which can widen the potential number of investors who can purchase these securities. While insurance companies may have difficulty convincing their regulators to allow them to invest in hedge funds, there will clearly be no issue purchasing investment-grade rated tranches of CFO issues.

EMERGING MARKETS HEDGE FUNDS

Most emerging markets managers will only purchase securities, as many young stock markets do not allow traders to short securities. The only hedging opportunities may be in American depository receipts (ADRs) listed on the U.S. stock markets or in the currency markets. However, these hedges can be extremely illiquid and expensive and can dramatically reduce the potential return to these investments.

Emerging markets managers may focus on Latin American or Asian markets, leveraging their specific experience or residence in a country with rapidly growing financial markets. In many markets, research may only be available in the local language, or to investors with personal contacts at the companies or in the markets. If a country has less transparent markets, or a focus on local accounting standards, the local manager will have a larger advantage in that market compared to international competitors. Regional managers may have an advantage, in that they can reallocate assets between countries within their region, depending on their view of relative returns within their region. Emerging markets managers have the ability to buy high-growth companies at value stock prices, but the market volatility in emerging regions can lead to extreme losses and low levels of liquidity.

Most emerging markets funds can only purchase securities, as short selling and options strategies are often not available in these less developed markets. Because it is difficult or impossible to hedge the risks of emerging markets investments, these hedge funds have volatility and correlations similar to those found in developed stock markets.

From January 1994 to June 2003, the CSFB/Tremont Emerging Markets Index returned an annual average of 7.80 percent, with a standard deviation of 18.17 percent and a Sharpe ratio of 0.19. (See Fig. 8-2.) This high volatility and low Sharpe ratio demonstrates the long-only nature of these funds. Emerging markets investments are subject to boom and bust cycles, with a 1998 return of −37.66 percent

FIGURE 8-2

CSFB/Tremont Emerging Markets Index performance, 1994 to 2003. (MSCI, reprinted by permission; TASS, CSFB/Tremont, http://www.hedgeindex.com.)

The CSFB/Tremont Emerging Markets Index measures the return to hedge fund managers investing in the stocks and bonds of emerging countries. Typically these hedge funds are long only, due to liquidity and short selling constraints in these nascent markets.

	CSFB/Tremont Emerging Markets
1994	12.50
1995	-16.90
1996	34.48
1997	26.57
1998	-37.66
1999	44.83
2000	-5.51
2001	5.85
2002	7.36
Annual Return	7.80
Annual Standard Deviation	18.17
Skewness	-0.58
Kurtosis	3.62
Sharpe Ratio	0.19
Sortino Ratio	0.31
Alpha vs. S&P 500	1.64
Beta vs. S&P 500	0.54
Alpha vs. MSCI World Debt	11.80
Beta vs. MSCI World Debt	-0.67
Best Monthly Return	16.42
Worst Monthly Return	-23.03
Best Annual Return	44.83
Worst Annual Return	-37.66
% Winning Months	57.0%

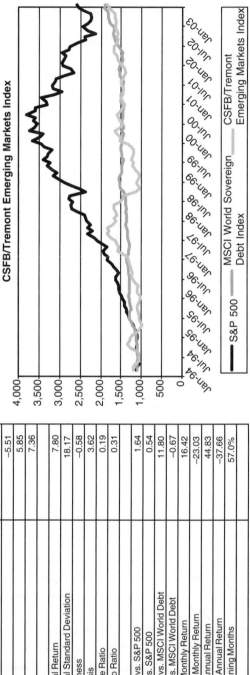

CSFB/Tremont Emerging Markets Index

S&P 500 — MSCI World Sovereign Debt Index — CSFB/Tremont Emerging Markets Index

FIGURE 8–2

Continued. (MSCI, reprinted by permission; TASS, CSFB/Tremont, http://www.hedgeindex.com.)

Distribution of one-month return

Correlation to	CSFB/Tremont Emerging Markets
TASS Fund of Funds	0.74
CSFB/Tremont Hedge Fund Index	0.65
CSFB/Tremont Convertible Arbitrage	0.32
CSFB/Tremont Ded Short Bias	-0.57
CSFB/Tremont Emerging Markets	1.00
CSFB/Tremont Equity Mkt Ntrl	0.23
CSFB/Tremont Event Driven	0.68
CSFB/Tremont Distressed	0.59
CSFB/Tremont E.D. Multi-Strategy	0.68
CSFB/Tremont Risk Arbitrage	0.42
CSFB/Tremont Fixed Inc Arb	0.30
CSFB/Tremont Global Macro	0.41
CSFB/Tremont Long/Short Equity	0.58
CSFB/Tremont Managed Futures	-0.14
CSFB/Tremont Multi-Strategy	-0.05
MSCI Discretionary Trading	0.54
MSCI Systematic Trading	-0.15
3 mo Tbills	-0.09
S&P 500	0.48
MSCI World Sovereign Bond	-0.23
Average to Hedge Fund Strategies	0.31
Average to Traditional Investments	0.05
Conditional Correlations	
S&P 500 Up Markets (71 mo)	0.14
S&P 500 Down Markets (43 mo)	0.50
MSCI Debt Up Markets (65 mo)	-0.15
MSCI Debt Down Markets (49 mo)	0.16

139

followed by a 1999 return of 44.83 percent. Many investors believe they can profit from emerging markets by owning these funds during bull markets, yet selling out before the inevitable crash occurs. Unfortunately, these are very small markets, which can be easily overwhelmed by investment flows from U.S. and European investors. Once the hot money starts to leave these markets, they tend to crash very quickly, as the size and liquidity of these markets aren't nearly sufficient to quickly redeem such large investments. Hedge funds in this category housed about 3.3 percent of hedge fund assets in 2001, up from 0.4 percent in 1990.

Emerging markets funds had an average correlation of 0.48 to the S&P 500 between 1994 and 2003. (See Fig. 8-3.) Unfortunately, the correlation to the S&P was 0.50 in down markets and only 0.14 in up markets. If investors are selling stocks in developed countries, they are also likely to be reducing their investments in emerging markets. We can better visualize this correlation between monthly returns by examining Figure 8-4.

Figure 8-5 clearly shows us that emerging markets offer little protection during times of declining prices in world equity markets.

FIGURE 8 – 3

CSFB/Tremont Emerging Markets Index: 24-month rolling correlation to traditional investments.

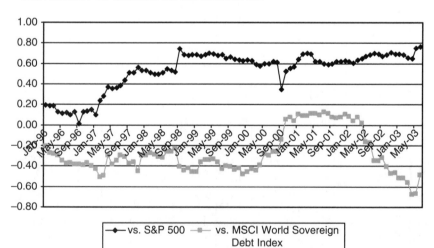

FIGURE 8−4

CSFB/Tremont Emerging Markets Index versus S&P 500: monthly return pairs, January 1994 to June 2003.

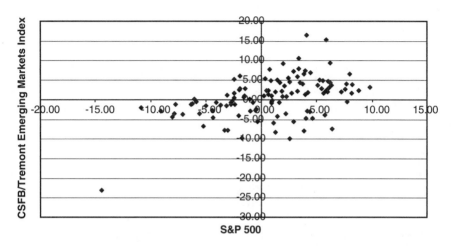

FIGURE 8−5

CSFB/Tremont Emerging Markets Index versus MSCI World Equity Index: monthly returns sorted by quintiles, January 1994 to June 2003.

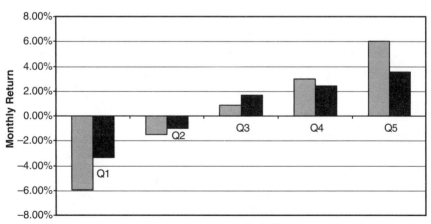

Whenever world equities decline, emerging markets funds are also likely to decline. When stocks worldwide increase in value, emerging markets investments will also grow in value, but at a much slower rate.

ENDNOTES

1. A. B. Colter, "Bermuda Boosting Oversight to Attract More Hedge Funds," *Wall Street Journal,* September 24, 2003.
2. M. Fothergill and C. Coke, "Funds of Hedge Funds: An Introduction to Multi-Manager Funds," *Journal of Alternative Investments* 4 (2001): 7–16.
3. S. McCrary, *How to Create and Manage a Hedge Fund: A Professional's Guide.* Hoboken, NJ: Wiley, 2002.
4. All country specific regulations are described in N. Dogniez, "Fund of Hedge Funds Regulation" in S. Jaffer (ed.), *Funds of Hedge Funds for Professional Investors and Managers.* London: Euromoney Books, 2003.
5. All insured products are described in B. F. Cole and C. M. Kailus, "Investing in Hedge Funds through Insurance Products" in S. Jaffer (ed.), *Funds of Hedge Funds for Professional Investors and Managers,* op. cit.
6. All guaranteed principal products are described in M. Mattoo, "Structured Alternative Investment Products" in S. Jaffer (ed.), *Funds of Hedge Funds for Professional Investors and Managers,* op. cit.
7. All CFO information is described in M. Anson, "Collateralized Fund Obligations" in S. Jaffer (ed.), *Funds of Hedge Funds for Professional Investors and Managers,* op. cit.

CHAPTER 9

Equity Hedge Fund Strategies

Equity hedge fund strategies are extremely popular. Undiscovered Managers estimates that 37.9 percent of all hedge fund assets are managed in long-short equity funds, with 5 percent in equity market–neutral and 11.3 percent in long-only equity funds. Many of the other categories, including event-driven, risk arbitrage, and convertible arbitrage, also include equity securities as part of a portion of their trading strategies. While most investors understand the purchase of stocks, many equity hedge fund managers spend a significant amount of effort on short sales of securities. We will take some extra time to analyze short selling because it is important as a hedge fund strategy and also because most investors are unfamiliar with it.

Managers who specialize in a specific sector can be long-only, long-short, or market-neutral managers. Some managers may be sector experts, confining their trading to only a small portion of the stocks available in a market. One example may be a trader with a background as a chemist, physician, or pharmacist who is able to separate the winners from the losers in the biotech and pharmaceutical sectors. Long-only funds, which often focus on a particular sector, are likely the most profitable hedge fund sector. Long-only sector funds can experience a high volatility of returns, which can lead to large gains for investors and large fees for fund managers. Of course, volatile funds may not be acceptable for some investors, especially those seeking absolute returns.

Because of their industry expertise, sector fund managers may be successful in distinguishing between successful and unsuccessful new products. They may also understand the implications of competitive changes in the industry and be able to forecast the next firm to be acquired or declare bankruptcy. These managers are in the best position to understand which catalysts will best contribute to the future growth prospects (or lack thereof) of each firm in a given industry.

These long-only managers purchase undervalued stocks in hopes that they will outperform the market. They may make decisions in a similar manner to market-neutral or long-short managers, but they don't typically hedge or short sell securities. Equity nonhedge funds have a similar return to long-short funds, but with significantly higher levels of risk.

SHORT SELLING

The short selling of stocks is a very different, and much less popular, process than the purchase of stocks. Even during the bear market of 2000 to 2002, the average stock on the NYSE and NASDAQ had less than 3 percent of its shares outstanding borrowed and sold short. The short seller must complete his or her own original research without relying on investment banking equity research departments, as most equity analysts publish a sell rating on less than 10 percent of their covered stocks.

When you own a stock, you have the ability to earn unlimited gains, and your losses are limited. Everyone wants to own the next Microsoft, while the most you can lose on a fully paid long-stock position is 100 percent. Managers who sell stock short face an opposite scenario, where they can earn limited gains, but experience unlimited losses. When you short the stock, the most you can gain is 100 percent, when the stock expires worthless. In unfortunate situations, especially Internet stocks in 1999, stocks can rise 500 percent or more in a year, leaving short sellers exposed to potentially large and catastrophic losses. It is important to implement a much stronger risk management policy when trading stocks from the short side. It is imperative that you limit your losses and not allow the stock to increase dramatically in value when you are short. You may wish to use options much more aggressively when trading short stocks. For example, if you have a 30 percent gain in a short position, you could purchase call options with perhaps one-third of that gain. You have now created a synthetic long put position, which locks in a portion of your profits and truncates the ability of the short position to post large losses, at least until the expiration of the option.

The first obstacle to executing the short sale of a stock is the uptick rule. In the United States, all orders to short sell a stock must be marked as a short sale and can only be executed on an uptick. You cannot sell a stock short at a price lower than the previous price, which means that you must wait for the price of the stock to rise since its previous trade. On the NASDAQ, short selling is allowed as long as the bid price is higher than the previous bid price. This prevents short sellers from staging a "bear raid," continuously selling stock on the bid price to drive the stock significantly lower.

It is extremely risky to use market orders to sell stock short. I have seen stocks fall continuously for over one hour, where a market order to sell long would be executed at a price 10 percent higher than the market order to sell short, which had to wait for the eventual uptick. To be safe, I would suggest a marketable limit order, placed perhaps 3 percent below the bid price of the stock. This ensures a fill if an uptick comes quickly, but avoids the much lower fills that can occur after a long series of consecutive downticks. In other markets, specifically in Europe, there is no uptick rule to make short selling more risky and more expensive.

In order to sell a stock short, you must first borrow the stock. Your broker must find an investor who owns the stock in a margin account and agrees to transfer the stock to your broker's firm. When you are short the borrowed stock, you must pay all dividends to the owner of the stock. In many cases, stocks may be placed on the "difficult to borrow" list. A manager may be unable to borrow a stock on this list, especially when the firm has a small market capitalization, heavy short interest, or a small number of publicly floating shares. Perhaps the most difficult situation that a short seller can experience is when your broker is unable to guarantee the continued borrow of the stock. If the person you borrowed the stock from decides to sell the stock, your broker must deliver the stock to complete that transaction. If your broker is unable to borrow the stock from another owner, you will be forced to buy back the stock, covering your short position at the current market price. When you own a stock that has been completely paid for, you can hold the stock indefinitely, and it is only sold when you decide to sell it. When you are short the stock, the stock can get "called away," meaning that you are unable to continue borrowing the stock. This lack of control over the timing of closing positions can be quite risky for the short seller, as the owners of the stock are more likely to sell, and force you to close your position, when the stock is rapidly rising in price.

When you short a stock, the proceeds of the sale of that stock are credited to your brokerage account, but are held as security against the short stock position. As the price of the stock falls, more funds are available for you to open new positions. Institutional investors are able to earn interest on the proceeds of short sales. This interest earned is called the "short stock rebate," which can be a significant source of return to short sellers. This interest rate is correlated to the risk-free rate, but lower interest rates may be earned when the manager is short stocks that are difficult to borrow.

Given the importance of the size and availability of the short stock rebate and stock borrowing, many short sellers consider the choice of their prime broker to be one of their most important decisions. When choosing a prime broker, short sellers are careful to choose the broker that pays the highest interest rate on short stock proceeds, pays interest on the highest portion of short stock positions, and is the most successful at borrowing stocks to sell short. You may also ask the broker how frequently his or her short sellers lose the ability to borrow the stock after executing a trade from the short side, as this is an indication of potential risk.

Kathryn Staley, in her excellent book *The Art of Short Selling*, gives us a number of important attributes of stocks that are likely to decline in price. Unfortunately, short selling is often a labor-intensive process, where the manager must ferret out secrets that firm managers want to keep hidden and focus on footnotes to accounting statements and cryptic notes in SEC filings.

The first sign that a stock is likely to decline in price is that the company is using nontraditional or aggressive accounting practices. A comprehensive treatment of the techniques for detecting accounting risk can be found in Howard Schilit's book *Financial Shenanigans: How to Detect Accounting Gimmicks and Fraud in Financial*

Reports. The techniques of accounting fraud are generally meant to overstate revenue, understate expenses, overvalue assets, or conceal the true extent of liabilities. Any time that an analyst has a conviction that improper accounting techniques are being used, it is fairly certain that the stock will decline in price once these gimmicks are revealed. Some particularly aggressive short sellers, such as Manuel Asensio, will publish their research to hasten corporate disclosure and cause other investors to sell the stock. The publication of short sellers' research can cause the eventual declines in the stock to come more quickly but can invite negative press and lawsuits from the target company.

The next sign of a good stock to short is insider greed and sleaze. If the managers of a firm are combative with analysts, earn unreasonable levels of compensation, or have conflicts of interest, they may not be running the company honestly and for the exclusive benefit of stockholders. When Enron was trading above $30 per share, short sellers already had detected conflicts of interests and special-purpose entities through their careful reading of the firm's SEC filings. The shorts became even more certain of their research when Enron's CEO refused to answer analyst questions about the transparency of the firm's financial statements.

Many short sellers will focus on the valuation of the stock. The higher the valuation of a stock relative to its competitors, the larger the potential returns to a short sale. Enron might be a good short at 6 times book value or 55 times earnings when Goldman Sachs was trading at 3 times book value and 20 times earnings and other energy and utility companies were trading at 2 times book value and 15 times earnings. Enron was overvalued relative to both trading companies and energy companies. A simple reversion to the average valuation in those industries would have earned significant returns for the short sellers.

Many short sellers are excellent accountants, and most of them focus on the cash flow statement and the balance sheet. One of the better short sales of 2002 was Edison Schools, a firm with a gluttonous appetite for cash. The firm has experienced negative cash flows from operations in every year since it became a public company. During that time, the firm repeatedly came back to Wall Street for new infusions of equity and debt capital. One of the quickest ways for a firm to go bankrupt, and provide large returns to short sellers, is to have a need for new cash and be denied new financing to continue its operations.

When reading the balance sheet, short sellers will be looking for overvalued assets or understated debt. A recent focus has been on the liability side, where investors are carefully searching for special-purpose entities and other off-balance-sheet financings that serve to reduce the amount of debt the firm reports on its financial statements. Overvalued assets can be found in a number of places, such as a technology company with obsolete inventory or a company that needs to write down the value of a failed merger.

Large and rising levels of short interest, exclusive of merger arbitrage activity, have been empirically proven to predict the future underperformance of a stock. Managers who short stock have typically completed much more research than those who have purchased stocks. The combination of short seller sentiment is seen in the short interest, the number of shares that have been borrowed and sold short. As more and more shorts understand the story, the larger the short interest becomes. Stocks that are difficult to borrow have extremely high levels of short interest and a significant probability of underperforming the market.

From January 1994 to June 2003, funds in the CSFB/Tremont Dedicated Short Bias index returned an annual average of 0.09 percent, with a standard deviation of 18.26 percent and a Sharpe ratio of −0.23. (See Fig. 9-1.) This is the lowest Sharpe ratio of all hedge fund categories, due to the style's low returns and high risk levels. Due to the large negative correlation between short funds and equity benchmarks, investments in these funds are meant as a hedge and are most appropriate when investors expect negative returns to equity markets. We would expect these funds to lose assets to more neutral or bullish funds when markets are expected to have large positive returns.

Figure 9-2 illustrates the correlation structure of short funds. Dedicated short bias funds have the largest negative correlation to equity markets of all hedge fund strategies, averaging −0.76 between 1994 and 2003. This includes a −0.48 conditional correlation in times of rising stock prices and a −0.57 conditional correlation when stock prices are falling. The average correlation is remarkably stable, ranging from −0.70 to −0.90 over the last five years.

CSFB/Tremont Dedicated Short Bias Index performance, 1994 to 2003. (MSCI, reprinted by permission; TASS, CSFB/Tremont, http://www.hedgeindex.com.)

The CSFB/Tremont Dedicated Short Bias Index measures the returns to hedge funds that consistently hold net short positions in equity securities.

CSFB/Tremont Dedicated Short Bias Index

	CSFB/Tremont Dedicated Short Bias
1994	14.91
1995	–7.37
1996	–5.48
1997	0.43
1998	–5.99
1999	–14.22
2000	15.77
2001	–3.58
2002	18.15
Annual Return	0.09
Annual Standard Deviation	18.26
Skewness	0.90
Kurtosis	2.10
Sharpe Ratio	–0.23
Sortino Ratio	–0.46
Alpha vs. S&P 500	9.46
Beta vs. S&P 500	–0.86
Alpha vs. MSCI World Debt	–1.09
Beta vs. MSCI World Debt	0.19
Best Monthly Return	22.71
Worst Monthly Return	–8.69
Best Annual Return	18.15
Worst Annual Return	–14.22
% Winning Months	47.4%

FIGURE 9-1

Continued. (MSCI, reprinted by permission; TASS, CSFB/Tremont, http://www.hedgeindex.com.)

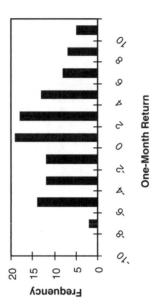

Distribution of one month returns

Correlation to	CSFB/Tremont Dedicated Short Bias
TASS Fund of Funds	-0.61
CSFB/Tremont Hedge Fund Index	-0.48
CSFB/Tremont Convertible Arbitrage	-0.23
CSFB/Tremont Ded Short Bias	1.00
CSFB/Tremont Emerging Markets	-0.57
CSFB/Tremont Equity Mkt Ntrl	-0.37
CSFB/Tremont Event Driven	-0.64
CSFB/Tremont Distressed	-0.63
CSFB/Tremont E.D. Multi-Strategy	-0.55
CSFB/Tremont Risk Arbitrage	-0.48
CSFB/Tremont Fixed Inc Arb	-0.09
CSFB/Tremont Global Macro	-0.13
CSFB/Tremont Long/Short Equity	-0.73
CSFB/Tremont Managed Futures	0.26
CSFB/Tremont Multi-Strategy	-0.03
MSCI Discretionary Trading	-0.48
MSCI Systematic Trading	0.22
3 mo Tbills	0.09
S&P 500	-0.76
MSCI World Sovereign Bond	0.06
Average to Hedge Fund Strategies	-0.33
Average to Traditional Investments	-0.20
Conditional Correlations	
S&P 500 Up Markets (71 mo)	-0.48
S&P 500 Down Markets (43 mo)	-0.57
MSCI Debt Up Markets (65 mo)	0.03
MSCI Debt Down Markets (49 mo)	-0.17

150

FIGURE 9-2

CSFB/Tremont Dedicated Short Bias Index: 24-month rolling correlation to traditional investments.

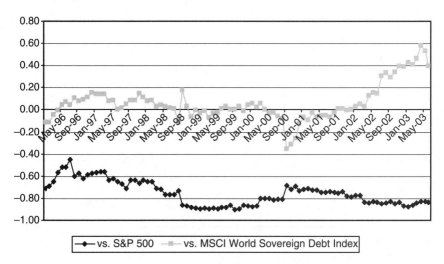

The scatter plot found in Figure 9-3 shows the strong negative correlation pattern between short bias funds and the S&P 500. There are few outliers in this plot, showing that the returns to short bias funds are quite predictable once the return to the equity market is known. You can also see that the percentage of winning months in this strategy is the lowest among all hedge fund strategies, 47.4 percent.

Perhaps the most redeeming quality of short funds is their positive skewness of 0.90. Because stock markets tend to decline more quickly than they rise, and short funds have a strong negative correlation to stock prices, the largest returns to short bias funds tend to be on the profitable side. This inverse relationship is also illustrated in Figure 9-4, where the gains to short stock funds during falling stock markets are much larger than the losses these funds post in the strongest bull markets.

Many managers prefer to short stocks because they feel that this is a less efficient market sector. If all investors and analysts are searching for undervalued stocks, there are likely to be very few stocks that are undervalued by a wide margin. If only 3 percent of investors short stocks, there is a much higher probability that short sellers can find overvalued stocks, as fewer investors are researching and trading from the short side.

FIGURE 9−3

CSFB/Tremont Dedicated Short Bias Index versus S&P 500: monthly return pairs, January 1994 to June 2003.

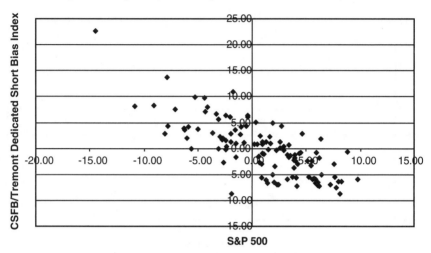

FIGURE 9−4

CSFB/Tremont Dedicated Short Bias Index versus S&P 500: monthly returns sorted by quintiles, January 1994 to June 2003.

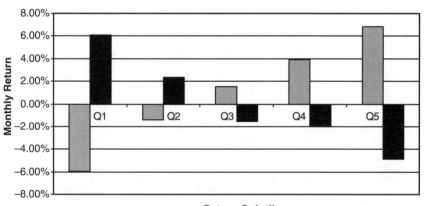

Short sellers contribute to improved market efficiency and liquidity. Shorts sell stocks at high prices and buy stocks at low prices, reducing stock price volatility and providing improved liquidity to investors who trade on the price momentum of stocks. Shorts improve market efficiency by reducing the potential overvaluation of stocks and publishing independent research that is often contrary to the reports published by investment banking analysts.

Given the weak history of these funds, there are few surviving funds that exclusively short stocks. The bull market of the 1990s made dedicated short selling a tough and risky business. At the end of 2001, dedicated short selling funds held only 0.1 percent of total hedge fund assets. If the bear market of 2000 to 2002 continues, we would expect a comeback of aggressive and dedicated short sellers. However, it is likely that we will see more short biased funds, which are long-short equity funds with a consistent short bias. Because it is difficult to have a fund that only shorts stocks, many funds will carry both long and short stock positions. In fact, long-short equity funds are the most popular hedge fund strategy, controlling 37.9 percent of all hedge fund assets at the end of 2001.

LONG-SHORT EQUITY FUNDS

Long-short equity hedge funds both buy and short sell stocks, with the ability to adjust their positions given their views on the direction of the equity market. Ideally, these funds would have net long positions when stocks are rising, and net short positions when stock prices are in a bear market. For managers with market-timing skill, long-short equity funds provide the strategy where they can best take advantage of their skill. On average, the CSFB/Tremont Long-Short Equity Index has a beta exposure to the S&P 500 of 0.41, demonstrating that these funds typically carry a net long position. A typical long-short fund, then, would have an average long position of 100 percent of assets and a short position of 59 percent of assets. This would result in a beta of 0.41 and a mild 59 percent leverage factor.[1]

Funds tracked by the CSFB/Tremont Long-Short Equity Index have been quite successful over the last nine years. (See Fig. 9-5.) Funds in this strategy posted average annual returns of 12.47 percent after fees, with a risk of 11.27 percent and a Sharpe ratio of 0.72. These managers are providing significant value to investors

F I G U R E 9 – 5

CSFB/Tremont Long-Short Equity Index performance, 1994 to 2003. (MSCI, reprinted by permission; TASS, CSFB/Tremont, http://www.hedgeindex.com.)

The CSFB/Tremont Long/Short Equity Index measures the return to hedge funds that invest in equity securities. These funds are typically not fully hedged, so they may hold substantial net long or net short positions. These funds may also take significant exposures to a given sector, market capitalization, or value vs. growth.

	CSFB/Tremont Long/Short Equity
1994	–8.10
1995	23.03
1996	17.14
1997	21.46
1998	17.19
1999	47.22
2000	2.08
2001	–3.67
2002	–1.60
Annual Return	12.47
Annual Standard Deviation	11.27
Skewness	0.22
Kurtosis	3.19
Sharpe Ratio	0.72
Sortino Ratio	1.47
Alpha vs. S&P 500	7.38
Beta vs. S&P 500	0.41
Alpha vs. MSCI World Debt	11.62
Beta vs. MSCI World Debt	0.03
Best Monthly Return	13.01
Worst Monthly Return	–11.43
Best Annual Return	47.22
Worst Annual Return	–8.10
% Winning Months	64.9%

CSFB/Tremont Long/Short Equity Index

Legend: S&P 500 — MSCI World Sovereign Debt Index — CSFB/Tremont Long/Short Equity Index

Continued. (MSCI, reprinted by permission; TASS, CSFB/Tremont, http://www.hedgeindex.com.)

Distribution of one-month returns

Correlation to	CSFB/Tremont Long/Short Equity
TASS Fund of Funds	0.85
CSFB/Tremont Hedge Fund Index	0.78
CSFB/Tremont Convertible Arbitrage	0.26
CSFB/Tremont Ded Short Bias	–0.73
CSFB/Tremont Emerging Markets	0.58
CSFB/Tremont Equity Mkt Ntrl	0.35
CSFB/Tremont Event Driven	0.65
CSFB/Tremont Distressed	0.57
CSFB/Tremont E.D. Multi-Strategy	0.63
CSFB/Tremont Risk Arbitrage	0.49
CSFB/Tremont Fixed Inc Arb	0.21
CSFB/Tremont Global Macro	0.43
CSFB/Tremont Long/Short Equity	1.00
CSFB/Tremont Managed Futures	–0.08
CSFB/Tremont Muliti-Strategy	0.13
MSCI Discretionary Trading	0.48
MSCI Systematic Trading	–0.02
3 mo Tbills	0.11
S&P 500	0.58
MSCI World Sovereign Bond	0.02
Average to Hedge Fund Strategies	0.33
Average to Traditional Investments	0.24
Conditional Correlations	
S&P 500 Up Markets (71 mo)	0.25
S&P 500 Down Markets (43 mo)	0.40
MSCI Debt Up Markets (65 mo)	0.05
MSCI Debt Down Markets (49 mo)	0.25

who choose these funds over an investment in the S&P 500, which offered returns of 11.46 percent, with an annual standard deviation of returns of 16.11 percent and a Sharpe ratio of 0.44.

Long-short equity funds have an average correlation of 0.58 to the S&P 500, the highest among all hedge fund strategies presented in this book. The conditional correlations are relatively unfavorable, averaging 40 percent in down markets and only 25 percent in periods of rising stock prices. Figure 9-6 gives us the idea that managers may have reduced their net long positions during the bear market of 2000 to 2002. During these three years, long-short funds nearly broke even, largely avoiding the carnage inflicted on the U.S. equity markets.

Figure 9-7 shows that long-short equity funds post profits in 64.9 percent of all months, a slight improvement to the S&P 500, which gained in 62.3 percent of the time. Figure 9-8 shows that long-short funds lose only one-third as much as the stock market in the most bearish times, while gaining more than one-half of the increase in the equity index during the strongest periods for stock prices. Funds in this style tend to have positive skewness (0.22), much better than the negative skewness (-0.60) of the S&P 500. The ability to avoid losses in the weakest stock markets shows up clearly in this statistic.

FIGURE 9—6

CSFB/Tremont Long-Short Equity Index: 24-month rolling correlation to traditional investments.

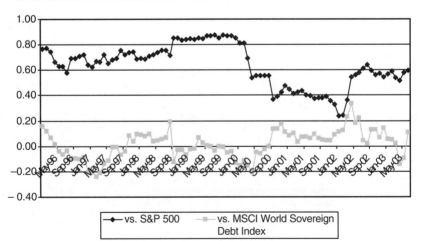

FIGURE 9-7

CSFB/Tremont Long-Short Equity Index versus S&P 500:
monthly return pairs, January 1994 to June 2003.

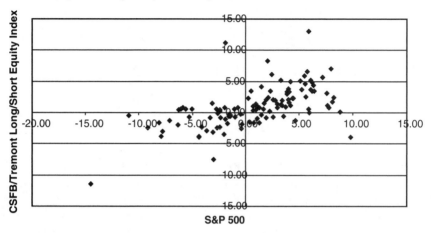

FIGURE 9-8

CSFB/Tremont Long-Short Equity Index versus S&P 500:
monthly returns sorted by quintiles, January 1994 to June 2003.

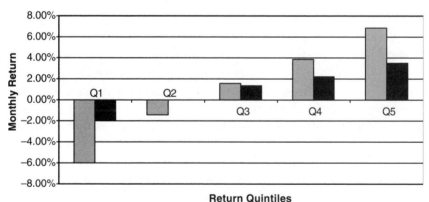

Because investors in long-short equity funds are generally tolerant of higher volatility investments, managers in these hedge funds may not carefully match the characteristics of their long and their short positions. If the manager has a view that small stocks are undervalued or growth stocks are overvalued, they may fill their long portfolio with small value stocks, while selling short large-capitalization growth stocks. If their style timing is accurate, these funds will perform very well. However, taking risks relative to the sector, industry, size, or value characteristics of a portfolio can significantly increase the volatility of a fund.

EQUITY MARKET-NEUTRAL FUNDS

Equity market–neutral funds are by far the most successful hedge fund strategy tracked by the CSFB/Tremont Hedge Fund Index when measured by the Sharpe ratio. (See Fig. 9-9.) From January 1994 to September 2002, funds in this category returned 10.86 percent, with a standard deviation of 3.14 percent and a Sharpe ratio of 2.07. This Sharpe ratio is more than double that of the entire hedge fund index, helped by an ultra stable time series of returns. These funds held 5 percent of all hedge fund assets at the end of 1998.

CSFB defines this investment strategy as being "designed to exploit equity market inefficiencies and usually involves being simultaneously long and short matched equity portfolios of the same size within a country. Market neutral portfolios are designed to be either beta or currency neutral, or both. Well-designed portfolios typically control for industry, sector, market capitalization, and other exposures. Leverage is often applied to enhance returns."[2]

Market-neutral funds separate stock picking from asset allocation decisions. A manager who only buys stocks can show positive returns simply because the stock market is rising. A market-neutral manager can only show positive returns when the stocks he buys outperform the stocks he has sold short. This means that a market-neutral fund manager can only be successful when he demonstrates skill in picking stocks. Many long-only managers may focus on their benchmark, perhaps owning the same percentage of energy stocks as the index. Market-neutral managers hedge all risks and therefore have no need to follow the benchmark.

In fact, some sectors are less lucrative than others for the market-neutral managers. In order for a manager to earn returns from market-neutral trades, there must be a significant return difference between the top and bottom performing stocks in a sector. In sectors where there is significant external price risk, such as energy, chemicals, or metals, there may not be enough spread between the returns to stocks in the sector to interest the market-neutral manager.

FIGURE 9-9

CSFB/Tremont Equity Market–Neutral Index performance, 1994 to 2003. (MSCI, reprinted by permission; TASS, CSFB/Tremont, http://www.hedgeindex.com.)

The CSFB/Tremont Equity Market Neutral Index measures the return to hedge funds that invest in both long and short equity securities. Due to their attempt to match the beta, sector exposures, market capitalization, and growth/value exposures of their long to their short positions, these funds feature very low volatilities and high Sharpe ratios.

CSFB/Tremont Equity Market Neutral Index

	CSFB/Tremont Equity Market Neutral
1994	-2.02
1995	11.04
1996	16.60
1997	14.82
1998	13.32
1999	15.32
2000	14.98
2001	9.30
2002	7.44
Annual Return	10.86
Annual Standard Deviation	3.14
Skewness	0.13
Kurtosis	0.18
Sharpe Ratio	2.07
Sortino Ratio	8.02
Alpha vs. S&P 500	9.50
Beta vs. S&P 500	0.08
Alpha vs. MSCI World Debt	10.20
Beta vs. MSCI World Debt	0.03
Best Monthly Return	3.26
Worst Monthly Return	-1.15
Best Annual Return	16.60
Worst Annual Return	-2.02
% Winning Months	83.3%

FIGURE 9-9

Continued. *(MSCI, reprinted by permission; TASS, CSFB/Tremont, http://www.hedgeindex.com.)*

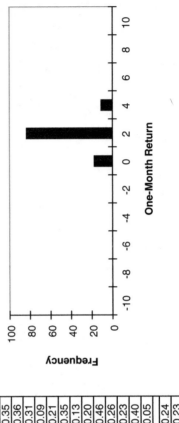

Distribution of one-month returns

	CSFB/Tremont Equity Market Neutral
Correlation to	
TASS Fund of Funds	0.45
CSFB/Tremont Hedge Fund Index	0.33
CSFB/Tremont Convertible Arbitrage	0.31
CSFB/Tremont Ded Short Bias	−0.37
CSFB/Tremont Emerging Markets	0.23
CSFB/Tremont Equity Mkt Ntrl	1.00
CSFB/Tremont Event Driven	0.38
CSFB/Tremont Distressed	0.35
CSFB/Tremont E.D. Multi-Strategy	0.36
CSFB/Tremont Risk Arbitrage	0.31
CSFB/Tremont Fixed Inc Arb	0.09
CSFB/Tremont Global Macro	0.21
CSFB/Tremont Long/Short Equity	0.35
CSFB/Tremont Managed Futures	0.13
CSFB/Tremont Multi-Strategy	0.20
MSCI Discretionary Trading	0.46
MSCI Systematic Trading	0.26
3 mo Tbills	0.23
S&P 500	0.40
MSCI World Sovereign Bond	0.05
Average to Hedge Fund Strategies	0.24
Average to Traditional Investments	0.23
Conditional Correlations	
S&P 500 Up Markets (71 mo)	0.31
S&P 500 Down Markets (43 mo)	0.21
MSCI Debt Up Markets (65 mo)	0.28
MSCI Debt Down Markets (49 mo)	−0.10

A market-neutral portfolio may simply be a combination of a number of pairs trades. In each paired trade, the manager selects one long and one short stock. Ideally the long stock will rise in value and the short stock will experience falling prices, leading to a positive return that is uncorrelated to the direction of the equity market. The pairs are designed to have a high correlation, meaning that both stocks are often of the same market capitalization and industry or sector membership. It would not be possible to reduce annual volatility to 3.14 percent if the long and the short positions were not highly correlated. These funds have clearly taken steps to reduce their risk exposures to sector, industry, market capitalization, and value versus growth. Most funds will attempt to have a similar beta (or similar dollar amount) of their long and short positions, which can be seen in a net beta of 0.08 to the S&P 500.

A good example of a paired trade may be between Best Buy and Circuit City, two U.S. home electronics retailers. Assume Best Buy trades at 40 times trailing earnings, even after a negative earnings surprise and a price decline of 30 percent. Their competitor, Circuit City, has already reported earnings and trades at 20 times earnings. The manager may buy CC and short BBY, in the hopes that the valuation will converge. Note that these two stocks are in the same business, are of similar size, and have the same factors affecting their profitability. The market-neutral manager only needs the valuation of the two firms to converge, so she doesn't care whether that convergence comes from a decline in the price of the stock she has shorted or from an increase in price of the stock she has purchased.

Market-neutral funds are the least volatile of all hedge fund strategies. Because of this low volatility, many investors will leverage their investment in these funds or trade with a futures overlay. The goal of a market-neutral portfolio is to earn the risk-free rate (from the short stock rebate), an alpha from the long stock selections, and an alpha from the short stock selections. An equitized investment in a market-neutral fund will include the hedge fund investment and the purchase of equity index futures. If the manager is truly providing alpha, many investors will prefer to add this alpha to the return on stocks, rather than to the return of risk-free securities. In fact, a good market-neutral manager may allow his "transportable alpha" to enhance the return of any asset class. The market-neutral manager can outperform the Japanese stock market or the U.S. Treasury bond market simply by purchasing the appropriate futures contract in addition to pairs trading. Most market-neutral funds have leverage at or less than two times their equity capital, so there are significant resources available to use for margins on the long futures positions.

Long futures contracts are a good match for market-neutral portfolios. Long futures positions require additional margin as prices fall, which is exactly when the gains to short positions increase the equity in an account. Similarly, the gains from long futures contracts in rising markets can be used to offset the rising margin requirements as the short stock positions are losing money. Market-neutral funds with a futures overlay do not require rebalancing of positions due to margin requirements, as the change in futures margin is expected to closely offset the margin needed for the short sales.

Without the futures overlay, a market-neutral portfolio will require rebalancing due to changes in the margin on short sales. This will allow an increase in the size or number of positions when the market is falling. As the market is rising, the short positions will require extra margin, which will cause the manager to reduce the size or number of trades. Most managers will open long positions with 90 percent of their capital, and short positions with 90 percent of their capital, which gives an unlevered fund open positions of 1.8 times their total capital. Managers within a broker-dealer may be allowed to use leverage of up to six times their total capital.

Risk management is extremely important to market-neutral managers. The fund strives to remain neutral to as many risk factors as possible, which allows them to focus on earning returns from their skillful stock selection. However, there are many questions about the proper way to measure and manage the market neutrality of a fund.

First, the dollars of long positions should equal the dollars of short positions. Equity funds should have zero beta exposure, and market-neutral bond funds should have zero duration exposure. Of course, every day of market movements conspires to move your fund away from a market-neutral position. Managers who trade in multiple countries will try to keep a currency-neutral position in each country. If the fund was net long Japanese stocks and net short Korean stocks, this could create a higher volatility fund that could be correlated to equity and currency markets.

There are many other risks inherent in equity market–neutral funds. Consider a trade that is long IBM and short Amazon.com. Even though this trade may be dollar-neutral, sector-neutral and beta-neutral, there are still several exposures in this trade. While both of these firms may be in the computer sector, one is an Internet retailer, while the other is a hardware manufacturer. If these specific industries have different returns, the risk of the portfolio could increase. Amazon.com has a much smaller market cap than IBM, which can affect the portfolio in times when the return to small stocks is significantly different than the return to large stocks. Finally, Amazon.com is a high-growth stock with negative earnings, while IBM is a slower growth company with many characteristics of a value stock. When value and growth have different returns and volatilities, this can also create issues in the portfolio. The better matched your long and short positions, the lower the risk, and the lower the likely return. The more trades like AMZN/IBM you have in your portfolio, the higher your risks and the higher your potential returns.

The CSFB/Tremont Equity Market–Neutral Index has an average correlation to the S&P 500 of 0.40, with conditional correlations of 0.21 in down markets and 0.31 in up markets. (See Fig. 9-10.) The

FIGURE 9–10

CSFB/Tremont Equity Market–Neutral Index: 24-month rolling correlation to traditional investments.

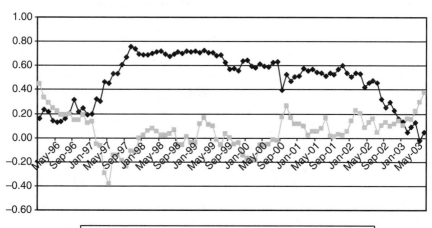

relatively low correlation can be seen from the scatter plot shown in Figure 9-11. Market-neutral equity funds profit in an astounding 83.3 percent of all months, far surpassing the S&P, which gains in 62.3 percent of all months. Perhaps the most important statistic for these funds is that the largest monthly loss is -1.15 percent, while the worst annual return is a loss of -2.02 percent. Clearly these hedge fund managers have created an attractive money machine, capable of earning nearly 1 percent per month in profits, net of fees, with extremely low risk. The distribution of the returns to this strategy is nearly normal, with skewness of 0.13 and kurtosis of only 0.18.

The consistency of returns can be seen in Figure 9-12, where equity market–neutral funds show positive returns in all equity market return patterns.

Capacity is an important concern of the market-neutral or short-selling manager. Because many managers may have correlated ideas for short-selling stocks, and the ability to borrow and sell short stocks is limited, managers will try to keep a high level of secrecy in their operations. Managers with the largest number of short stock positions, or with the largest number of small-cap stock positions, should be the quickest to close their fund to new investors. These managers are likely to close their fund before assets reach $100

FIGURE 9–11

CSFB/Tremont Equity Market–Neutral Index versus S&P 500: monthly return pairs, January 1994 to June 2003.

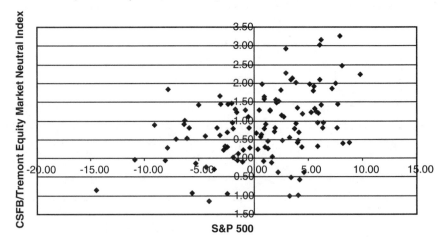

FIGURE 9-12

CSFB/Tremont Equity Market–Neutral Index versus S&P 500: monthly returns sorted by quintiles, January 1994 to June 2003.

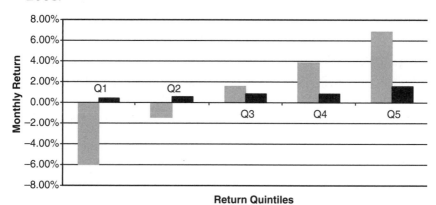

Return Quintiles

S&P 500   CSFB/Tremont Equity Market Neutral Index

FIGURE 9-13

Capitalization size in equity strategies. *(MSCI, reprinted by permission.)*

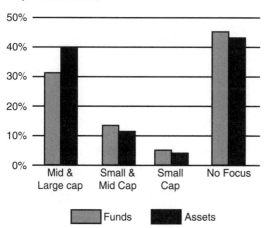

Funds   Assets

million, as a $1 billion fund that shorts stocks or trades small-caps would be quite unmanageable. As you can see from Figure 9-13, over 15 percent of equity hedge funds have an exclusive focus on small- and mid-cap stocks, while over 40 percent of funds may mix small- and mid-cap stocks with other larger-capitalization holdings.

Hedge funds trade small- and mid-cap stocks much more frequently than most other investors, which means that many managers are accepting liquidity risk in their equity hedge funds. The more the fund focuses on smaller stocks, the more it should be concerned about the capacity and liquidity of the fund.

ENDNOTES

1. These strategies are discussed in more detail in J. G. Nicholas, *Market Neutral Investing: Long/Short Hedge Fund Strategies.*
2. Viewed at CSFB/Tremont Web site, http://www.hedgeindex.com.

CHAPTER 10

The Building Blocks of Fixed-Income Trading

THE YIELD CURVE

Many fixed-income arbitrage strategies require an intimate knowledge of the yield curve. Also called the *term structure of interest rates,* we can simply graph the yields to Treasury securities ordered by maturity. The shape and slope of this graph can be the basis of a number of different types of hedge fund trades. While many fund managers will have no exposure to changes in the general level of interest rates, they may take massive bets based on an anticipated change in the yield curve (Fig. 10-1).

An inverted yield curve is a relatively infrequent, but very important occurrence. When short-term interest rates exceed long-term interest rates, it is likely that the Central Bank is tightening monetary policy. These restrictive actions are usually meant to slow down high levels of economic growth in order to control the level of price inflation. Inverted yield curves, therefore, usually precede significant economic slowdowns or recessions.

When yield curves are inverted, many traders will place a flattening trade, betting that short-term interest rates will fall and/or long-term interest rates will rise. In order to implement this view, the fund can purchase short-term bills or notes and sell short long-term notes or bonds. This trade should be duration-neutral, or volatility-balanced, so that there will be no profit or loss from the trade if there is a parallel shift in the yield curve. A parallel shift in

FIGURE 10−1

Yield curves.

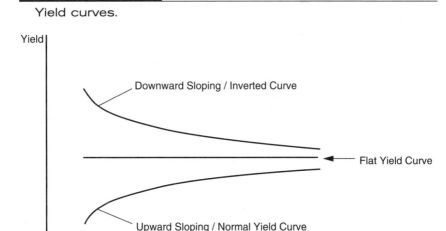

the yield curve occurs when interest rates change by the same amount across the yield curve, where the slope remains unchanged. If a trader buys 2-year notes and sells 10-year notes, he may need to purchase over four times the value of notes as he sells, which will equate price volatility between the long and short positions.

When the curve is inverted, fixed-income positions will have to be financed at negative carry. Negative carry occurs when the cost of financing the position exceeds the coupon income earned from the purchased securities. For example, if short-term interest rates dictate that a position can be financed at an 8 percent annual rate of interest, and long-term securities pay interest at a 5 percent annual rate, the position will have a negative cash flow of 3 percent per year. In order for this trade to be profitable, the fund needs interest rates to fall. The bet, therefore, is that the cost of financing the position will fall or that the long-term security will rise by over 3 percent in price over each year of the trade. As the trader must pay for every day that he stays with a negative carry position, we may find that the number of traders borrowing to finance positions in times of high short-term interest rates may be very small.

A flat yield curve is found when interest rates are relatively equal across all maturities.

An upward sloping yield curve is also called a normal-yield curve, as interest rates generally assume this shape. Interest rates frequently increase with the maturity of the security in order to compensate long-term investors for the long time to maturity and the larger level of interest rate risk that accompanies these securities.

Hedge fund managers may be expected to reach their maximum profitability when the yield curve has its steepest slope. For example, in late 2003, 10-year U.S. Treasury securities yielded 4.5 percent, with coupons as high at 6.5 percent, when short-term interest rates were less than 1 percent. This creates a positive carry trade. The more traders borrow, the more they can be expected to profit. If you borrow at 1 percent and invest the proceeds at 4.5 percent, you are earning positive carry at an annual rate of 3.5 percent. This can tempt hedge fund managers to increase their leverage, which can lead to astounding profits if interest rates continue to fall. As long as interest rates fall or remain stable, your profits grow the more you borrow and invest. However, we know that longer maturity securities also have higher levels of interest rate risk. If the yields on 10-year Treasuries increased by 1 percent to 5.5 percent, the notes are expected to lose over 7 percent in value, wiping out two years of positive carry. If the trader has high leverage when yields increase sharply, the losses are magnified by increased borrowings.

THE REPURCHASE MARKET

One of the most important skills of hedge fund managers may be in knowing how to properly finance their positions. Futures have a significant degree of natural leverage, as the exchange may only require a performance margin of 5 to 10 percent of the notional value of the contract. Retail stock investors are allowed 2-to-1 leverage when they borrow the maximum 50 percent of the trade value from their broker by opening a margin account. In fixed-income trading, the repurchase market allows financing of positions, usually by requesting a collateralized loan from a major bank or bond dealer. Leverage available in the repurchase market can be extremely high, in some cases allowing investors to finance 100 percent of new bond purchases.

The repurchase, or repo, market allows large investors to borrow money to finance the purchase of fixed-income securities. In order to access this market, the trader contacts the bank or bond dealer to arrange a short-term collateralized loan, usually in an amount exceeding $10 million. Technically, the trader borrows money from the bank and sends high-quality fixed-income securities to the bank as collateral. The trader then promises to repurchase the securities at a fixed date in the future at a fixed price. For example, a repo agreement can be arranged at a 1 percent annual interest rate with a fixed term of four weeks. At the end of the four weeks, the trader repurchases the securities at 100 percent of the loan amount, while adding 1/13 of 1 percent, or 0.0769 percent, to pay the interest due on the financing transaction. In practice, many traders will continually roll over their loans, agreeing to a new interest rate and a new transaction at the end of each day, each week, or each month, depending on the maturities available and their view on interest rates.

Notice that the price of redeeming the securities is fixed in advance and is not related to the actual value of the collateral at the end of the repurchase term. If interest rates rise, the collateral will fall in value. This makes the loan less secure, and the bank increases its credit risk to the trader. If interest rates decline, the collateral becomes more valuable, creating counterparty risk to the fund manager.

Generally, repo agreements are very short term in nature. While the positive carry trade is very attractive, borrowing at 1 percent to invest in notes yielding 4.5 percent, the borrowing rate cannot be locked in for long periods of time. This positive-carry trade can become unprofitable in a hurry if interest rates rise. Consider the losses that can be sustained if the borrowing rate rises to 3 percent while the note yield rises to 6 percent in a short time period. Not only is the trader losing money on his long note investment, he is also paying higher financing costs on his position.

Different securities may have different financing rates in the repo market. The lowest rates are generally reserved for the most liquid collateral, such as short-term U.S. Treasury securities. It is likely that less liquid or more risky bonds, such as corporate bonds or mortgage-backed securities, will have to be financed at higher interest rates, in order to compensate the bank for the higher probability that the collateral will be insufficient to repay the loan at the end of the repurchase term.

Consider the example of Robert Kessler, manager of the $1.2 billion Kessler Investment Advisers.[1] Since 1989, the firm has delivered average annual returns of 13.3 percent, beating the average long-term U.S. government bond fund by nearly 4 percent a year. In 2002, his fund returned 24 percent after fees, far in excess of the average bond fund's 16.2 percent.

Kessler can offer returns to investors that exceed the returns to Treasury securities, even without taking additional interest rate risk. Assume that 3-year Treasuries yield 2.5 percent while 10-year Treasuries yield 4.5 percent. The long-only investor could invest $10 million in 10-year Treasuries to earn 4.5 percent. Kessler can buy $30 million 3-year securities with an initial investment of $10 million and borrow $20 million in the repo market. Given that 3-year securities have only one-third the interest rate risk of 10-year securities, the interest rate risk of the two positions is equal. However, the leverage obtained in the repo market increases the yield on the notional investment. Earning 2.5 percent interest on $30 million in securities is like earning 7.5 percent interest on $10 million in securities. After subtracting costs of financing these positions in the repo market, the net yield can exceed 6 percent, a dramatic increase in yield relative to the long-only scenario, even without increasing interest rate risk.

As you can see, the profits of leveraged strategies increase with the steepness of the yield curve. When the yield curve is very steep, short-term financing rates are very low compared to the interest rates available on longer-term investments. As the difference between long-term yields and the short-term financing costs increase, the profits to a repo-financed bond position also increase.

The record low federal funds rate prevailing in 2003 has allowed some of the most profitable carry trades in recent memory. Any time you can borrow at 1 percent and invest in 10-year Treasuries with yields exceeding 4 percent, the profit opportunities are tremendous. Of course, you want yields to remain stable or fall, as the risk of rising interest rates can lead to falling bond prices, which can wipe out your profits from the positive carry trade.

In such a positive-yield curve environment, a trader can borrow at lower short-term rates and earn a higher coupon on the longer-term note. This positive carry situation, where it is profitable to finance notes in the repo market, will cause those with short futures positions to deliver the notes toward the end of the delivery period.

The opposite occurs during times of a negative, or inverted-yield, curve, when short rates are higher than long rates. In this situation, deliveries will tend to be concentrated earlier in the delivery period, for it is not profitable for the trader to hold a negative carry position any longer than he has to. The short chooses which notes to deliver and when to deliver that note. This is of value to the trader with the short futures position. We can call this option the switch option or the strategic delivery option. This option value increases with the volatility of interest rates and the probability of a change in the cheapest to deliver note. Because the seller of the future earns this valuable delivery option, we would expect futures to trade at a lower price than if the contract did not contain this potential arbitrage opportunity.[2]

DURATION

How can we calculate that the 10-year Treasury notes have three times the interest rate risk of 3-year Treasury notes? How can we know that the interest rate risk of our short positions is equal to the interest rate risk of our long positions, leaving our profits unchanged after a parallel shift in the yield curve? The answer lies in the most popular measure of interest rate risk, duration.[3]

Duration measures the sensitivity of a bond price to a change in yields, which varies with the maturity date, coupon rate, and yield of the bond. Duration can be interpreted as the weighted average time that it takes for the investor to receive the promised cash flows of the bond. Cash flows received in the near future have a lower weight, while distant cash flows have a much larger weight in the duration calculation.

An understanding of the time-weighting factor in duration can yield several intuitive properties. The longest possible duration for a bond will be the maturity of the bond. The duration will only be equal to the maturity when there are no cash flows received before maturity, which is the case for a zero coupon bond. Therefore, a zero coupon bond has a duration equal to its maturity. Bonds that pay interest before maturity will have a duration shorter than the maturity of the bond. For two bonds with a similar maturity, the bond with the higher coupon payment will have a shorter duration, as the higher coupon payments mean that the average cash flows are received at an earlier time.

The formula for Macaulay duration is the sum of the weighted average time to receive the cash flows, multiplied by the value of each cash flow, and divided by the price of the bond.

$$\text{Macaulay duration} = D = \frac{\displaystyle\sum_{t=1}^{n} \frac{C_t(t)}{(1+i)^t}}{\displaystyle\sum_{t=1}^{n} \frac{C_t}{(1+i)^t}}$$

The Macaulay duration of a three-year security, with a 3 percent semiannual coupon, priced at par of $1000, yielding 6 percent can be calculated as follows:

Time (years)	Cash Flow	Present Value	Time	×	Cash Flow	×	Present Value	=	Subtotal
0.5	$30 coupon	1/(1.03)	0.5	×	30	×	0.9709	=	14.56
1.0	$30	1/(1.03)²	1.0	×	30	×	0.9456	=	28.28
1.5	$30	1/(1.03)³	1.5	×	30	×	0.9151	=	41.18
2.0	$30	1/(1.03)⁴	2.0	×	30	×	0.8885	=	53.31
2.5	$30	1/(1.03)⁵	2.5	×	30	×	0.8626	=	64.70
3.0	$30	1/(1.03)⁶	3.0	×	30	×	0.8375	=	75.37
3.0	$1000 maturity	1/(1.03)⁶	3.0	×	30	×	0.8375	=	2512.45

The sum of these values is equal to 2789.85. Divide this value by the price of $1000 to find the Macaulay duration of 2.79 years. Once we know the Macaulay duration, which is the weighted average time to cash flows, we will need to calculate the modified duration of the bond and then take one more step to be able to determine the bond's sensitivity to changes in yield.

Modified duration = Macaulay duration / [1 + (yield to maturity / coupon frequency)]
= 2.78985 / [1 + (.06/2)]
= 2.78985 / 1.03
= 2.7086

To find the approximate percentage price change for a bond, we simply multiply the modified duration by -1 and the change in yield. Multiplying the modified duration by -1 shows that bond prices and bond yields have an inverse relationship. As bond yields increase, bond prices decline. Assuming a 0.50 percent increase in yields, we calculate that the approximate price change of this bond is -1.3543 percent.

$$\text{Approximate percentage price change} = 2.7086 \times -1 \times 0.5 \text{ percent}$$
$$= -1.3543 \text{ percent}$$

Duration is a linear estimate of the change in the price of a bond given a changing yield, which is a nonlinear function. Therefore, duration is most accurate when we estimate small changes in bond yields. Because duration changes as time passes, coupons are paid, and as yields change, we should recalculate the duration of our portfolio whenever these variables have made a significant change.

Because duration is a linear measure, the duration of a portfolio can be calculated simply by taking the dollar-weighted average of the duration of each bond in the portfolio. Hedge fund managers can use duration to implement their views on the future course of interest rates. Traders who expect rates to decline will lengthen duration, swapping into securities with longer maturities and/or lower coupon rates. When rates are expected to increase, you should reduce the duration of your portfolio by buying securities with shorter maturities and/or higher coupons. Buying bond futures increases duration, while selling bond futures reduces duration. It is important to note that the change in duration is related to the duration of the bond that is most closely tracked by the futures contract, which is the cheapest-to-deliver bond. Selling futures on U.S. Treasury bonds will reduce your duration, and your exposure to an increase in Treasury interest rates of the stated maturity. Be careful, though, as selling Treasury bond futures does not hedge you relative to changes in credit spreads to corporate bonds or changes in shorter-term Treasury bill interest rates.

Duration is a vital risk measure used by hedge funds and bond traders worldwide. For a fund to be market-neutral, the duration of the long bond positions must be equal to the duration of the short bond positions.

Another use of duration has proven very helpful to those who are charged with managing both an asset and a liability portfolio, or hedge funds desiring to manage a market-neutral fund. Hedge funds or financial institutions can generally eliminate interest rate risk from their portfolio by setting the duration of their assets, or their long portfolio, equal to the duration of their liabilities, or their short portfolio. Once the fund is duration-neutral, attention must be paid to maintain this neutrality, as duration changes with time and changes in yield.

As illustrated in Figure 10-2, the linear measure of duration is quite an accurate approximation of the change in a bond price given small changes yield. However, a linear function cannot accurately predict the changes in the nonlinear price/yield graph for

FIGURE 10-2

Bond convexity and duration.

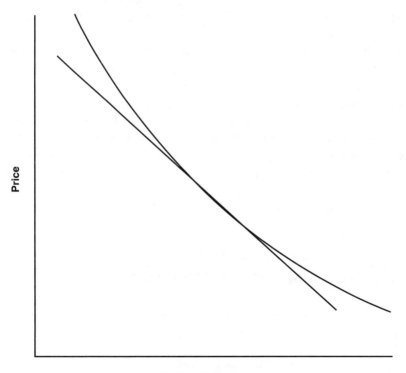

Yield-to-Maturity

large changes in yield. To compensate for this difference between the linear and the nonlinear function, we will need to add a term called *convexity.*

Option-free bonds, such as all noncallable corporate and Treasury bonds, have positive convexity, where price rises more quickly as yields decline and prices fall more slowly as yields rise. Investors would always prefer to own bonds with large positive convexity, as their portfolio gains value quickly as rates fall and loses value slowly as rates rise. Because investors value convexity, bonds with higher levels of convexity will usually trade at higher prices and lower yields.

Callable bonds and mortgage-backed securities have negative convexity. Because bond issuers and homeowners have the ability to refinance their debt, prices of callable and mortgage-backed bonds will rise more slowly as rates fall. Once the borrower chooses to refinance the debt, the investor is usually repaid at the face value, or the remaining principal value, of the note. Therefore, bonds with negative convexity will not typically trade at values far above this repayment value, especially when interest rates are lower than the coupon rate and the bond is eligible to be called at the current time. As interest rates fall, there will be a widening difference in the price between callable and noncallable securities. Investors assume that callable bonds will soon be refinanced, so prices do not rise much above the face value. Noncallable bonds can trade at significant premiums to the face value, as investors know that they cannot be redeemed before maturity. For example, a 20-year Treasury bond with an 8 percent coupon and a yield of 5 percent can trade at a price of over $137 per $100 face value. Investors will be earning 8 percent yields in a 5 percent market, so they are willing to pay dearly for the privilege of earning above market yields for the remaining 20-year life of the bond.

We can see, then, that negative convexity approximates a short option position, while positive convexity approximates a long option position. Because investors of callable bonds have sold a put option on interest rates, which is a call option on bond prices, to the borrower, the investor will demand a higher yield to compensate for the sale of this option.

Similarly, investors will pay higher prices for the most convex bonds, as they have the opportunity to earn large gains in falling rate environments. Similar to an option, the price of convexity increases with the volatility of interest rates, as these extreme price-yield scenarios have a higher probability of occurring.

Let's continue our example of the three-year security, with a 3 percent semiannual coupon, priced at par of $1000, yielding 6 percent. This is the same bond used in the above example, so we know that the modified duration of this security is 2.7086 years.

Convexity estimates the nonlinear portion of the change in bond prices using the following formula.

$$\text{Convexity} = \frac{\dfrac{1}{(1 + i)^2}\left[\displaystyle\sum_{t=1}^{n}(t^2 + t)\dfrac{CF_t}{(1 + i)^t}\right]}{PV(CF)}$$

Period (t)	Cash Flow	PV Factor$^{(t+2)}$	t × (t + 1) × Cash Flow/PV Factor	=	Subtotal
1	$30 coupon	$1/(1.03)^3 = 0.9151$	$1 \times 2 \times 30 \times 0.9151$	=	82.36
2	$30	$1/(1.03)^4 = 0.8885$	$2 \times 3 \times 30 \times 0.8885$	=	213.24
3	$30	$1/(1.03)^5 = 0.8626$	$3 \times 4 \times 30 \times 0.8626$	=	388.17
4	$30	$1/(1.03)^6 = 0.8375$	$4 \times 5 \times 30 \times 0.8375$	=	602.99
5	$30	$1/(1.03)^7 = 0.8131$	$5 \times 6 \times 30 \times 0.8131$	=	853.75
6	$1000 + $30	$1/(1.03)^8 = 0.7894$	$6 \times 7 \times 1030 \times 0.7894$	=	39028.39

After summing these values, we divide by our price of par and the time until maturity of three years. The result is convexity of 41168.90 / (1000 × 3) = 13.723. To estimate the price change from convexity, we multiply this result by 0.5 and the change in yield squared.

To get the total estimated price change from both duration and convexity, we add together the linear estimate of the price change given duration to the nonlinear estimate of price change approximated by convexity.

Total price change for a 0.5 percent increase in yield is calculated as follows:

$(-1 \times \text{modified duration} \times \text{yield change})$
$+ (0.5 \times \text{convexity} \times \text{yield change}^2)$
$= (-1 \times 2.7086 \times 0.5\%) + (0.5 \times 13.723 \times 0.5\%^2)$
$= -1.354\% + 0.017\%$
$= -1.337\%.$

Repeating the exercise for a much larger 200 basis point increase in yield:

$(-1 \times$ modified duration $\times$ yield change$)$
$+ (0.5 \times$ convexity $\times$ yield change$^2)$
$= (-1 \times 2.7086 \times 2\%) + (0.5 \times 13.723 \times 2\ \%^2)$
$= -5.417\% + 0.274\%$
$= -5.143\%.$

The actual price changes given these yield changes are -1.34% and -5.24%. While the calculation of duration estimated price changes of -1.354% and -5.417%, including convexity in the calculation allows us to come much closer to the true price changes.

When yields rise by 50 basis points, we see less than a 2 basis point contribution from convexity. When yields increase by a much larger 200 basis points, convexity is worth over 17 basis points, a substantial difference in portfolio return. We can see then, that convexity is most valuable when interest rates are moving quickly. Therefore, we can anticipate that the price of convexity will be correlated to the prices of options on the underlying bonds. As volatility increases, the price of convexity also increases.

It is vital for managers of hedge funds to understand duration and the optionality embedded in bond prices. In order to fully eliminate risk to the general level of interest rates in the economy, fund managers need to match the duration of their long portfolio to the duration of their short portfolio. Investors with accurate options pricing models may be able to buy cheap convexity or sell overvalued mortgage-backed securities, significantly increasing the returns to their fixed-income trading.

ENDNOTES

1. Kimberly Allers, "Repo Man," *Fortune Magazine*, September 15, 2003.
2. G. Burghardt, and Belton, T., *The Treasury Bond Basis: An In-depth Analysis for Hedgers, Speculators and Arbitrageurs*, New York: McGraw-Hill, 1993.
3. F. Fabozzi, *Bond Market Analysis and Strategies*, 2d ed. Englewood Cliffs, NJ: Prentice Hall, 1993.

CHAPTER 11

Fixed-Income Hedge Fund Strategies

Fixed-income arbitrage managers firmly believe that the yields between all fixed-income securities are related in some way. Specifically, they believe that the spreads between the yields on related securities are mean-reverting. When yield spreads are wide relative to their history, traders will bet on the convergence of the spread. When yield spreads are narrow, funds can assume that the spread will widen back toward historical levels. By tracking the differences between yields of different types of fixed-income securities, arbitrage managers attempt to capture small pricing anomalies, while maintaining a market-neutral position with respect to changes in the overall level of interest rates. This type of trading is likely the most quantitatively sophisticated and data intensive strategy employed by hedge funds. Not only does the manager need to track thousands of bonds worldwide, they must also understand credit risks, embedded options, liquidity and issuance schedules, and the strategies of government and corporate debt issuers.

When an equity fund is market-neutral, the manager is matching the beta of the short positions to the beta of the long positions to eliminate the influence of the return to equity markets on a fund's returns. When a fixed-income fund is market-neutral, the fund seeks to have a zero duration, which allows the fund to have returns that are uncorrelated to the direction of interest rates. It is also important to have a balance of currency exposures in your portfolio, matching the duration of bonds in each currency. The standard calculation of duration assumes a parallel shift of the yield curve. If you are duration-hedged and yields on government securities increase by 50 basis points, your portfolio is market-neutral. Many managers will also insist on hedging their portfolio using rotational duration. As parallel duration only hedges your portfolio against parallel shifts in the yield curve, you must also consider the portfolio risks when the shape of the yield curve shifts and interest rate changes are not parallel. Rotational duration seeks to be duration-neutral at each sector of the yield curve, where long duration equals short duration at the 3-year, 10-year, and 30-year sectors of the yield curve.

A key to understanding, and profiting from, fixed-income arbitrage trading strategies, is the operation of the repo market, where repurchase agreements are executed. Most fixed-income arbitrage trades involve significant amounts of leverage, so it is vital for a fund to have continued access to the lowest financing rate available. To take full advantage of these financing opportunities, a fund should have at least $25 to $50 million in assets under management, as well as a good credit rating. In a repurchase agreement, traders sell their long bond positions to a bond dealer and agree to repurchase those securities at a fixed price at a stated time in the future. The difference between the purchase price and the sale price is simply the cost of the financing, which is related to the level of short-term interest rates. The owner of the securities has taken out a loan collateralized by its fixed-income securities and is entitled to keep all income and gains from those securities while the lender holds them. The levered purchase of fixed-income securities can be extremely profitable during times of a steep yield curve. Assume a situation typical of the markets of late 2002. A trader can purchase 10-year Treasury notes at a yield of 4.23 percent, while the repo rate is only 1.23 percent, leaving the trader to earn positive carry at an annual rate of 3 percent. Of course, as interest rates rise the position becomes less profitable, with losses on the Treasury note positions and increases in the cost of the financing. The dealers who lend against fixed-income collateral will only provide such low rates to the most liquid and highest-quality collateral. Less liquid bonds or those with more risky credit ratings are likely to be viewed as lower-quality collateral, which can cause the interest rate on the borrowed funds to increase. Similarly, you would like your bond dealer to pay you the highest interest rate possible on the proceeds from the short sale of fixed-income securities. Unfortunately, if a bond is in tight supply, and therefore difficult to borrow, the interest rate paid on the proceeds of that sale is likely to fall, which compensates the dealer for the borrowing of a difficult bond on your behalf.

The government bond futures contracts offered by the Chicago Board of Trade provide interesting trading, spreading, and arbitrage opportunities for sophisticated traders. The 10-year futures contract at the CBOT tracks U.S. government notes with 6½ to 10 years until maturity. Assume that you purchased the bond that is currently the cheapest to deliver, financed the purchase in the repo market, and have done so at an annual positive carry of 3 percent. Once you sell short a duration-weighted equivalent number of CBOT 10-year futures contracts, you have hedged away the risk of interest rate changes of Treasury notes followed by the futures contract. However, you now have purchased the delivery option embedded in the futures contract. When the physical delivery future is in the expiration month, the bonds can be delivered to anyone holding a long futures position. Typically, there will be a number of securities that can be delivered against a contract, but the sellers of the futures will usually deliver the cheapest security that fits the future's delivery specifications. In addition to earning the positive carry in this trade, you can earn extra profits when the cheapest-to-deliver bond changes. Obviously, if you own the bond that used to be the cheapest to deliver and a new bond becomes cheaper, you can sell the bond you own, buy the new cheapest-to-deliver bond, and profit from the difference in these prices.

The value of this embedded option depends on the volatility of interest rates, the level of interest rates, and the similarities or differences between the bonds that are eligible to be delivered against the futures contract. Basis traders will seek to purchase the option (buy bonds and sell futures) when the option is cheap, and sell short the option (sell bonds and buy futures) when the option is overvalued.

Any government bond dealer will also have an interest rate swaps desk. These asset swaps can be valuable to hedge fund managers, as changing the characteristics of a package of securities can likely lead to profitable trading opportunities. A typical asset swap trade would be to purchase a fixed-rate bond, finance the purchase in the floating-rate repo market, and then swap the fixed-rate cash flows of the bond for floating-rate cash flows. In this example the trader pays a fixed-interest rate, earns a floating interest rate, and pays a floating repo rate. You can see that this trade is profitable when the floating rate earned in the swaps market exceeds the floating rate paid in the repo market. However, government bond dealers and swaps market makers are smart traders and will not allow these opportunities to become too profitable for other dealers or hedge fund managers. Therefore, these profit opportunities are often very small, especially when government securities are used as collateral. To increase the size of the profit opportunity, hedge fund managers may increase the level of leverage or implement the strategy with less liquid or more risky securities.

Historically, the term *TED spread* denoted the spread between the yield on Treasury bills and Eurodollars. Today, this term can be applied to the spread between government and corporate yields in any currency. This trade could be implemented in the futures market at the Chicago Mercantile Exchange, simply by buying one futures contract and short-selling another. We would expect Eurodollars, the yield at which prime corporate credits can borrow in the Eurocurrency market, to always trade at a higher yield than Treasury bills. Remember that Treasury bills are our definition of the risk-free asset, and trade at the lowest yield of any fixed-income security. When you lend to any corporate credit, even those determined to be investment grade, you are taking more risk than lending funds to the U.S. government. We would never expect Eurodollars to trade at lower yields than Treasury bills, so this spread can never go negative. When the spread is trading at extremely low levels, often during a strong economy where confidence in corporate profits is high and the perception of credit risk is very low, fund managers may purchase the spread, anticipating that a corporate credit scandal is inevitable at some time in the near future. During times of a flight to quality, the perception of risk of corporate securities is very high, and investors are selling risky securities and purchasing safe government securities. TED spreads can widen significantly, as government yields are falling while yields on risky securities are rising. Managers that are confident that the worst of the crisis has passed will sell the spread, assuming that the high yields on risky securities will attract buyers once confidence returns to the markets.

Credit spread trading is a more general term than TED spread trading. While TED spreads are typically used to describe the spread between corporate and government yields, credit spreads can be implemented between any two types of securities. For example, a credit spread trader may purchase AAA bonds and sell short A-rated bonds, assuming that some of the lower rated bonds will be downgraded to noninvestment grade and spreads will widen.[1]

This type of trading may also arbitrage the liquidity differences in narrow sectors of the government bond curve. The most recently issued Treasury security at a benchmark maturity (5, 10, 30 years) is called the *on-the-run security*. This security is by far the most liquid in this part of the yield curve and trades at a lower yield than other securities, meaning that many traders will pay to be able to trade a more liquid security. Once the Treasury auctions the next security three to six months later, the on-the-run bond becomes the old bond and the newly issued bond becomes the on-the-run liquid issue. Shorting the old bond before the next auction could be profitable, as this trade can benefit from the declining liquidity in this issue.

Not only is it important to understand the issuance schedule, traders must watch the Treasury policies for retiring debt. From 1997 to 2000, the U.S. government was running budget surpluses and retiring government debt. The presence of the Treasury in the open market repurchase of securities around 20 years in maturity significantly changed the dynamics of this part of the yield curve. When the Treasury is a big buyer at a specific portion of the yield curve, the prices of those bonds will increase, and their yields will decline. This will likely cause the yield curve to have some kinks and noncontinuous shape that will lead to arbitrage opportunities.

Yield curve arbitrage is a popular activity that seeks to profit from changing spreads between Treasury securities of different maturities. The shape and steepness of the yield curve can be influenced by technical, market and political influences such as supply and demand at each maturity on the curve, central bank trading and monetary policy, Treasury security issuance and buybacks, and preferences for liquidity.

The two general types of trades are bets that the curve will either steepen or flatten. A steepening trade benefits when the spread between short-term and long-term securities increases, which typically happens when the Fed is easing. A steepening trade was profitable in 2001 when the Fed was easing, as short-term rates such as the 2-year fell by over 4 percent, while long-term rates such as the 10-year, fell by only 2 percent. A duration-neutral spread that purchased the 2-year and sold short the 10-year would have been very profitable during this time period.

Conversely, a flattening trade can be profitable when monetary policy is tight and short-term rates are rising more quickly than long-term rates. Exactly the opposite trade would be profitable in this situation: long 10-year and short 2-year securities.

Not all yield curve spreads require as wide a maturity difference as our example of 2-years versus 10-years. A trader could easily profit by buying the old bond and shorting the new bond, expecting this spread to tighten at the next issuance of the new bond.

Finally, there could be large returns to rolling down the yield curve. Assume a steep yield curve, where 5-year notes yield 5 percent and 4-year notes yield 4 percent. We would expect that the 5-year note will yield 4 percent one year in the future, which earns traders large capital gains given that they purchased the bonds at today's 5 percent yield.

These trades are often highly levered, as the potential gains from this type of spread trading can be small, especially in the most narrow maturity differences. In some low-risk trades, such as the spread between more liquid and less liquid Treasury securities of similar maturities, fixed-income arbitrageurs may be satisfied with earning profits as small as 7 basis points. It takes a large number of highly levered trades to earn a 10 percent annual return by entering arbitrage trades of this type.

While many types of fixed-income arbitrage trades have factors that guarantee the convergence of spreads, riskier relative-value trades offer no such guarantee. These types of trades have been derived from a long-term study on the correlation of the price behavior of many different types of bonds. If the bonds are of different maturities, different issuers, or even from different countries, there are no fundamental factors that mandate the convergence of yield spreads. These pricing disparities simply come from market activity, and arbitrageurs believe that spreads that have been highly correlated in the past will revert to their long-term mean after the temporary market imbalances have passed.

Relative-value trades should be entered with a positive carry and a positive skew of returns. Every day that you are in a positive carry trade, your interest income exceeds your financing expenses, meaning that you earn a small interest rate profit as you wait for the spreads to converge. Entering trades with a positive skew means that you have studied the historical yield spread between these two bonds and believe that the expected gains to the spread are significantly higher than the expected losses. The larger the number of these trades that you enter, the higher your statistical chances of earning a profit, especially if your estimates of the reward-to-loss ratios are correct.

The largest risk to fixed-income arbitrageurs is interest rate risk. Interest rates can move by much larger magnitudes than interest rate spreads, especially during times of active decisions by monetary policymakers. Because this risk is so large, traders make sure to hedge away the interest rate risk by ensuring that their portfolio is duration neutral, that is the duration of the short securities in the portfolio is equal to the duration of the securities owned.

Credit risk is both a source of risk and return for fixed-income managers. Some managers will accept credit risk, betting on a large change in yields between bonds of different credit qualities. Other managers, however, will make sure that they own equal dollars of long and short bonds within a given credit rating, hedging away the vast majority of the credit risk in their portfolio.

When you borrow and lend securities in the repo market, you are taking a risk that your counterparty is less than creditworthy. Most bond dealers and investment banks covet their AAA rating and make sure that they keep this highest credit rating. As the credit rating of a counterparty declines, the universe of potential trading partners dwindles rapidly.

As the trading strategies become more complex or funds become more highly leveraged, model risk becomes more important. When valuing embedded options, or placing bets on esoteric spreads, the trading strategies simply become bets on the accuracy of the model designed by your financial engineers. The most accurate model will earn the most profits, while an inaccurate model can lead a manager to take large positions at unprofitable levels.

Perhaps the biggest downfall of models is their inability to estimate tail risk. Consider the trading record of mortgage-backed securities (MBS) arbitrage managers. From 1993 to 1997, these funds averaged annual returns of over 14 percent, with a range between 11.6 percent and 17.3 percent. This strategy produced extremely stable returns, where monthly returns ranged from 0.32 percent to 2.29 percent, with 64 consecutive months of positive returns. A standard mean-variance analysis of this time series would show this to be a very stable strategy, with just a 3 percent annual standard deviation. Unfortunately, extreme events happen much more frequently in financial markets than are implied in statistical distributions. No amount of statistical analysis that ignored the problem of tail risk could have anticipated that MBS arbitrage managers could lose 12.5 percent in three months, including a loss of 9.24 percent in October 1998, coinciding with the crisis at Long-Term Capital Management.

The CSFB/Tremont Fixed Income Arbitrage Index earned an average annual return of 7.02 percent between January 1994 and June 2003, with a standard deviation of 4.01 percent and a Sharpe ratio of 0.66. (See Fig. 11-1.) Without the disastrous year of 1998, the Sharpe ratio of this strategy would have been dramatically higher, with larger returns and lower risks. The returns over the last three years have been positive and less volatile, earning 6.29 percent, 8.03 percent, and 5.73 percent in calendar 2000, 2001, and 2002, respectively.

Notice that fixed-income arbitrage funds have some of the least desirable exposures to skewness (−3.58) and kurtosis (19.43) of any hedge fund strategy. Fixed-income arbitrage funds earn small profits in 81.6 percent of all months but can post extremely large losses in times of market stress.

Figure 11-2 shows the correlation between fixed-income arbitrage hedge funds and the returns to traditional investments. While the average correlation between these funds and equity investments is 0.03, we see that this correlation is quite volatile, ranging between −22 percent and +57 percent. Correlation between arbitrage funds and the MSCI World Sovereign Bond Index averages −17 percent, and is usually negative. However, this correlation ranges from −65 percent in the aftermath of the LTCM crisis to a high of 40 percent in 2003. While this correlation has generally been negative over the last nine years, arbitrage funds and world bonds have had a positive correlation during 2002 and 2003, when interest rates have been falling.

Figure 11-3 shows the scatter plot of returns between fixed-income hedge funds and traditional investments. While the returns

CSFB/Tremont Fixed Income Arbitrage Index performance, 1994 to 2003. (MSCI, reprinted by permission; TASS, CSFB/Tremont, http://www.hedgeindex.com.)

The CSFB/Tremont Fixed Income Arbitrage Index measures the return to hedge funds which attempt to profit from changing spreads between the yields on different bonds. While these funds are generally neutral duration, they may take significant exposure to changes in credit spreads, yield curve spreads, swap spreads and the changing value of mortgage backed securities.

	CSFB/Tremont Fixed Income Arbitrage
1994	0.33
1995	12.48
1996	15.93
1997	9.35
1998	–8.16
1999	12.10
2000	6.29
2001	8.03
2002	5.73
Annual Return	7.02
Annual Standard Deviation	4.01
Skewness	-3.58
Kurtosis	19.43
Sharpe Ratio	0.66
Sortino Ratio	0.92
Alpha vs. S&P 500	6.71
Beta vs. S&P 500	0.01
Alpha vs. MSCI World Debt	7.49
Beta vs. MSCI World Debt	–0.11
Best Monthly Return	2.02
Worst Monthly Return	–6.96
Best Annual Return	15.93
Worst Annual Return	–8.16
% Winning Months	81.6%

CSFB/Tremont Fixed Income Arbitrage Index

Legend: S&P 500 — MSCI World Sovereign Debt Index — CSFB/Tremont Fixed Income Arbitrage Index

FIGURE 11-1

Continued. (MSCI, reprinted by permission; TASS, CSFB/Tremont, http://hedgeindex.com.)

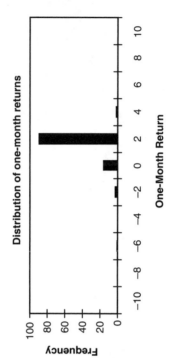

Distribution of one-month returns

Correlation to	CSFB/Tremont Fixed Income Arbitrage
TASS Fund of Funds	0.42
CSFB/Tremont Hedge Fund Index	0.45
CSFB/Tremont Convertible Arbitrage	0.54
CSFB/Tremont Ded Short Bias	–0.09
CSFB/Tremont Emerging Markets	0.30
CSFB/Tremont Equity Mkt Ntrl	0.09
CSFB/Tremont Event Driven	0.40
CSFB/Tremont Distressed	0.31
CSFB/Tremont E.D. Multi-Strategy	0.44
CSFB/Tremont Risk Arbitrage	0.13
CSFB/Tremont Fixed Inc Arb	1.00
CSFB/Tremont Global Macro	0.45
CSFB/Tremont Long/Short Equity	0.21
CSFB/Tremont Managed Futures	–0.09
CSFB/Tremont Multi-Strategy	0.27
MSCI Discretionary Trading	0.15
MSCI Systematic Trading	0.01
3 mo Tbills	0.07
S&P 500	0.03
MSCI World Sovereign Debt	–0.17
Average to Hedge Fund Strategies	0.24
Average to Traditional Investments	–0.02
Conditional Correlations	
S&P 500 Up Markets (71 mo)	–0.21
S&P 500 Down Markets (43 mo)	0.27
MSCI Debt Up Markets (65 mo)	–0.16
MSCI Debt Down Markets (49 mo)	–0.09

FIGURE 11-2

CSFB/Tremont Fixed Income Arbitrage Index: 24-month rolling correlation to traditional investments.

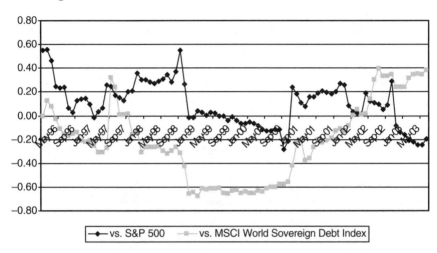

FIGURE 11-3

CSFB/Tremont Fixed Income Arbitrage Index versus MSCI World Sovereign Debt Index: monthly return pairs, January 1994 to June 2003.

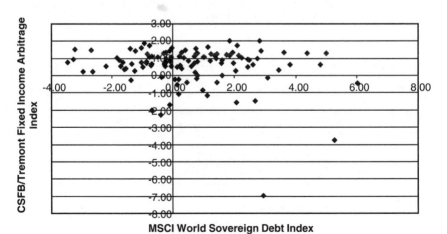

are generally uncorrelated, we can see that the largest losses to fixed-income arbitrage funds typically come in months when the MSCI World Sovereign Fixed Income Index has returns greater than 1 percent. (See Fig. 11-4.)

The most liquid bonds will earn the lowest returns, while one can earn higher returns in less liquid bonds. However, during a flight to quality, risky, illiquid bonds may be unable to be sold at any price. This risk during times of market crisis may overwhelm the promise of higher returns from the purchase of less liquid securities.

It makes sense, then, that fixed-income arbitrage funds have their lowest returns during the flight-to-quality markets that dominate the fifth quartile of returns to the MSCI World Sovereign Bond Index.

Because of the relatively low risk profile of fixed-income arbitrage funds, their managers can afford to use a significant amount of leverage. Ineichen estimates that fixed-income arbitrage hedge fund managers can control 20 to 30 times the assets contributed by their investors.[2] Of course, these managers must consider the example of LTCM and understand the impact that these high levels of

FIGURE 1 1 – 4

CSFB/Tremont Fixed Income Arbitrage Index versus MSCI World Sovereign Debt Index: monthly returns sorted by quintiles, January 1994 to June 2003.

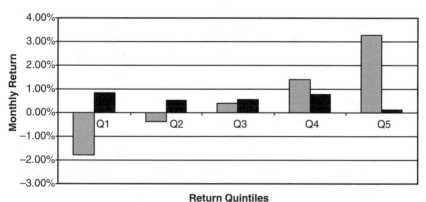

Return Quintiles

□ MSCI World Sovereign Debt Index ■ CSFB/Tremont Fixed Income Arbitrage Index

leverage can have on the risk profile of the fund. Fixed-income arbitrage funds easily have the most levered funds, as no other strategy is estimated to invest more than 10 times its investor capital.

An important part of the analysis of fixed-income arbitrage funds is their extreme levels of skewness and kurtosis. With skewness of −3.58 and kurtosis of 19.43, we see that these funds have significant exposure to event risk. The tendency of these funds to have large negative returns in a short period of time is certainly related to the leverage and liquidity risks these funds incur. The only other hedge fund styles with such extreme levels of skewness and kurtosis are diversified event-driven funds and those that trade distressed securities.

ENDNOTES

1. This chapter benefits from the discussion in J. G. Nicholas, *Market Neutral Investing: Long/Short Hedge Fund Strategies,* Chapters 5 and 6.
2. A. M. Ineichen, *Absolute Returns: The Risk and Opportunities of Hedge Fund Investing.* Hoboken, NJ: John Wiley & Sons, 2003.

CHAPTER 12

Mortgage-Backed Securities Hedge Fund Strategies

The percentage of Americans who own their own homes is perhaps the largest in the world, and this universal access to cheap mortgage financing is directly attributable to the mortgage-backed securities (MBS) market. A typical homebuyer will visit a local bank to apply for a home mortgage. Before MBS, the amount of mortgage lending by a bank was typically limited to the amount of capital saved by customers of the local bank.

Government-sponsored agencies purchase the mortgages originated by the banks, securitize the cash flows, and sell the resulting MBS to institutional investors. Three government agencies—the Government National Mortgage Association ("Ginnie Mae"), the Federal National Mortgage Association ("Fannie Mae"), and the Federal Home Loan Mortgage Corporation ("Freddie Mac")—assist banks in the securitization of mortgage loans. Once these loans are packaged into securities, they are sold to institutional investors to place in their bond portfolio. This participation of institutional investors and the credit guarantee provided by the government agencies dramatically increases the capital available to banks for mortgage lending.

Other types of loans packaged into asset-backed securities include credit cards, auto loans, and commercial mortgages.

Mortgage-backed securities pool loans of similar coupons and maturities. All of the 15-year mortgages issued in the first half of 2002 may be packaged into GNMA 5 percent of 2017. The coupon on the MBS is likely to be 50 to 75 basis points below the consumer's interest rate on the mortgage, as the issuing bank earns servicing fees and the government agency earns an insurance fee. Even though MBSs have a fixed coupon, they have an uncertain maturity. While it is easy to value a fixed-rate bond, it can be quite challenging to value a bond of uncertain maturity. MBSs are pass-through securities, where the owner of the bond earns the principal and interest payments of the homeowner. If the loan is paid off early, the life of the bond is shorter and the total interest earned on the bond decreases.

When consumers borrow money to buy a home, the mortgage contract typically allows them to prepay the loan at any time without penalty. This means that not all 15-year mortgages are repaid in exactly 15 years; many of these loans may be paid much earlier than the stated maturity of the loan. Homeowners can repay their mortgage for either economic or noneconomic reasons. The most common noneconomic reason is the sale of the home to enable the family to relocate to a new home. The mortgage may also be repaid before maturity if there is an insurance payout as a result of the house being destroyed by a storm, earthquake, or fire, or if the death or divorce of the homeowner causes the sale of the home. While these noneconomic factors may be relatively constant over time, it can be quite difficult to determine the number of prepayments that will be generated for these reasons.

The economic prepayment of a home mortgage, caused by a decline in the market level of interest rates, is an important and difficult modeling problem. The fund with the most accurate estimates of prepayment levels will be the most profitable, while inaccurate assumptions about prepayment rates can cause disastrous losses, especially when you are valuing structured products. Prepayment rates are a function of the current level of interest rates relative to the coupon rate of the mortgage, interest rate volatility, path of interest rates, and age of the mortgage. As interest rates fall, homeowners prepay their mortgages and the principal value of the bond is reduced. As interest rates rise, homeowners are less likely to refinance or move, lengthening the duration relative to the original prepayment assumptions.[1]

Investors are likely to demand a higher yield from MBS than from noncallable bonds due to the negative convexity of MBS. As shown in Figure 12-1, the value of noncallable bonds rises quickly as rates fall, for investors will be earning above market interest rates on their bond holdings. However, the price of the MBS is unlikely to rise far above par value as interest rates fall. As interest rates decline, the homeowners will refinance, replacing their mortgages with new lower rates, refusing to pay the higher coupon rate of the original mortgage. Homeowners are exercising their call option on MBS when they refinance, keeping investors from earning large price returns on these bonds in times of falling rates.

If you were thinking that prepayment modeling and the value of convexity sounded like an options-pricing problem, you are right. In fact, some of the smartest financial engineers spend their time valuing options embedded in fixed-income securities, including convertible bonds and mortgage-backed securities.

The yield on MBSs should be higher than the yield to Treasuries of similar maturities for several reasons. First, MBSs are less liquid and have more credit risk than government bonds. Second, the owner of the MBS has sold a call option on the bond to the homeowner. If the bond will be retired early as interest rates fall, the MBS owner wants to earn a higher yield before negative convexity takes

FIGURE 12−1

Price yield relationship: callable versus noncallable bonds.

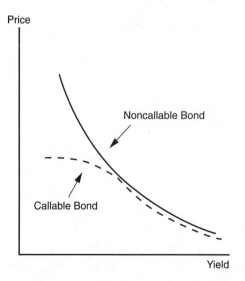

its toll. To own the most profitable portfolio of MBS, the investor should purchase the bond with the largest option-adjusted spread (OAS).

You might want to visit the Web site contingencyanalysis.com, where you can find over 1000 pages of information on financial risk management. I especially enjoyed their glossary, where they offer this definition of OAS:

> Option-adjusted spread (OAS) measures the yield spread of a fixed-income instrument that is not attributable to imbedded options. For example, a callable bond might be trading at a spread to Treasuries of 200 basis points. Of that, 60 basis points might be attributable to the bond's call feature, with the remaining 140 basis points attributable to such factors as the bond's credit risk, liquidity, etc. For that bond, the option-adjusted spread would be 140 basis points.
>
> The value of option-adjusted spread is that it enables investors to directly compare fixed-income instruments which have similar characteristics, but trade at significantly different yields because of imbedded options. For example, an investor might be comparing a callable bond to a mortgage backed security. If the two had comparable credit risk and liquidity, the investor might purchase whichever one had the higher option-adjusted spread-, it would offer the higher compensation for the risks being taken.

Obviously, OAS can be difficult to calculate, and the values can differ between analysts. Traders with the most accurate valuations earn the highest profits. MBSs are some of the most complex securities, so there is definitely a return to having technology and financial engineering capabilities to apply to investments in this sector.

If you think that plain vanilla pass-through MBSs are complex, wait until you see what they do with structured products based on MBS.

Structured products based on mortgage-backed securities are responsible for some of the most spectacular gains and losses in Wall Street history. Once you understand the structure of these securities, and the importance of the modeling process and assumptions, you will see why.

The cash flows to all fixed-income securities are composed of interest and principal. Some financial engineers at Wall Street firms found out a way to sell MBSs where separate pieces of the bond could be sold for more than the total bond. Thus, interest-only (IO) and principal-only (PO) strips were born. The MBS is stripped into two separate securities: one derives its cash flows from the interest payments from the bond, while the other derives its cash flows solely from the principal payments. For a noncallable, fixed-maturity bond, IO and PO strips are straightforward to value. For MBSs of unknown maturity, the eventual value of the strips can be dramatically different than the original price, depending on how the actual prepayments of the mortgage pool compare to the prepayment assumptions priced into the bond. If prepayments are very high compared to assumptions, the PO strips rise in value as the loan is immediately repaid, while the IO strips lose their entire value as the loans are no longer generating interest payments. The PO strips can be compared to a zero coupon, or a low-coupon bond. As the majority of the principal is paid far into the future, the present value of this strip increases dramatically as prepayments increase and principal is paid much more quickly than assumed. IO strip owners earn all of the interest paid over the life of the MBS. If prepayments are high, homeowners are refinancing and will no longer pay interest on their original loan. If the IO strip owner assumed 10 years of interest payments and only earns 5 years of interest payments, the losses can be quite severe.

While IO and PO strips increase the prepayment risk relative to standard pass-through MBS, other structured products are designed to reduce the prepayment risks inherent in MBS. Collateralized mortgage obligations (CMOs) use pools of pass-through securities as collateral for this MBS product. While all CMO owners earn interest, the principal prepayments are not distributed equally to all investors. The bond is sold in tranches, where investors can choose whether they want to be the first or last bondholders to be prepaid. The first tranche will have a very short average life, as all prepayments will be sent to owners of this tranche until this bond is paid in full.

Planned amortization class (PAC) bonds are similar to these sequential pay CMOs, but with a support bond structure. PAC bonds are built to create a stable, fixed-maturity bond-like amortization schedule that is relatively insensitive to prepayments in an assumed range. Support bonds are used to generate or absorb excess cash flows, making the PAC bonds less sensitive to prepayments than CMOs. The shortest maturity PAC bonds are the most stable, but the longest maturity PAC bonds may be as volatile as CMOs, as the support bonds may have paid out before this tranche is reached. For even more volatility and investment options, the support bonds can be stripped from PACs.

Because there is a strong demand for floating-rate securities, floaters and inverse floaters have been created from MBSs. Both types of securities receive principal payments, but the coupon payments change with the level of market interest rates. Floaters earn higher interest rates when interest rates increase. However, because the MBS is paying a fixed rate of interest that is split between the holders of the two securities, all additional interest payments paid to the owners of the floater directly reduce the interest payments to the owner of the inverse floater. Therefore, inverse floaters earn lower coupon payments as the market rates of interest increase.

Even more complicated securities can be derived, such as stripped floaters and inverse floaters with embedded interest rate caps and floors. Other structures include inverse IOs, where a premium bond with high interest rates is stripped. Bonds with higher interest rates are even more sensitive to prepayment risks.

Long MBS positions are exposed to changes in interest rates, and have a long, positive duration. To hedge a long duration portfolio, you simply hedge with short Treasury bonds of a similar duration. You must be careful with your hedges, because short Treasury bonds only hedge for a change in government bond interest rates of the maturity of the cheapest-to-deliver bond. A portfolio of long MBSs and short Treasuries is hedged against changes in interest rates, but not against changes in option values, credit spreads, nonparallel shifts in the yield curve, or liquidity premiums.

A trader may prefer to hedge the effective duration of the MBS, which is the duration of the bond after adjusting for prepayments. If managers feel that their portfolio is sensitive to changes in the shape or the slope of the yield curve, they will hedge using partial duration. To use partial duration, managers divide their portfolio into several parts, placing separate hedges against their bonds that are sensitive to changes in the 1-year, 5-year, 10-year, and 30-year bond rates.

MBSs have negative convexity, where the price of these callable bonds rises much more slowly than noncallable bonds as interest rates rise. This is harder to hedge than duration, and these hedges will reduce your returns in times of rising interest rates. In order to hedge negative convexity, you need to buy some positive convexity to add to your portfolio. This usually takes the form of buying call options on bonds that increase in value as rates fall and economic prepayments increase.

While it is nice to understand the price sensitivity of your portfolio to changes in prepayments, it is very difficult to hedge prepayment duration.

ENDNOTE

1. This chapter benefits from the discussion in J. G. Nicholas, *Market Neutral Investing: Long/Short Hedge Fund Strategies*, Chapter 6.

CHAPTER 13

Global Macro Hedge Fund Strategies

Macro funds were once the largest hedge fund strategy, representing over 71 percent of all hedge fund assets in 1990. However, these funds were so large and so successful that they were unable to profitably trade the large amount of assets invested in their funds. After losing more than half of their assets over the last five years, while other hedge fund strategies grew assets quickly, macro funds only controlled 15.4 percent of hedge fund assets at the end of 2001. (See Fig. 6-1.) We can tell that macro funds are, on average, much larger than other styles of hedge funds, as macro funds are only 4 percent of hedge funds yet control over 15 percent of assets. Perhaps macro funds became less popular relative to other strategies given hedge fund investors' preference for low-risk, low-correlation hedge funds, especially in light of the extended bull market in U.S. stocks during the 1990s.

Global macro fund managers are often categorized as the "gunslingers" of the hedge fund industry. Rather than hedging their positions, most macro fund managers take outright long and short positions. These funds can be extremely volatile, as they often increase the size of their positions with derivatives and leverage.

By far the most famous global macro fund manager is George Soros. Soros multiplied his investors' funds by over 400 times by making large bets in the global equity, fixed-income, commodity, and currency markets. A $1000 investment with Soros in 1969 would have compounded to over $4 million by the year 2000. The Quantum Fund earned a 31 percent compounded annual return over a 30-year period, before the Internet stock mania of 2000 caused him to close his fund. His most famous trades found him short the British pound in 1992 and the Thai baht in 1997, just in time for each currency to announce a devaluation. Gains of 30 to 60 percent on the devaluations could be magnified through derivatives trading. Soros became a billionaire by managing the Quantum Fund, which he now donates to numerous charitable causes in Eastern Europe.

Some market participants and governments believe that macro traders and other investors actually caused the Thai and British devaluations, which were very painful for those countries in the short run. A 1998 study by the International Monetary Fund titled "Hedge Funds and Financial Market Dynamics" concluded that there is empirical evidence that hedge funds and other investors were herding. Herding means that a large number of market participants took similar positions. The study concluded that herding by hedge funds did not cause the currency crises, and that "herding is unlikely to pose a systemic risk." Macro funds may have actually reduced the volatility of currency prices after the devaluation, as the funds were buying the currency as it was falling in order to cover their short positions, and this likely reduced the severity of the price decline.

Macro funds trade in the most flexible hedge fund style, as these managers are free to pursue nearly any trading opportunity that interests them. Ideally, their trades would be designed as the result of macroeconomic analysis that results in a top-down view. A view that a specific currency will be weak or U.S. interest rates will fall can be traded in a number of ways. It is the job of the macro fund manager to develop these views and execute them in the most profitable way. Because of their large size, many macro fund managers may feel that they must focus their trading on the most liquid markets.

Global macro funds, according to CSFB/Tremont, earned an average annual return of 15.37 percent between January 1994 and June 2003, with a standard deviation of returns of 12.40 percent and a Sharpe ratio of 0.89. (See Fig. 13-1.) These funds have little exposure to the skewness (-0.04) and kurtosis (1.99) problems that affect other hedge fund strategies, as global macro managers typically seek to profit from event risk. Many other hedge fund strategies seek to profit in more stable markets, while accepting risk in the relatively rare situations where event risk is prevalent in the markets.

FIGURE 13-1

CSFB/Tremont Global Macro Index performance, 1994 to 2003. (MSCI, reprinted by permission; TASS, CSFB/Tremont, http://www.hedgeindex.com.)

The CSFB/Tremont Global Macro Index measures the return to hedge funds that seek to profit from political and economic changes in the world markets. While global macro funds may hold long and short positions, their trades are often separate positions and are not meant to hedge market movements. These managers often take very concentrated positions, seeking to profit from major changes in currency, equity, interest rate and commodity markets.

	CSFB/Tremont Global Macro
1994	-5.70
1995	30.70
1996	25.60
1997	37.11
1998	-3.63
1999	5.81
2000	11.69
2001	18.38
2002	14.67
Annual Return	15.37
Annual Standard Deviation	12.40
Skewness	-0.04
Kurtosis	1.99
Sharpe Ratio	0.89
Sortino Ratio	1.74
Alpha vs. S&P 500	12.38
Beta vs. S&P 500	0.18
Alpha vs. MSCI World Debt	16.60
Beta vs. MSCI World Debt	-0.35
Best Monthly Return	10.60
Worst Monthly Return	-11.55
Best Annual Return	37.11
Worst Annual Return	-5.70
% Winning Months	70.2%

CSFB/Tremont Global Macro Index

S&P 500 — MSCI World Sovereign Debt Index — CSFB/Tremont Global Macro Index

FIGURE 13-1

Continued. *(MSCI, reprinted by permission; TASS, CSFB/Tremont, http://www.hedgeindex.com.)*

Correlation to	CSFB/Tremont Global Macro
TASS Fund of Funds	0.65
CSFB/Tremont Hedge Fund Index	0.86
CSFB/Tremont Convertible Arbitrage	0.29
CSFB/Tremont Ded Short Bias	–0.13
CSFB/Tremont Emerging Markets	0.41
CSFB/Tremont Equity Mkt Ntrl	0.21
CSFB/Tremont Event Driven	0.37
CSFB/Tremont Distressed	0.31
CSFB/Tremont E.D. Multi-Strategy	0.42
CSFB/Tremont Risk Arbitrage	0.12
CSFB/Tremont Fixed Inc Arb	0.45
CSFB/Tremont Global Macro	1.00
CSFB/Tremont Long/Short Equity	0.43
CSFB/Tremont Managed Futures	0.25
CSFB/Tremont Multi-Strategy	0.10
MSCI Discretionary Trading	0.20
MSCI Systematic Trading	0.37
3 mo Tbills	0.09
S&P 500	0.24
MSCI World Sovereign Bond	–0.18
Average to Hedge Fund Strategies	0.31
Average to Traditional Investments	0.05
Conditional Correlations	
S&P 500 Up Markets (71 mo)	–0.03
S&P 500 Down Markets (43 mo)	0.10
MSCI Debt Up Markets (65 mo)	–0.08
MSCI Debt Down Markets (49 mo)	–0.08

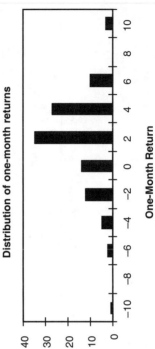

Distribution of one-month returns

Macro traders often seek out the most volatile situations possible, investing only when they view prices as far from equilibrium. They take advantage of market psychology, stepping into booming and busting markets, where spread relationships are often two or more standard deviations away from their historical relationships. Funds that can focus on the true value of an asset without focusing on the market price, and have the assets and patience to stick to this view, can earn significant profits when prices revert to their long-term relationships.

Many macro trades are inspired by an understanding of government-mandated changes in the currency and bond markets. Perhaps no currency market changes are more dramatic than those surrounding the creation of the Eurocurrency. In order for a common currency to be feasible, each member of the European Monetary Union (EMU) must subscribe to a common set of monetary and fiscal policy goals. If each country were to independently pursue its own goals, excess inflation in some countries could stress the common economic relationships between the member countries. To prove worthy of membership in the EMU, a country must meet the standards of the Maastricht Treaty, where each country must have a government debt of less than 60 percent of GDP, an annual government budget deficit of less than 3 percent of GDP, and an inflation rate that is less than 1.5 percent above the average inflation rate of the lowest three countries in the union.

Because of the benefits expected to accrue to the members of the EMU, countries are willing to make large changes in their financial position in order to take advantage of this opportunity to surrender their currency and monetary policy to the Euro. Among the original 11 member countries, Germany was the one whose monetary and fiscal policy most closely matched the criteria of the Maastricht Treaty. Other countries, notably Italy and Spain, had fiscal and economic conditions that fell far short of the requirements of the treaty.

Macro traders have been very profitable trading on the convergence between the strongest members and weakest candidates for inclusion in the Euro. Before Italy and Spain joined the union in 1998, and before Greece joined in 2001, there were tremendous opportunities in the convergence trade. The convergence trade, buying the stocks and bonds of these high-yielding countries while selling short the bonds of the current member countries, became very profitable when the inflation rates fell quickly as each country prepared for convergence.

The convergence trade has recently been rekindled, with a 2002 announcement that 10 new countries are eligible for EMU membership if they meet the Maastricht criteria by May 2004. Many traders will place large bets on whether or not Latvia, Lithuania, Estonia, Poland, Hungary, the Czech Republic, Slovakia, Slovenia, Malta, and Cyprus will qualify to adopt the Eurocurrency. The best bets may be Poland and Hungary, with short-term interest rates at the end of 2002 of 6.63 percent and 8.37 percent, respectively. You can imagine the large gains to currency or bond trades if these rates converge to the short-term Euro interest rates of 2.85 percent. A trader can bet by taking a long or spread position that bets on the convergence. A long position may simply buy the stocks or bonds of these countries, while a spread position would short Euro-denominated stocks or bonds against the long position. Long positions can be more volatile and less profitable, especially if Euro interest rates move significantly higher, toward 6 percent, in 2004. Spread trades simply bet on the spread, which is likely to be less volatile than an outright long-bond position. Should Hungary and Poland take the steps necessary to reduce their government debt and inflation rates and be accepted for membership, this will be a very profitable trade.[1]

An example of a more bearish macro trade would be a bet that the Eurocurrency will not be able to survive the tension between the fiscal policies of the member countries. In 2002, the average Euro country had a government budget deficit of 2.2 percent of GDP, while Germany had a deficit of 3.7 percent of GDP. At the end of 2003, France expects to have a budget deficit in excess of 4 percent. Traditionally the strongest member of the union, Germany is not currently in compliance with the Maastricht Treaty. Should other members press Germany on this issue, the currency could meet an untimely end. The European Central Bank has also been accused of moving too slowly to implement changes in monetary policy. The ECB reduced rates much more slowly than the United States in 2001–2002, which likely deepened the recession among Euro members. Should this tension over monetary policy increase, we may see the dissolution of the currency or the ECB. Macro traders who believe either of these scenarios would like to short the Euro currency or

Euro-denominated bonds. Of course, dissolving the Eurocurrency in its fifth year would be a dramatic, and quite unexpected, development. While this trade is not frequently discussed in the financial mainstream, traders who expect the unexpected are those who can produce the largest gains or avoid the extreme losses of other market participants who weren't prepared for such an event.

Some of the most spectacular gains earned by global macro funds have come from the devaluations of fixed-rate currencies, such as the Argentine peso and the Thai baht. It is possible to predict which of the few remaining fixed-rate currencies will devalue by a careful understanding of politics and economics, the strong points of a global macro manager.

The key to understanding currency markets is to follow the size of international trade and investment flows, as well as inflation rate differentials. Let's focus first on trade flows, as measured by the current account. If a country imports significantly more goods and services than it exports, it is running a current account deficit. In order to pay for this excess of imported goods, citizens must sell their home currency and purchase foreign currency. The capital account measures investment flows and is expected to balance the currency supply-and-demand situation caused by current account transactions.

As in all other markets, the prices of currencies are usually determined by supply and demand. However, if a government declares an official price for the currency, the supply-and-demand situation for that currency can stray far from the free market equilibrium. When a country has a large current account deficit, it is creating a large supply of its currency. There will be little pressure on a currency to devalue if there is an offsetting demand for the currency, which can offset the selling pressure of imported goods with the buying pressure for domestic investments. This brings us to the capital account, which measures the amount of investment capital entering and exiting each country. If foreign investors find attractive investments in a country, they must buy that currency to purchase these investments. Ideally, there will be a balance of payments, where the outflow of currency to pay for net imports will be exactly offset by the inflow of currency from foreign investors.

If the current account deficit is larger than the capital account surplus, the currency will typically decline in value, as the demand for foreign currency exceeds the demand for the domestic currency. Many countries with fixed exchange rates, however, are reluctant to devalue and see the price of their currency fall. Therefore, many countries will defend the value of their currency by using government reserves and monetary policy. This is when global macro funds may get involved. A government may spend its cash and gold reserves to compensate foreign traders for the difference between the imported goods and the exported investments. Unfortunately, many governments do not have enough savings to defend the currency for long periods of time. If there is still an imbalance between the current account and the capital account when the government has depleted its reserves, the country is forced to abandon the official currency rate and trade at a much lower price.

Each week *The Economist* publishes a table showing the current account and foreign reserves of emerging markets countries. Countries with large current account deficits and small foreign reserves can be the most likely candidates for devaluation, especially if their foreign investors suddenly lose faith and leave the country. For example, in late January 2003, we saw that Hungary had an annual current account deficit of $3.3 billion, with foreign reserves of only $9.8 billion. Similarly, Brazil had a current account deficit of $9.4 billion with reserves of $35.6 billion. While both of these countries have floating currencies, we would expect the value of these currencies to decline given these trade flows if investment flows are not sufficiently positive.

Rather than depleting their reserves, some governments will use restrictive monetary policy to attract foreign investment flows. By restricting the money supply available to the domestic economy, the Central Bank forces interest rates to very high levels in the hopes of making their investments more attractive to foreign investors. While this strategy can be successful in stalling the devaluation of a currency, it often comes at a very high cost to the domestic economy, as very tight monetary policy often leads to a domestic recession.

The Chinese yuan, or renminbi, has been pegged to the U.S. dollar at a rate of 8.28 yuan to US$1 since 1997. In order to manage this peg, the Chinese government must constantly intervene in the currency market. Because the United States has a large trade deficit with China, U.S. dollars are flowing into China at a record rate. As each purchase of Chinese goods creates a demand for yuan, the

Chinese government must buy U.S. dollars and dollar-denominated assets, and sell or print yuan, to keep the currency at the pegged price. The Chinese government may be willing to keep this strategy in place, as an undervalued yuan makes Chinese goods cheaper in foreign markets. As long as the currency trades at a pegged value, the Chinese economy can continue to grow GDP at annual rates in excess of 8 percent by selling large quantities of goods into the export market. China's exports to the world totaled $326 billion in 2002, up 22 percent from the previous year. Now that China is the world's fifth largest exporter, the world has certainly taken notice of its manufacturing prowess.[2] There are significant political implications of this rapid export growth, as other countries are pressuring China to abandon the peg, which can help the export economies of other countries.

Many analysts expect the Chinese yuan to increase in value from its official rate, given its huge current account surplus and foreign reserves of $346.5 billion as of June 2003. With foreign reserves rising at over $60 billion in the first half of 2003, there is tremendous economic pressure to break this peg. With Chinese Treasury bonds yielding 2.7 percent, this could be a popular positive carry trade for those who can borrow at low rates in the U.S. dollar market.[3] There is also increasing evidence that foreign manufacturers with Chinese operations are increasing their cash positions in China in anticipation of the revaluation.

The undervalued yuan is an important political issue in the United States, as 15 percent of U.S. manufacturing jobs disappeared in 2002 and 2003, many of them moving to low-wage countries such as China. While the United States is placing pressure on China to break the peg and increase the value of its currency, China was still resisting that notion at the end of 2003. However, it is likely that a revaluation will come sooner rather than later, as China promised to float its currency by 2008 as a condition of its membership in the World Trade Organization.[4]

There may come a point, however, where the economic pressure to break the peg may exceed the political pressure. As China exports massive quantities of goods to the United States, and speculators worldwide attempt to buy the Chinese currency, the Chinese government must continue to sell or print yuan while buying the currencies and assets of its North American and European trading partners. As the Chinese money supply increases, this can lead to price inflation in China. If the government sees excessive levels of speculation in the real estate and equity markets, they may finally realize that the threat of domestic inflation or an asset price bubble may be more dangerous than breaking the peg. The government has already raised the reserve requirements of banks by over 16 percent, a dramatic move that tightens loan availability and effectively reduces the money supply.

An important part of the strategy for keeping the Chinese yuan at a stable price is that the currency is only convertible for current account transactions. The Chinese government will allow foreign citizens to buy the yuan to facilitate direct investments and the trade of goods and services. However, the yuan is not convertible for capital account transactions. This means that foreign investors are unable to buy the yuan to facilitate investments in Chinese stock, bonds, and currency. Similarly, Chinese citizens have a limited ability to invest their assets outside of the Chinese markets. However, many Chinese have already invested in U.S. assets. If a large number of Chinese citizens choose to sell their U.S. assets and invest the proceeds in yuan-denominated assets, the currency controls may seem less effective. While the government restricts the purchase of dollars by Chinese citizens, there are no effective controls on Chinese citizens selling foreign holdings to increase their position in the yuan, which places pressure on the price of the currency to rise.

Many analysts believe that the Chinese currency will eventually have to rise in value by 20 to 40 percent to reach its equilibrium value against the U.S. dollar. It is unlikely that the Chinese government will immediately revalue its currency by this amount, as the immediate increase in the currency price may have negative implications for the export economy. What is more likely is that the government will revert to a managed float, allowing the currency to increase in value by 5 percent each year, or 0.1 percent each week, until it reaches the equilibrium value. At the end of July 2003, Merrill Lynch estimated that two-year forward contracts on the yuan were priced at a 3.6 percent revaluation, while five-year contracts were priced at a 9.9 percent revaluation.[5] Those who estimate a revaluation of up to 40 percent could be overestimating China's willingness to comply with worldwide political pressure or may be large buyers of Chinese currency in the forward market.

Because U.S. investors are not allowed to legally purchase and own Chinese yuan, they will need to earn this exposure in other ways. Most U.S. investors would purchase ADRs on Chinese stocks or mutual funds that own a significant stake in Chinese companies. Surprisingly, the Everbank Web site (http://www.everbank.com) now offers Chinese yuan-denominated accounts to U.S. citizens. Of course, this exposure is gained in the derivatives market, as the bank is unable to directly purchase the currency. This seems to be a popular alternative, as these accounts have earned over $100 million in deposits in their first year of availability.

A less obvious way to play the revaluation of the Chinese currency would be to short the stocks of U.S. companies that depend on importing cheap Chinese goods or to buy stocks of U.S. companies that compete with Chinese goods. With Chinese imports comprising over 70 percent of inventory purchases, Wal-Mart may be an interesting short candidate. With recent revenues of over $250 billion, Wal-Mart has much to lose from a revaluation of the Chinese currency. Fifty percent of all U.S. imports from China that are sold in U.S. retail stores are purchased by Wal-Mart, an estimated $15 billion in 2003. As Wal-Mart's main marketing strategy is low and falling prices, an increase in the price of Chinese goods in excess of 20 percent may dramatically reduce Wal-Mart's profit margins and revenues.[6]

Finally, you can forecast currency prices using inflation and interest rate differentials. Theoretically, the prices of tradable goods should be the same in all countries, and there is evidence that this is true in the long run. When the markets enforce this purchase power parity, countries with the highest inflation rates will see their currency decline in value. A global macro fund may short a currency if it predicts extremely high inflation rates combined with a strong or stagnant currency value, as the currency is not falling as predicted by interest rate theory. It is easy to see why the South African currency significantly declined in value in 2002. The inflation rate of 14.5 percent was larger than the interest rates of 13.5 percent. When investors experience negative real interest rates and the country has a small reserve balance, we expect the currency to fall in value.

George Soros had a very profitable way of trading currencies, which was counterintuitive to traditional economic theory.[7] If a country runs a large government budget deficit, economists often predict that this will lead to inflation. Some countries, however, will simultaneously implement tight monetary policy to offset these inflationary pressures. In this situation Soros would buy the currency, betting that inflation would not appear and that the currency would remain strong.

Global macro funds have typically been high-risk, high-reward funds that concentrated their positions in a few highly leveraged directional trades. However, we have seen macro funds lose assets in recent years, perhaps due to investor preferences for lower-risk hedge funds. Macro funds perform best in volatile markets with opportunities to ride trends in several areas. Unfortunately, some markets are quiet and trend less; this works against the global macro manager.

Gabriel Burstein's book *Macro Trading and Investment Strategies: Macroeconomic Arbitrage in Global Markets* explains how to reduce the volatility of macro funds. Burstein believes that funds that implement trades based on macroeconomic ideas do not have to take volatile directional bets. He also believes that macro funds do not have to flounder in quiet trendless markets.

Burstein suggests that macro funds can implement spread trades instead of taking directional bets. It still pays to build a macroeconomic forecast, but the trades are executed in a less risky way, similar to arbitrage-oriented hedge funds. While some fund managers would play European convergence by buying the high-yielding bonds of the candidate countries, a macro spread trader would also short the bonds of stronger members of the EMU to offset the risk of rising interest rates.

Spread traders may also choose to trade industry spreads to take advantage of their macroeconomic forecasts. If your forecast is for high oil prices, you can buy oil stocks or futures, while simultaneously shorting stocks in fuel-consuming industries, such as airlines and trucking companies. This spread reduces the risk of a falling U.S. equity market. If you believe that the U.S. dollar will trade to lower levels, you can buy the stock of U.S. exporters, while selling European export-oriented companies. This trade is less risky than a simple purchase of U.S. exporting companies, as you have hedged away the risk of a global equity bear market.

A fund may wish to combine the traditional directional plays of a macro fund with the idea of macroeconomic spread trading.

While the traditional positions can generate large returns in volatile, trending markets, the spread positions can reduce the volatility of the fund and produce profits in quiet markets when the directional positions are less profitable.

Figure 13-2 shows us that while global macro funds had an average correlation of 0.24 to the S&P 500 and −0.18 to the MSCI World Sovereign Bond Index over the last nine years, the correlation structure has changed markedly in recent years. While the correlation between macro funds and sovereign bonds averaged −40 percent from 1994 to 2000, the correlation has generally been positive over the last three years. Similarly, the correlation between macro funds and stocks generally exceeded +20 percent until 2001, the correlation has been negative over the last two years, showing that macro funds can profit in equity bear markets.

Figure 13-3 shows the monthly return pairs between global macro funds and the S&P 500. This graph illustrates the idea that losses to global macro funds can occur in any equity market environment.

Figures 13-4 and 13-5 illustrate the superior hedging properties of global macro funds. Macro traders earn their highest profits

FIGURE 13-2

CSFB/Tremont Global Macro Index: 24-month rolling correlation to traditional investments.

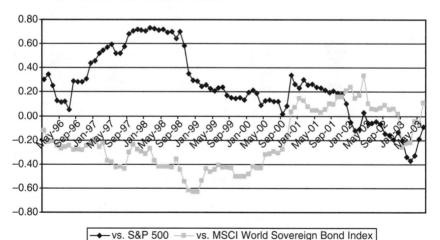

vs. S&P 500 — vs. MSCI World Sovereign Bond Index

FIGURE 13-3

CSFB/Tremont Global Macro Index versus S&P 500: monthly return pairs, January 1994 to June 2003.

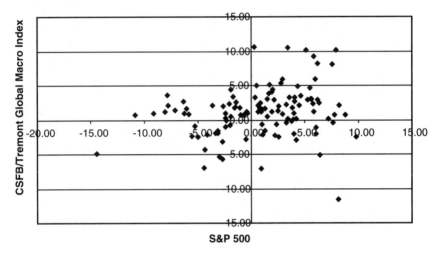

FIGURE 13-4

CSFB/Tremont Global Macro Index versus MSCI World Sovereign Debt Index: monthly returns sorted by quintiles, January 1994 to June 2003.

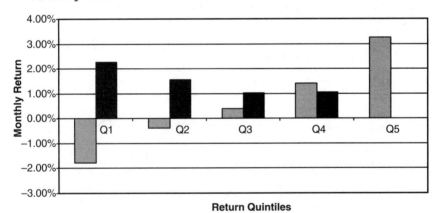

FIGURE 13-5

CSFB/Tremont Global Macro Index versus S&P 500: monthly returns sorted by quintiles, January 1994 to June 2003.

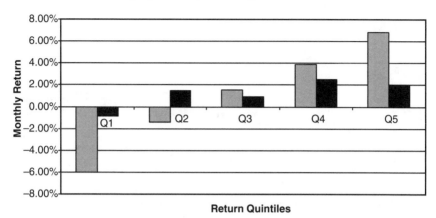

in the weakest times for fixed-income investors. As governments default on their debt and devalue their currencies, macro traders earn their most spectacular gains. While macro funds earn profits in over 70 percent of all months, they are generally unable to profit during the most profitable periods of sovereign bond markets. Macro funds are able to earn profits in most equity market environments, posting only small losses during the worst periods for equity market investments.

Figure 13-6 shows a similar pattern of profits relative to the MSCI World Equity Index that we saw when sorting by returns to the S&P 500. However, global macro funds have slightly lower profits in times of slightly weak world equity markets (second quintile) than is experienced in similar periods of returns for the S&P 500.

Brooks and Kat calculate the correlation between five hedge fund indices within a given trading style.[8] Many fund styles have very high correlations between indices, showing that managers in some hedge fund styles have returns that are highly correlated to each other. For example, managers within fund-of-funds, emerging-markets, distressed trading, and long-short equity markets typically show a high correlation, as the various hedge fund indices generally

FIGURE 13−6

CSFB/Tremont Global Macro Index versus MSCI World
Equity Index: monthly returns sorted by quintiles, January
1994 to June 2003.

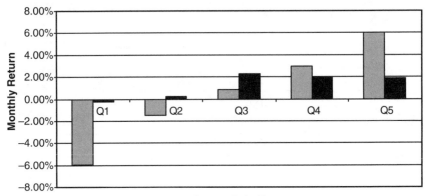

have correlations above 80 percent. Global macro managers have a much lower correlation of returns within their style, showing that there is a wide diversity of positions and opinions in the global macro community. This is evidenced by correlations between macro hedge fund index returns, which can be as low as 8 percent, and averaging only 45 percent. Therefore, we can assume that some global macro players, at any given time, may be long oil and short dollars, while other funds in the same strategy are simultaneously short oil and long dollars.

The implication of this diversity of opinion means that it can be very difficult to replicate the returns to a global macro index, as the returns to individual funds will often have a large tracking error, or a volatility of returns, relative to the index return. Investors wanting to replicate the returns to the hedge fund style index will need to invest in at least 10 global macro funds, while an investment in only 3 emerging-market funds will offer the same capability of tracking the index returns.

ENDNOTES

1. Keith Black, "Reaching for Yield? Try the European Convergence Trade," *Journal of Global Financial Markets*, 2003.
2. Peter Wonacott and Neil King, Jr., "China Moves Quietly to Push Trade Goals," *Wall Street Journal*, September 15, 2003.
3. Peter Wonacott and James T. Areddy, "Hope of Revaluation Drives Yuan Demand," *Wall Street Journal*, August 29, 2003.
4. Jeff D. Opdyke and Jane J. Kim, "The China Bet: How to Play a Rising Yuan," *Wall Street Journal*, September 10, 2003.
5. Leslie P. Norton, "Behind the Debate Over China's Currency," *Barron's*, July 28, 2003.
6. Peter Wonacott and Leslie Chang, "As Fight Heats Up over China Trade, Business Is Split," *Wall Street Journal*, September 4, 2003.
7. George Soros, *The Alchemy of Finance*. New York: John Wiley & Sons, 1994.
8. C. Brooks and H. M. Kat, "The Statistical Properties of Hedge Fund Index Returns and Their Implications for Investors," *Journal of Alternative Investment* 5: 26-44 (Fall 2002).

CHAPTER 14

Managed Futures Funds

The business of building hedge fund and managed futures databases and indices is large and crowded. While it may be nice to have a choice of benchmarks, the sheer number of indices can make comparisons difficult. Managers will prefer to be judged by a benchmark that makes their performance seem more favorable, while investors will choose benchmarks that provide the best improvement in their portfolio characteristics.

Let's first consider three commodity indices. Commodity indices differ from CTA and hedge fund indices in one very important way: you can invest directly in a commodity index, whereas you are unable to exactly match the performance of CTA or hedge fund indices. Commodity indices replicate the return to holding long positions in agricultural, metals, and energy futures markets. There are three sources of return to a futures-based index: price, roll, and collateral. Remember that futures positions require collateral, which is typically posted using Treasury bills, which will earn a return equal to the risk-free rate. The price return to a futures position is simply the changes in the price of the futures contract since the trader initiated the position. Finally, a trader can earn returns to rolling futures, where futures are likely to trade lower than spot prices. As the future converges to the spot price, traders earn a higher return than if they held a position in the cash commodity.[1]

Each index includes different commodities and different weighting strategies. Most indices use arithmetic weighting of the included commodities, which requires rebalancing the underlying positions on a monthly basis. It is important that the weights in the commodity index reflect economic reality, as it makes little sense to give equal weight to cocoa futures and crude oil futures, given their dramatically different importance in the world economy and inflation indices. Unfortunately, the CRB index is equally weighted, which detracts from its usefulness as a hedge against overall inflation rates. In some cases, especially meats, the cash market is significantly larger than the futures market. Any large investment in these commodity indices may not be able to be perfectly hedged or replicated, given the limited liquidity of some futures contracts.

Perhaps the most popular commodity index is the Goldman Sachs Commodity Index (GSCI). This is an arithmetic index weighted by the world production levels of each commodity. Commodities in this basket include agricultural and energy products, industrial and precious metals, and livestock. The total return for this index assumes that the notional value of the index is invested at the risk-free rate. As of November 19, 2003, the weights of the GSCI allocated 65.7 percent to energy products, 6.8 percent to industrial metals such as copper and aluminum, 2.4 percent to gold and silver, and 17.1 percent to agricultural products, mainly wheat, corn, and soybeans.[2] The Dow Jones-AIG commodity index is similar in composition to the GSCI.

The JP Morgan Commodity Index (JPMCI) includes only energy and metals commodities and excludes the agricultural goods that are included in other indices. Investors would expect this index to have the best portfolio characteristics, as the weighting scheme uses an optimization process that seeks to maximize the Sharpe ratio of the index, as well as a positive correlation to unexpected inflation and GDP growth and a negative correlation to the return on traditional investments.

Both the GSCI and JPMCI are highly correlated to each other, and both experienced a negative Sharpe ratio during the 1990s. While underperforming Treasury bills for a decade may not seem attractive, we must realize that the 1990s were a period of low inflation and strong financial market returns. Commodity indices can best be viewed as a hedge against inflation, where the prices of commodities obviously increase in value most quickly when prices are rising economy-wide. This investment is an excellent hedge against a portfolio of fixed-income securities, as commodity prices rise and bond prices fall during periods of rising inflation. The GSCI Collateralized Futures Index earned 24.0 percent, with a risk of 27.1 percent, in the inflationary 1970s, outperforming the S&P 500's lackluster return over this decade. In times of lower inflation, such as the 1980s, the GSCI underperforms stocks (11.9 percent vs. 18.2 percent) while offering higher annual volatility (16.8 percent vs. 12.7 percent).[3] Performance in the 1990s was similar, when the GSCI underperformed Treasury bills, despite having a significant annual volatility. Commodity indices, then, are more attractive as portfolio diversifiers or hedging vehicles than as stand-alone return enhancers.

There is a wide range of differences between indices that measure the performance of commodity trading advisers (CTAs) and commodity pool operators (CPOs). The index composition can vary by the type of fund, the index weighting scheme, and the track record of included funds. Unfortunately, none of the CTA benchmarks are investable, so the investor must invest in individual funds or funds of funds to attempt to replicate the risk-return characteristics of the benchmarks.[4]

Managed futures funds, managed by CTAs or CPOs, can trade in over 150 equity, commodity, futures, options, and currency markets worldwide. Many investors prefer to place assets with these funds, as almost all of their trading is executed on futures exchanges that require their traders to follow significant regulations. Futures trading typically requires participants to have their gains and losses marked to market on a daily basis, which can reduce the counterparty risk. Managed futures, therefore, are viewed as a safer, more regulated area when compared to many other hedge fund styles.

The Managed Account Reports (MAR) Index tracks performance of individual CTAs, as well as CTA funds and pools. MAR computes returns on both an equal-weighted and a dollar-weighted basis. A dollar-weighted benchmark is preferable; the largest funds have the highest weighting, rebalancing is unnecessary, and the index is easier to replicate. Dollar-weighted indices should usually outperform equal-weighted indices, as the funds with the highest returns have the best ability to increase the amount of assets under management. Equal-weighted indices require monthly rebalancing, but this may not be feasible, as most CTAs have policies on fund withdrawals that may only allow quarterly liquidity or require a one- to three-month notice before withdrawing funds.

Similar indices include the TASS dollar-weighted index of individual CTAs and the Barclay equal-weighted index of the performance of individual CTAs. These indices each have several subindices, where the investor can track the performance to managers in currency markets, financial products, or those with systematic or discretionary trading styles. CTA return indices are highly correlated, each having returns that have a correlation of at least 90 percent to the other indices. Each of these indices may have some biases, as each allows CTAs to report their own returns. When managers have the discretion to report their own returns, we may find a significant lag between the actual performance and the time that the returns are included in the database. A larger problem is that only funds with "acceptable" returns will choose to have their returns included in the index. This means that the index returns are likely to be higher than the returns to all CTAs, as the funds with the worst performance will choose not to report their returns.

A very different index is offered by Evaluation Associates Capital Management. The EACM CTA index is equal-weighted, but rebalancing of the index is completed on an annual basis, because monthly rebalancing is not feasible in these funds. The returns to each fund are calculated and reported by the index manager, not the manager of the constituent funds. The most important characteristic of the EACM index might be its high level of survivor bias: the index includes funds available today and then calculates the track record of the index using the hypothetical track record of those funds. MAR allows all funds that report returns to be included in the index, whereas the EACM only includes a relatively small number of funds, based on the size of their assets and their track record, including their returns and the length of time the fund has existed. An EACM index may outperform a MAR index of similar construction by an average of 3.5 percent per year, which demonstrates the potential magnitude of survivor and selection bias.

The CSFB/Tremont Managed Futures Index is a dollar-weighted index that typically measures the returns to 85 percent of the assets managed under this objective. This index has earned an average annual return of 7.9 percent with a risk of 12.28 percent and a Sharpe ratio of 0.29 since its inception in 1994. (See Fig. 14-1.)

Managed futures are extremely diversifying to traditional portfolios, as the correlation between the S&P 500 and the managed

FIGURE 14 – 1

CSFB/Tremont Managed Futures Index performance, 1994 to 2003. (MSCI, reprinted by permission; TASS, CSFB/Tremont, http://www.hedgeindex.com.)

The CSFB/Tremont Managed Futures Index measures the returns to alternative investment funds managed by commodity trading advisers (CTAs). CTAs can be categorized as following a discretionary or systematic strategy. Discretionary CTAs rely on the fund manager to design and implement trades while systematic CTAs rely almost exclusively on computer programs to make their trading decisions.

	CSFB/Tremont Managed Futures
1994	11.95
1995	−7.09
1996	11.98
1997	3.11
1998	20.66
1999	−4.70
2000	4.25
2001	1.92
2002	18.34
Annual Return	7.90
Annual Standard Deviation	12.28
Skewness	0.01
Kurtosis	0.49
Sharpe Ratio	0.29
Sortino Ratio	0.54
Alpha vs. S&P 500	9.69
Beta vs. S&P 500	−0.19
Alpha vs. MSCI World Debt	3.20
Beta vs. MSCI World Debt	0.70
Best Monthly Return	9.95
Worst Monthly Return	−9.35
Best Annual Return	20.66
Worst Annual Return	−7.09
% Winning Months	55.3%

CSFB/Tremont Managed Futures Index

Legend: S&P 500 — MSCI World Sovereign Debt Index — CSFB/Tremont Managed Futures Index

FIGURE 14-1

Continued. (MSCI, reprinted by permission; TASS, CSFB/Tremont, http://www.hedgeindex.com)

Correlation to	CSFB/Tremont Managed Futures
TASS Fund of Funds	0.05
CSFB/Tremont Hedge Fund Index	0.09
CSFB/Tremont Convertible Arbitrage	-0.23
CSFB/Tremont Ded Short Bias	0.26
CSFB/Tremont Emerging Markets	-0.14
CSFB/Tremont Equity Mkt Ntrl	0.13
CSFB/Tremont Event Driven	-0.24
CSFB/Tremont Distressed	-0.17
CSFB/Tremont E.D. Multi-Strategy	-0.28
CSFB/Tremont Risk Arbitrage	-0.26
CSFB/Tremont Fixed Inc Arb	-0.09
CSFB/Tremont Global Macro	0.25
CSFB/Tremont Long/Short Equity	-0.08
CSFB/Tremont Managed Futures	1.00
CSFB/Tremont Multi-Strategy	-0.06
MSCI Discretionary Trading	-0.02
MSCI Systematic Trading	0.82
3 mo Tbills	-0.10
S&P 500	-0.25
MSCI World Sovereign Debt	0.36
Average to Hedge Fund Strategies	0.00
Average to Traditional Investments	0.00
Conditional Correlations	
S&P 500 Up Markets (71 mo)	-0.08
S&P 500 Down Markets (43 mo)	-0.47
MSCI Debt Up Markets (65 mo)	0.39
MSCI Debt Down Markets (49 mo)	-0.14

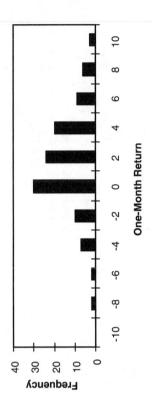

Distribution of one-month returns

FIGURE 14-2

CSFB/Tremont Managed Futures Index: 24-month rolling correlation to traditional investments.

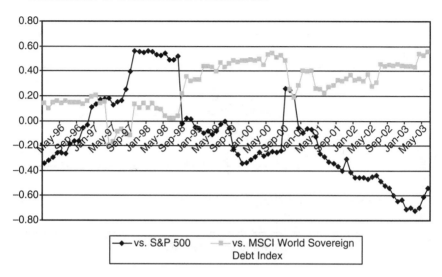

futures index is −0.25. As you can see in Figure 14-2, this correlation varies over time. Perhaps the most attractive property of managed futures is the negative correlation to stock prices when the S&P 500 is falling. The conditional correlation to stocks when the S&P 500 is rising is −0.08, while the conditional correlation falls to −0.47 when stocks are falling, making managed futures an excellent diversifier for equity portfolios.

The correlation to the MSCI World Sovereign Bond Index averages 0.36, with conditional correlations of 0.39 when interest rates are falling and −0.14 when interest rates are rising. These higher correlations come from the reliance of funds on the T-bill return from futures collateral, which have returns similar to government bonds.

Figure 14-3 illustrates that the managed futures index produces trading gains in 55.3 percent of all months, and that the correlation to bond prices is inversely related to interest rate changes. Figure 14-4 shows that gains to managed futures funds are more prevalent when government bond prices are rising. Due to this return pattern, managed futures funds do not add significant diversification to a fixed-income portfolio.

FIGURE 14-3

CSFB/Tremont Managed Futures Index versus MSCI World
Sovereign Debt Index: monthly return pairs, January 1994 to
June 2003.

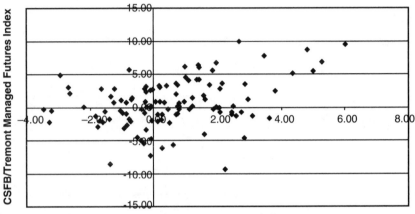

MSCI World Sovereign Debt Index

FIGURE 14-4

CSFB/Tremont Managed Futures Index versus MSCI World
Sovereign Debt Index: monthly returns sorted by quintiles,
January 1994 to June 2003.

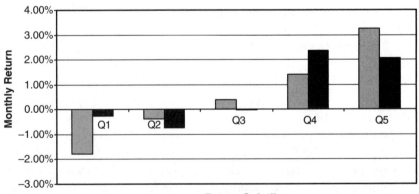

Return Quintiles

However, Figure 14-5 shows the significant diversification power of managed futures when added to a global portfolio of stocks. Managed futures provide larger improvements to a portfolio of stocks than to a diversified portfolio of stocks and bonds, because the addition of bonds to an equity portfolio has already made the portfolio more efficient. Adding CTAs to either a stock portfolio or a stock-and-bond portfolio is likely to increase the Sharpe ratio, as the diversification power of managed futures reduces the portfolio risk. Managed futures are more appropriate for diversifying a portfolio than for increasing the return to a portfolio, as these funds typically have returns lower than those of equity indices.

CTAs and commodity indices have low correlations around 0.25, largely due to the fact that commodity indices are passive investments in long futures contracts, whereas CTAs are actively managed portfolios of both long and short futures contracts. Managed futures funds also trade currencies, fixed-income, and equity index futures, which are not included in commodity indices.

During the 1980s, managed futures had a 0.12 correlation to the S&P 500, while posting a correlation of 0.33 to the U.S. stock

FIGURE 14-5

CSFB/Tremont Managed Futures Index versus MSCI World Equity Index: monthly returns sorted by quintiles, January 1994 to June 2003.

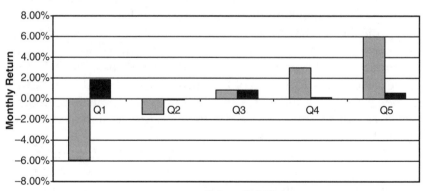

index during the 1990s. These funds also have a low correlation to U.S. bonds, averaging only 0.33 over the last decade. Managed futures funds have an important and unique correlation to traditional investments. This is the only hedge fund strategy that has a positive correlation to equities during bull markets and a negative correlation to equities during bear markets. This return structure acts like a put option on S&P 500 funds, a valuable return profile for traditional investors. As managed futures have earned profits in 17 of the last 20 years, despite varying market conditions, this style of hedge fund may make the highest contribution to improving the efficiency of traditional investment portfolios.

While we can find an improvement in the risk-return characteristics of our portfolio by investing in managed futures, it may be difficult to replicate the return to CTA indices. We would like to earn the return to a CTA index, but this return is the average return to between 20 and over 200 funds. It is difficult to earn this return because managers within a given CTA style index may have returns that are only 30 percent correlated to other managers within the same style. In order to minimize the tracking error between our CTA portfolio and the CTA index, we may need to invest in a large number of funds. Complete diversification is typically found by an investment in 10 to 20 separate funds. Five randomly selected managers have a 40 percent correlation to the benchmark, 10 managers gives an 80 percent correlation, and investments with 20 different CTAs is likely to have a correlation of 90 percent to the returns of the benchmark. Obviously, investors would prefer to replicate the return to the benchmark, and reduce their manager risk. By investing in a larger number of funds, each manager becomes a smaller portion of the portfolio and the CTA style has a larger impact on the return of the portfolio. The best diversification comes from a portfolio of CTAs with low correlations to each other, selected from a number of different styles of managed futures funds.[5]

Typically, efficient frontiers are estimated using mean-variance optimization, which helps us allocate assets between different asset classes based on their risk, return, and diversification characteristics. Once the efficient frontier is estimated, investors simply selects the portfolio that best matches their risk tolerance and desired return. When we are building portfolios of CTAs, however, we would rather select the funds randomly rather than through mean-variance optimization. Mean-variance optimization can overweight funds with strong recent performance, even when this performance may be unlikely to continue. When adding a portfolio of alternative investments to our traditional investments, we find that optimal portfolios include around a 20 percent allocation to alternatives.

Because each index is designed in different ways, there can be large differences in risk or return measurements between indices. The first major design difference is the selection criteria, or how the index chooses to include hedge funds. The criteria for inclusion in an index may be related to the length of the fund's track record, the size of the assets managed by the fund, or whether the fund is open to new investors. MAR and Hedge Fund Research (HFR) indices include nearly all hedge funds, while EACM selects 100 large funds.

The way returns are weighted and the rebalancing methodology of the indices can also be very different. MAR reports the results of the median fund, which does not require rebalancing. HFR indices are equally weighted and rebalanced monthly, while EACM indices are equally weighted at the beginning of the year and rebalanced only once per year. If you are an investor who would like the performance of your fund to track an index, EACM may offer the lowest tracking error, as investments in large funds rebalanced annually are the closest to an actual trading strategy. Benchmarking to the median manager, the MAR methodology, certainly does not make for an investable benchmark. Funds that limit the ability of investors to deposit and withdraw assets will make the monthly rebalancing assumed in the HFR indices difficult to practically implement. CSFB/Tremont may have the most realistic weighting, as dollar-weighted indices do not require rebalancing.

Survivor bias can be a major problem with hedge fund databases. CSFB/Tremont started tracking funds in January 1994, MAR in May 1994, while EACM and HFR began in January 1996. All returns subsequent to this date are likely to represent actual returns to fund investors. Survivor bias can be large before the inception of the databases, as many indices backfilled data to 1990 using funds in existence when each index was initially formed. Funds that liquidated prior to database inception were likely not included in the indices. This biases the returns upward, as the funds that ceased operations likely had significantly lower returns than funds that survived until they could be included in the databases.

Selection bias is more of an issue with EACM, as other indices include nearly all hedge funds. In the EACM database, the included funds were able to gather large amounts of assets under management because of their track record of excellent returns. Including only funds with excellent returns means that the returns to the EACM funds are higher than the returns to funds not included in this index. This selection bias is even larger during the period before the inception of the database.

At the end of 1999, there were over 800 commodity trading advisers (CTAs) registered with the NFA. At that time, CTAs managed around $44 billion, not much more than the assets under management in this strategy than in 1994. The weak equity markets and strong opportunities to short dollars, buy oil, and buy bonds significantly boosted the inflows to managed futures funds in 2002, with assets rising to $50.7 billion at the end of the year.[6] In 2002, CSFB/Tremont reports that the average managed futures fund earned 18.34 percent.

Unfortunately, the best days of managed futures funds may be behind them. From 1985 to 1995, the MAR CTA dollar-weighted index earned average annual returns of 15.81 percent with a risk of 14.58 percent and a Sharpe ratio of 1.08. The CSFB/Tremont managed futures index returned only 7.9 percent, with a risk of 12.28 percent and a Sharpe ratio of 0.29 between 1994 and 2003. This difference could be due to a change in market conditions, or simply more reliable databases that were developed in the 1990s that reduce survivor bias. There may also be more competition today for the same type of trades, making these strategies more efficient and less profitable. Recent returns have improved, however, with pronounced bear markets in global equities and the value of the U.S. dollar.

Commodity pool operators (CPOs) are basically funds of funds that combine investments in a number of CTA funds. Many individual CTAs post volatile returns that may be relatively uncorrelated to the return of the average managed futures fund. Because correlations to style indices are especially low between CTAs, diversifying across a number of funds in the same style is extremely important. Schneeweis estimates that it can take an investment between 7 to 11 CTA funds before the portfolio of funds closely tracks the return and risk of CTA style indices and eliminates the majority of the manager-specific risk. CPOs will allow investors to earn returns much closer to CTA style indices, with lower risk and lower minimum investments. More than 1500 CPOs are registered with the NFA, showing that there is perhaps more demand for pools of CTA funds than for individual investments with single managers.

The fees charged by managed futures funds can be among the highest of all alternative investment categories. CTAs may charge a 3 percent management fee plus a 20 percent incentive fee, while CPOs may add an additional management and incentive fee to this cost structure. Many CPOs may be affiliated with futures commission merchants (FCMs), who earn the commissions that funds spend to execute their futures trades. Fees of managed futures funds vary widely, so investors must be careful to understand their investments before allocating funds, in order to avoid funds with management fees as high as 12 percent or incentive fees as high as 40 percent.

Systematic CTAs use computer models and/or technical analysis to implement their trading decisions. Typically, most CTAs implement their trades in a systematic, trend-following manner, focusing on the most liquid futures markets. CTAs keep 75 percent of their assets in currency and financial futures markets.[7] Focusing on the most liquid futures markets allows CTAs to maximize the asset size of funds that can be managed without capacity issues. However, CTAs focusing on energy and agricultural commodities may be more diversifying to traditional portfolios given their positive returns during inflationary times. CTAs that specialize in the financial markets may be long stocks or bonds when these traditional investments decline in value, which reduces the diversifying power of managed futures.

A typical trend-following strategy, such as that followed by the Turtles, is described in Chapter 5. Computer models will be programmed to search markets worldwide for trend-following opportunities, seeking to take long positions in an uptrend and open short positions in a downtrend. As markets become more volatile, the opportunities and profits of CTAs can dramatically increase. Unfortunately, trend-following strategies post small losses in most markets and spectacular gains in just a few trades each year. Because the vast majority of the profits come from a limited number of trades, it is very important to take advantage of these headline-grabbing market moves. If you were not short the stock market crash of 1987 or short Asian markets in 1997, you likely underperformed CTA indices, because you missed some of the best opportunities of each decade.

MSCI has separate indices to track the returns of systematic and discretionary CTAs. The MSCI Systematic Trading Index has earned average annual returns of 14.13 percent since 1994, with a volatility of 14.69 percent and a Sharpe ratio of 0.66. (See Fig. 14-6.) This index offers a correlation of 0.82 to the CSFB/Tremont Managed Futures Index.

Similar to the CSFB index, systematic traders tracked by MSCI offer near zero correlations to stock and bond markets over the last decade, with the attractive property of negative correlations and positive returns when traditional investment markets are posting losses. (See Fig. 14-7.) Both indices offer the bonus of positive skewness and near normal kurtosis.

Figure 14-8 shows that the MSCI Systematic Trading Index profits in 58.8 percent of all months, and the lack of correlation over all stock market return regimes.

Like the CSFB index, the MSCI index offers the largest profits in times when sovereign bonds have their highest returns. (See Fig. 14-9.) While the MSCI index shows returns averaging over 1 percent per month when bond prices are declining, this hedging property of CTA funds may simply be due to the differences between the funds tracked by the two indices. Figure 14-10 is similar to Figure 14-5, in that the highest returns to managed futures come at the best possible time for traditional investors, when stock prices are falling an average of 6 percent per month.

A much smaller portion of CTAs will implement their trades in a countertrend manner. These trades are designed to profit in quiet, trendless markets by selling rallies and buying dips, assuming that prices are trading in a narrow range. Some funds will trade both trend-following and countertrend strategies. This diversity of models and profit opportunities allows funds to produce more consistent returns, profiting in both high-volatility and low-volatility market conditions, as well as trending and nontrending markets.

MCSI Systematic Trading Index performance, 1994 to 2003. (MSCI, reprinted by permission; TASS, CSFB/Tremont, http://www.hedgeindex.com.)

The MSCI Systematic Trading Index measures the return to commodity trading advisers (CTAs) who generally delegate trading decisions to a computer model. These managers design technical analysis models to profit from large trends in a wide variety of worldwide futures, commodity, currency, equity and fixed income markets.

	MSCI Systematic Trading
1994	–5.56
1995	32.95
1996	21.18
1997	10.91
1998	21.35
1999	0.25
2000	13.65
2001	7.05
2002	17.19
Annual Return	14.13
Annual Standard Deviation	14.69
Skewness	0.74
Kurtosis	1.81
Sharpe Ratio	0.66
Sortino Ratio	1.55
Alpha vs. S&P 500	1.24
Beta vs. S&P 500	–0.15
Alpha vs. MSCI World Debt	0.72
Beta vs. MSCI World Debt	0.74
Best Monthly Return	18.65
Worst Monthly Return	–8.47
Best Annual Return	32.95
Worst Annual Return	–5.56
% Winning Months	58.8%

MSCI Systematic Trading Index

S&P 500 — MSCI World Sovereign Debt Index — MSCI Systematic Trading Index

FIGURE 14 – 6

Continued. (MSCI, reprinted by permission; TASS, CSFB/Tremont, http://www.hedgeindex.com.)

Correlation to	MSCI Systematic Trading
TASS Fund of Funds	0.20
CSFB/Tremont Hedge Fund Index	0.21
CSFB/Tremont Convertible Arbitrage	–0.06
CSFB/Tremont Ded Short Bias	0.22
CSFB/Tremont Emerging Markets	–0.15
CSFB/Tremont Equity Mkt Ntrl	0.26
CSFB/Tremont Event Driven	–0.16
CSFB/Tremont Distressed	–0.11
CSFB/Tremont E.D. Multi-Strategy	–0.17
CSFB/Tremont Risk Arbitrage	–0.17
CSFB/Tremont Fixed Inc Arb	0.01
CSFB/Tremont Global Macro	0.37
CSFB/Tremont Long/Short Equity	–0.02
CSFB/Tremont Managed Futures	0.82
CSFB/Tremont Multi-Strategy	0.06
MSCI Discretionary Trading	–0.02
MSCI Systematic Trading	1.00
3 mo Tbills	0.04
S&P 500	–0.16
MSCI World Sovereign Debt	0.32
Average to Hedge Fund Strategies	0.08
Average to Traditional Investments	0.07
Conditional Correlations	
S&P 500 Up Markets (71 mo)	–0.05
S&P 500 Down Markets (43 mo)	–0.51
MSCI Debt Up Markets (65 mo)	0.53
MSCI Debt Down Markets (49 mo)	–0.19

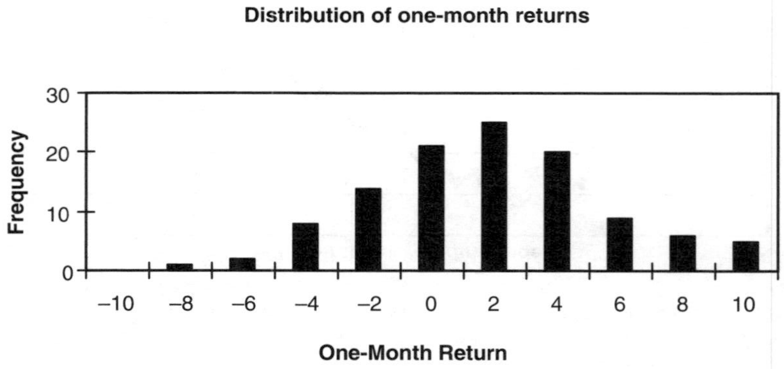

Distribution of one-month returns

FIGURE 14-7

MSCI Systematic Trading Index: 24-month rolling correlation to traditional investments.

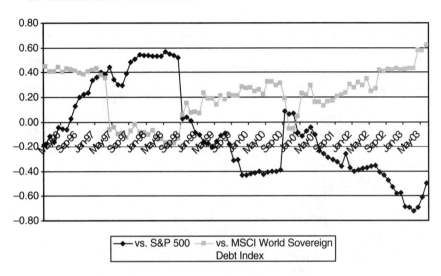

FIGURE 14-8

MSCI Systematic Trading Index versus S&P 500: monthly return pairs, January 1994 to June 2003.

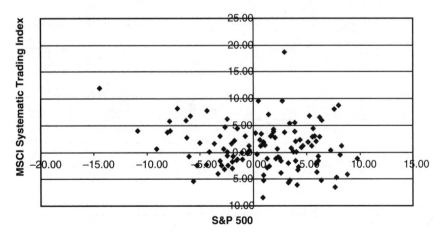

FIGURE 14-9

MSCI Systematic Trading Index versus MSCI World Sovereign Debt Index: monthly returns sorted by quintiles, January 1994 to June 2003.

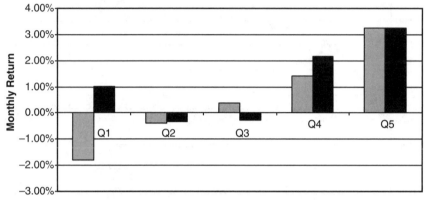

FIGURE 14-10

MSCI Systematic Trading Index versus MSCI World Equity Index: monthly returns sorted by quintiles, January 1994 to June 2003.

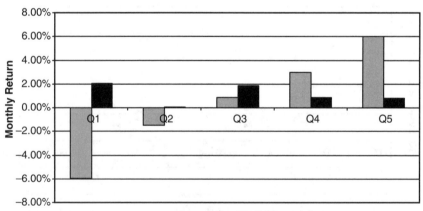

The term *black-box funds* was likely initially applied to systematic CTAs. Systematic managers typically build systems by backtesting trading ideas using historical data. If managers find a set of parameters that seem to be profitable in a given market over a specific period of time, they may add this model to their list of strategies. Many managers have a deep understanding of the caveats of backtested models. In order to build a successful trading model, you must be careful to include reasonable assumptions of liquidity and trading costs, you must understand that markets have constantly changing volatility and return patterns, and you must avoid the tendency to build overfitted systems that tend to be much more profitable in the past than they prove to be in the future. Many CTAs may design systems with the idea that one set of parameters should work for all major currency markets while another set of parameters works for all agricultural futures markets. The more markets and time periods over which a model seems to trade profitably, the less model risk the fund is taking.

Each manager will use different types of systems and parameters, but many traders base their systems on the common themes of technical analysis and moving average crossover or breakout systems. Many managers will not consider the fundamental developments in each market, but simply rely on the history of the price, volume, and open interest in each futures or options contract.

In order to define a trend, many managers may simply initiate a long position when the fast-moving average of a contract, measured over perhaps 1 to 10 days, rises above the slow-moving average of a contract, using perhaps 10 to 100 trading days. Conversely, the manager may initiate a short position when the fast-moving average drops below the slow-moving average. While these crossover systems will be quick to catch a trend, they cause the fund to always have a short or long position in each market. If a market is not trending, this crossover system may cause many trades with small losses, attempting to trade in the direction of a trend that may not exist.

In order to avoid these whipsaw trades that generate constant small losses in trendless markets some traders will use breakout systems. These systems will open long positions when the fast-moving average trades x percent above the slow-moving average, while shorting futures when the fast-moving average is x percent below the slow-moving average. When the fast-moving average is within x percent of the slow-moving average, the trader has no position in that market. As this threshold x percent increases, the trader is more likely to only trade in trending markets but capture a much smaller percentage of profits available from a specific trend. As the threshold decreases, the trader captures a higher percentage of profits from each trend, with the cost of opening more trades in trendless markets. Ideally managers can capture between one- and two-thirds of the total trend, as they are careful to buy after the uptrend has started and sell after the downtrend has begun.

In order to further diversify their systems, some managers may trade a variety of systems, such as three different systems on all currency markets, four different systems on energy markets, and two different systems in the agricultural sector. This way the trader has less risk if the parameters of a single model are less appropriate for the current market conditions. Managers will always search for models that are uncorrelated to their current algorithms, as uncorrelated systems can reduce the risk and increase the profits of systematic trading. Unprofitable periods can end up being valuable learning experiences for systematic managers if they are able to isolate a flaw in their system during losing periods and add a feature to their system that reduces losses during similar situations in the future.

Figure 14-11 shows the recent return history to the MSCI Discretionary Trading Index. These funds offer higher returns (14.45 percent) and lower risk (7.3 percent) than systematic traders, which increases the Sharpe ratio to 1.42.

However, these improved returns come at the cost of a strong positive correlation to stock prices that increases in bear markets. While systematic traders offer significant potential as portfolio diversifiers, discretionary traders are not nearly as effective in enhancing your efficient frontier. The correlation structure of discretionary trading funds is illustrated in Figure 14-12. Discretionary CTAs have a 0.40 correlation to the S&P 500, but a 0.01 correlation to investments in sovereign bonds. The conditional correlation is unfavorable relative to the S&P 500, averaging 0.27 in up markets, and rising to 0.52 in down markets.

Surprisingly, this index has a correlation of −0.02 to the MSCI Systematic Trading Index. Just because two fund managers can trade the same markets doesn't guarantee that they will produce similar returns.

Discretionary CTAs have a much more consistent track record, as shown in Figure 14-13. These managers post profits in

FIGURE 14–11

MSCI Discretionary Trading Index performance, 1997 to 2003. (MSCI, reprinted by permission; TASS, CSFB/Tremont, http://www.hedgeindex.com.)

The MSCI Discretionary Trading Index measures the returns to commodity trading advisers (CTAs) where fund managers make the trading decisions. These managers may consider fundamental and technical factors to make frequent trades in global currency, futures, commodity, equity and fixed income markets.

	MSCI Discretionary Trading
1994	
1995	
1996	
1997	
1998	3.78
1999	29.55
2000	28.06
2001	4.83
2002	6.76
Annual Return	14.45
Annual Standard Deviation	7.30
Skewness	-1.40
Kurtosis	6.69
Sharpe Ratio	1.42
Sortino Ratio	2.55
Alpha vs. S&P 500	1.03
Beta vs. S&P 500	0.16
Alpha vs. MSCI World Debt	1.12
Beta vs. MSCI World Debt	0.01
Best Monthly Return	5.41
Worst Monthly Return	-9.30
Best Annual Return	29.55
Worst Annual Return	3.78
% Winning Months	74.4%

MSCI Discretionary Trading Index

S&P 500 — MSCI World Sovereign Debt Index — MSCI Discretionary Trading Index

FIGURE 14–11

Continued. (MSCI, reprinted by permission; TASS, CSFB/Tremont, http://www.hedgeindex.com.)

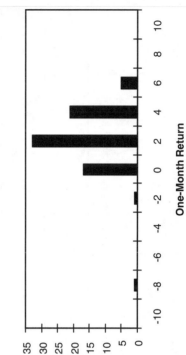

Distribution of one-month return

Correlation to	MSCI Discretionary Trading
TASS Fund of Funds	0.59
CSFB/Tremont Hedge Fund Index	0.44
CSFB/Tremont Convertible Arbitrage	0.37
CSFB/Tremont Ded Short Bias	–0.48
CSFB/Tremont Emerging Markets	0.54
CSFB/Tremont Equity Mkt Ntrl	0.46
CSFB/Tremont Event Driven	0.60
CSFB/Tremont Distressed	0.49
CSFB/Tremont E.D. Multi-Strategy	0.63
CSFB/Tremont Risk Arbitrage	0.52
CSFB/Tremont Fixed Inc Arb	0.15
CSFB/Tremont Global Macro	0.20
CSFB/Tremont Long/Short Equity	0.48
CSFB/Tremont Managed Futures	–0.02
CSFB/Tremont Multi-Strategy	0.05
MSCI Discretionary Trading	1.00
MSCI Systematic Trading	–0.02
3 mo Tbills	0.12
S&P 500	0.40
MSCI World Sovereign Debt	0.01
Average to Hedge Fund Strategies	0.29
Average to Traditional Investments	0.18
Conditional Correlations	
S&P 500 Up Markets (71 mo)	0.27
S&P 500 Down Markets (43 mo)	0.52
MSCI Debt Up Markets (65 mo)	0.17
MSCI Debt Down Markets (49 mo)	–0.12

FIGURE 14–12

MSCI Discretionary Trading Index: 24-month rolling correlation to traditional investments.

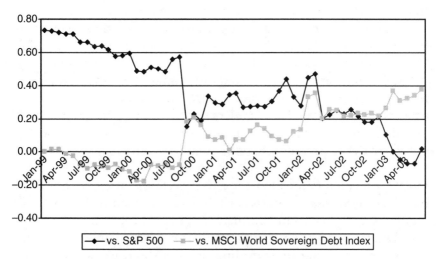

FIGURE 14–13

MSCI Discretionary Trading Index versus S&P 500: monthly return pairs, January 1997 to June 2003.

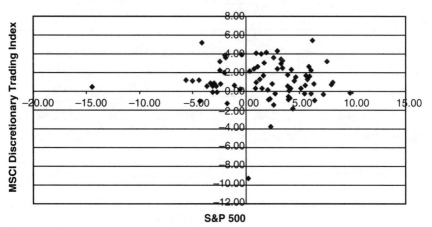

74.4 percent of all months, and have smaller annual losses than systematic traders. An interesting contrast comes in 1999, when discretionary traders earned 29.55 percent, while systematic traders offered a return below the risk-free rate (0.25 percent).

The consistency of discretionary trading profits is shown in Figures 14.14 and 14.15, where these CTAs offer profits in all possible stock and bond return quintiles.

Discretionary CTAs can trade the same set of markets as systematic CTAs, but leave all trading decisions to a trader rather than to a mechanized system. These traders may have much in common with global macro traders, as they may base their trades on political or economic developments. Other discretionary traders may have more fundamental systems based on trader judgment, which may have a lower correlation to the global macro style. Some discretionary CTAs may have a systematic component, but use the computer signals as a guide rather than a commandment that traders must follow.

Discretionary CTAs may consider many familiar economic statistics when making their trading decisions and market forecasts.

FIGURE 14-14

MSCI Discretionary Trading Index versus MSCI World Sovereign Debt Index: monthly returns sorted by quintiles, January 1997 to June 2003.

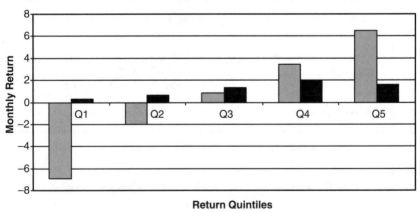

Return Quintiles

☐ MSCI World Sovereign   ■ MSCI Discretionary
Debt Index   Trading Index

FIGURE 14-15

MSCI Discretionary Trading Index versus MSCI World Equity Index: monthly returns sorted by quintiles, January 1997 to June 2003.

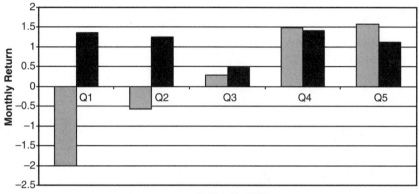

Return Quintiles

▫ MSCI World   ▪ MSCI Discretionary
  Equity Index   Trading Index

Many managers are intimately familiar with statistics from markets around the world, including GDP growth, employment trends, interest rates and inflation trends, Central Bank policies, trade flows and capital flows, as well as the valuation and growth statistics of the worldwide equity markets.

These funds may be less volatile than global macro funds, however, because they are regulated by the futures markets and may have less opportunity for leverage, concentrated positions, or customized OTC derivatives.

ENDNOTES

1. T. Schneeweis and J. F. Pescatore, *The Handbook of Alternative Investment Strategies.* New York: Institutional Investor, 1999.
2. "Goldman Sachs Commodity Index." Viewed at http://www.gs.com/gsci.
3. P. D. Kaplan and S. Lummer, "GSCI Collateralized Futures as a Hedging and Diversification Tool for Institutional Portfolios: An Update," *Journal of Investing* (1998): 7, 11–18.

4. T. Schneeweis and J. F. Pescatore, 1999, *The Handbook of Alternative Investment Strategies*, op. cit.

5. Ibid.

6. D. Strachman, "Managed Futures: Back in Vogue," *Futures Industry Magazine*, May-June 2003.

7. Ibid.

CHAPTER 15

Risk Arbitrage Hedge Fund Strategies

Event-driven strategies are defined as fund styles in which trading opportunities are created through changes in publicly traded companies, where hedge funds can take advantage of inefficiencies caused by announced corporate actions such as mergers, bankruptcies, and spin-offs.

The returns to event-driven strategies may be cyclical, as there may not be enough corporate actions in a given year to sustain the number of hedge funds dedicated to these trading styles. In 2002, there were fewer opportunities for merger arbitrage and more opportunities for distressed investing. For example, Kiplinger's reported that merger activity dropped from $1.4 trillion in announced deals in 2000 to only $350 billion in announced deals in 2002. Conversely, U.S. bankruptcies were at record levels in 2001 and 2002: BankruptcyData.com reported that 186 public companies declared bankruptcy in 2002 with total assets of $368 billion, while bankruptcies of U.S. firms totaled $259 billion in assets during 2001. Of course, not all of the event-driven trading opportunities are found in the United States. Firms in Europe or Asia may also announce mergers and bankruptcies, which may occur with different timing than in the U.S. market.

Figure 15-1 shows the correlation between Mergerstat's reported percentage change in the dollar value of annual merger activity and the return on the S&P 500 index. This correlation is 43.5 percent,

FIGURE 15-1

Merger activity by year. *(Mergerstat.)*

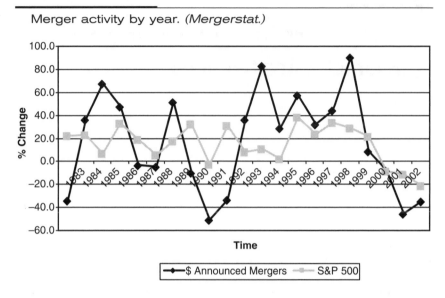

showing that the best years for merger arbitrage tend to be toward the end of bull markets, as acquiring firms have higher stock prices. For example, the large increase in merger activity in 1998 came in the fourth consecutive year that stock prices had risen at least 23 percent. Similarly, merger activity fell a cumulative 68 percent from 2000 to 2002, when the stock market had declined in three straight years.

The first event-driven strategy that we will discuss is risk arbitrage, also called merger arbitrage. Besides risk arbitrage funds, many other hedge funds, especially equity market–neutral and long-short funds, may also implement trading strategies based on merger activity. Because of the limited supply of merger arbitrage opportunities, most funds in this style will have very similar positions.[1]

The general idea of merger arbitrage is to purchase the stock of a target firm in an acquisition while shorting the shares of the acquiring firm. For example, assume that ABC is trading at $15 and agrees to be purchased for 0.5 shares of XYZ, which is trading at $40. If ABC stock immediately rises to $18 on the announcement of the merger, and XYZ is unchanged on the news, a merger arbitrage trade can be created. If you buy 1000 shares of ABC at $18, and short 500 shares of XYZ at $40, you can earn $2 per ABC share if and when the merger is completed. Your annualized return is 22.2 percent if you earn $2 on an $18 investment in a six-month period. You can also profit from the short stock rebate on the shares of the acquiring firm that you have shorted, and your return will improve if the dividend yield on the shares of the target firm is higher than the dividend yield on the acquirer's shares.

Not all mergers are announced as a simple stock swap transaction, which gives each target shareholder a fixed number of shares of the acquiring firm. Some mergers will be all cash transactions, such as a $20 all cash offer for ABC. Other deals will be structured as collar transactions to minimize the volatility of the stock of the target firm. For example, if XYZ wants to offer $20 per share for ABC, it may offer 0.5 shares of its own stock when it is trading between $35 and $45; 0.55 shares when its own stock is less than $35; and 0.45 shares when its own stock exceeds $45. The increased share ratio below $35 protects the target shareholders from a decline in the acquirer's stock, while the reduced share ratio above $45 protects the acquirer's shareholders from paying too much for the shares of ABC. While collared mergers may be more difficult to hedge, they add a complexity premium that may increase the spreads offered to arbitrageurs. However, target shareholders may value the put portion of the collar and reduce their selling pressure, thereby reducing the arbitrage spreads.

Of course, we must remember that this strategy is called *risk* arbitrage. Merger arbitrage is not a true arbitrage, as there are risks that a deal will not be consummated at the time or price anticipated, or may not even be consummated at all.

The best merger arbitrage managers will not necessarily invest in the deals with the highest spreads, as the wide spread compensates for a higher probability that the deal will not be completed. The most profitable managers may be the ones with the highest percentage of completed deals, or those who best manage the risk of failed deals. As Paulson notes, because the reward in a completed merger may be $2 per share, while the risk of a failed deal may be $10 per share or more, the true skill in risk arbitrage is shown by managers who have the best ability to avoid losses and failed deals.[2]

The first risk factor in merger arbitrage is the regulatory risk. Governments worldwide have antitrust rules that seek to prevent mergers that will reduce competition in an industry that will lead to higher prices or lower quality of goods and services offered by the newly merged firm. Other government agencies may be responsible for reviewing mergers in highly regulated industries, such as utilities or telecommunications. The more government agencies responsible for reviewing a merger transaction, the longer it may take to get the deal approved. Of course, as the time lengthens between the announcement and consummation of the merger, the lower the annual returns to the arbitrageur. Many arbitrageurs will closely follow regulatory proceedings and study applicable regulations to determine the probability and timing that the merger may be completed.

A recent merger that failed due to regulatory issues was General Electric's proposed purchase of Honeywell. The antitrust regulators in Europe believed that this merger would have created excess concentration in the market for certain aircraft engines and components. It is interesting to note that European regulators killed this merger, even though these are U.S. companies that had already been cleared for merger by the U.S. antitrust authorities. Companies may resubmit their merger proposal to regulators, especially if they offer to sell critical assets to competing firms to maintain a competitive industry. When GE first announced the bid for Honeywell in September 2000, HON rose from $36 to over $50, while you could have shorted GE around $53. When the deal finally fell apart nine months later in July 2001, HON fell back to $36, while GE stayed relatively constant around $50. This failed merger cost arbitrageurs over $10 per share. As it became clear that the merger might not be approved, the spread widened before the deal actually failed. Of course, many managers may have avoided this deal, as these companies were very large and subject to detailed regulatory investigations.

When deals involve cash, arbitrageurs must estimate whether the acquiring firm can finance the transaction. If the acquirer is a large capitalization firm that can afford to purchase the target for cash on hand, there is minimal financing risk. If the acquirer is a smaller firm or a firm with a marginal credit rating, it may be much more difficult for the firm to borrow the funds necessary to complete the buyout. If interest rates rise before financing is secured, the deal may also be at risk. You must also consider the size and reputation of the acquirer. If the firm is smaller than the target, or if it has previously failed in merger transactions, the financing risk may be quite significant.

Merger arbitrage can become much more profitable, as well as more risky, if a third party enters the discussion. Remember our example of XYZ buying ABC for $20 per share? If DEF comes along and bids $22 for ABC, the stock price of ABC may move higher, possibly increasing your profits from your original spread. However, if the market viewed XYZ's bid as being too high, the price of XYZ may rally on announcement of the competing bid, giving you a loss on your short position. You must now decide whether you want to be short XYZ or DEF against your ABC position. While DEF's bid may look better today, XYZ may gain the upper hand if the price of DEF falls or if ABC decides that XYZ has a stronger bid. The target company has a say in who purchases it, so it may prefer XYZ if XYZ has promised jobs for ABC management or if XYZ is viewed as a stronger firm that is more likely to complete the deal. The worst-case scenario may emerge if XYZ quits the competition because the price seems too high, and then DEF is unable to complete the deal. While XYZ may have been willing and able to complete the transaction on the original terms, the emergence of a competing bid may eventually lead to a failure of all merger bids.

Mergers also face risk from movements in the market or developments in the industry. If stock prices of the target and acquirer are relatively stable after the announcement, it may not be difficult to complete the merger at the announced price and date. If the market, or the price of stocks in your industry, moves up or down 25 percent or more over the course of a 6- to 12-month period, either the buyer ends up paying too much or the target is selling for a much lower price than it thought it had agreed to. If either party is sensitive to these price changes, it may choose to abandon its merger plans, simply due to price volatility of stocks in its market or industry. Similarly, if the growth prospects of the industry change dramatically, one party may cancel the transaction, as the merger may be more expensive than previously modeled, given the new dynamics of the industry.

A stock swap merger is self-liquidating when it is completed. If you are long the target and short the acquirer in the proper ratio, the completion of the deal will find you long and short the same number of shares in the acquiring firm. Ideally, you can open the trade with a $2 or higher spread, and close the trade at a zero spread when the deal is completed.

The Merger Fund is an SEC-registered mutual fund that invests in risk arbitrage trades for retail investors. This fund returned 7.6 percent per year over the five years ending 2002, beating the market by over 8.5 percent annually. Even better than this outperformance is the statistic that the fund has an annual standard deviation of less than one-third of the risk of the S&P 500 index. Of course, such a low-risk fund is likely to underperform during large bull markets.

The Merger Fund's fourth-quarter 2002 report contains an especially interesting and candid discussion of the risk-reward situation of the recent merger between Cardinal Health and Syncor. Merger transactions can fail if one company underperforms. The target may refuse to accept the shares of the acquirer after a negative earnings surprise or the revelation of aggressive accounting. Similarly, the acquirer may refuse to complete its acquisition if the target underperforms expectations or if negative developments are found during the due diligence process.

The Merger Fund bought shares of Syncor and shorted shares of Cardinal Health in the hopes of a declining spread. On June 14, 2002, Cardinal Health made a bid for Syncor, offering 0.52 shares of CAH for each share of SCOR. As Figure 15-2 shows, the stocks of the target and acquiring firms are closely correlated when the market expects the deal to be completed. From June 17 to October 30, 2002, we can see that the two stocks have a correlation close to 1; buying the target firm and short selling the acquiring firm would have earned a return of 2.76 percent over this period. This annualizes to a return of 7.76 percent, an acceptable return to risk arbitrageurs who make money as the spread slowly tightens.

When the spread fell to less than 25 cents per share long before the deal was expected to close, the fund closed its position based on a risk-reward analysis. This shows excellent risk management skills, as the potential reward of holding the spread was much smaller than the potential risk. While Long-Term Capital Management lost over $150 million on the failed takeover of Ciena, the Merger Fund seems more careful about deal risk. It was very fortunate that the

FIGURE 15-2

Close correlation between target and acquiring firm stocks when the deal is expected to be completed. (*Bloomberg.*)

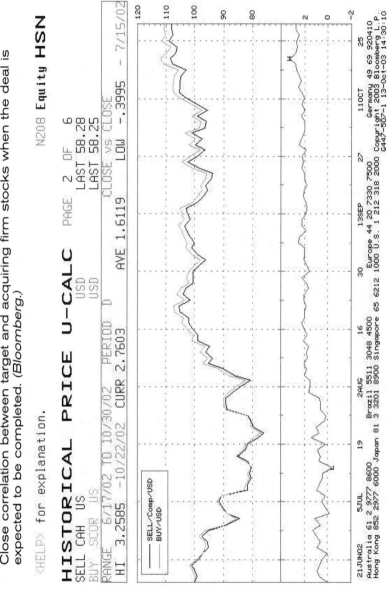

Merger Fund closed the spread in late October, as Cardinal Health later disclosed that its due diligence uncovered that executives of Syncor may have bribed Asian businessmen, a revelation that led to criminal charges. Upon this announcement in November 2002, the spread widened to $10; Syncor fell from $37 to $17 when many traders believed that the deal would be canceled. We can see this risk in Figure 15-3: the price of SCOR fell dramatically as these allegations were revealed. When the completion of the deal encounters significant uncertainty, we see that the correlation between the two stocks drops dramatically. Arbitrageurs who closed out this trade on this news locked in a loss of $10 per share. Of course, if the deal later failed, arbitrageurs who stayed with the trade could have posted even larger losses. The Merger Fund fortunately reopened the position at this widened spread. Cardinal later consummated the merger on December 31, 2002, but not before firing several executives of Syncor and cutting the deal price by about 10 percent, to 0.47 shares of CAH for each share of SCOR. In this trade the Merger Fund showed a keen understanding of the risk-reward relationships in merger arbitrage and made an even larger profit on its second trade than on its first.

A final risk to merger arbitrage is based on the reaction of the target and acquirer stocks to the merger announcement. Traders should look at the announcement price reactions to determine where the prices of the stocks will trade if the deal fails. If the target firm doubled while the acquiring firm fell by 30 percent upon the announcement of the deal, this can be a very risky trade if the merger is not consummated and the firms return to their predeal prices. A much less risky trade is one where the target firm increased 30 percent while the acquiring firm moved little as the merger was announced. While you may wish to hedge this exposure with stock options, the rest of the market also understands that failed deals can create large stock price volatilities, so these options may trade at very high prices, largely discounting the value of using derivatives for hedging merger breakups.

The CSFB/Tremont Risk Arbitrage Index averaged annual returns of 8.40 percent between January 1994 and June 2003, with a risk of 4.57 percent and a Sharpe ratio of 0.88. (See Fig. 15-4.) Risk arbitrage strategies have a high correlation of 0.44 to the S&P 500,

FIGURE 15–3

There can be significant risk to a merger arbitrage transaction if the market believes the transaction will not be completed. *(Bloomberg.)*

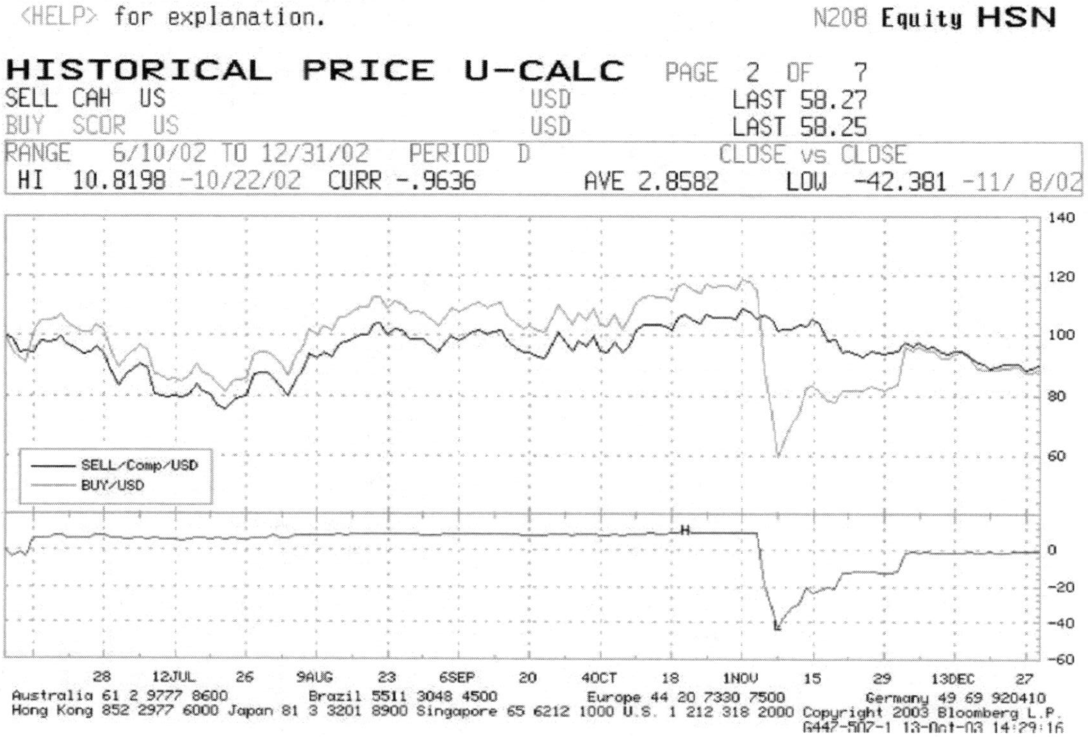
<HELP> for explanation.
N208 Equity HSN
HISTORICAL PRICE U-CALC PAGE 2 OF 7
SELL CAH US USD LAST 58.27
BUY SCOR US USD LAST 58.25
RANGE 6/10/02 TO 12/31/02 PERIOD D CLOSE vs CLOSE
HI 10.8198 -10/22/02 CURR -.9636 AVE 2.8582 LOW -42.381 -11/ 8/02
SELL/Comp/USD
BUY/USD
140
120
100
80
60
0
-20
-40
-60
H
L
28 12JUL 26 9AUG 23 6SEP 20 4OCT 18 1NOV 15 29 13DEC 27
Australia 61 2 9777 8600 Brazil 5511 3048 4500 Europe 44 20 7330 7500 Germany 49 69 920410
Hong Kong 852 2977 6000 Japan 81 3 3201 8900 Singapore 65 6212 1000 U.S. 1 212 318 2000 Copyright 2003 Bloomberg L.P.
G447-507-1 13-Oct-03 14:29:16

FIGURE 15−4

CSFB/Tremont Risk Arbitrage Index performance, 1994 to 2003. (MSCI, reprinted by permission; TASS, CSFB/Tremont, http://www.hedgeindex.com.)

The CSFB/Tremont Risk Arbitrage Index measures the return to hedge funds that anticipate the successful completion of corporate mergers. These funds purchase shares in the target comany while selling short shares in the acquiring firm.

CSFB/Tremont Risk Arbitrage Index

Legend: S&P 500 — MSCI World Sovereign Debt Index — CSFB/Tremont Risk Arbitrage Index

	CSFB/Tremont Risk Arbitrage
1994	5.26
1995	11.90
1996	13.83
1997	9.84
1998	5.59
1999	13.23
2000	14.67
2001	5.69
2002	−3.46
Annual Return	8.40
Annual Standard Deviation	4.57
Skewness	−1.30
Kurtosis	5.77
Sharpe Ratio	0.88
Sortino Ratio	1.58
Alpha vs. S&P 500	6.75
Beta vs. S&P 500	0.12
Alpha vs. MSCI World Debt	8.52
Beta vs. MSCI World Debt	−0.07
Best Monthly Return	3.81
Worst Monthly Return	−6.15
Best Annual Return	14.67
Worst Annual Return	−3.46
% Winning Months	78.9%

FIGURE 15-4

Continued. (MSCI, reprinted by permission; TASS, CSFB/Tremont, http://www.hedgeindex.com.)

Correlation to	CSFB/Tremont Risk Arbitrage
TASS Fund of Funds	0.49
CSFB/Tremont Hedge Fund Index	0.37
CSFB/Tremont Convertible Arbitrage	0.41
CSFB/Tremont Ded Short Bias	−0.48
CSFB/Tremont Emerging Markets	0.42
CSFB/Tremont Equity Mkt Ntrl	0.31
CSFB/Tremont Event Driven	0.68
CSFB/Tremont Distressed	0.56
CSFB/Tremont E.D. Multi-Strategy	0.65
CSFB/Tremont Risk Arbitrage	1.00
CSFB/Tremont Fixed Inc Arb	0.13
CSFB/Tremont Global Macro	0.12
CSFB/Tremont Long/Short Equity	0.49
CSFB/Tremont Managed Futures	−0.26
CSFB/Tremont Multi-Strategy	0.04
MSCI Discretionary Trading	0.52
MSCI Systematic Trading	−0.17
3 mo Tbills	0.25
S&P 500	0.44
MSCI World Sovereign Debt	−0.09
Average to Hedge Fund Strategies	0.25
Average to Traditional Investments	0.20
Conditional Correlations	
S&P 500 Up Markets (71 mo)	0.20
S&P 500 Down Markets (43 mo)	0.50
MSCI Debt Up Markets (65 mo)	0.02
MSCI Debt Down Markets (49 mo)	0.22

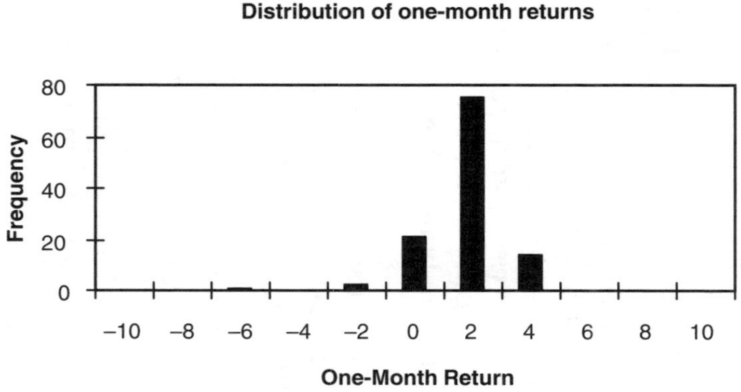

as deals tend to be announced and completed more often during bull markets. Merger arbitrage is an extremely popular strategy, estimated at 11.5 percent of hedge fund assets at the end of 2001.

While the average correlation between risk arbitrage funds and the S&P 500 is 0.44, this increases to 0.50 in falling stock markets and falls to 0.20 in rising stock markets. Figure 15-5 illustrates that this correlation can be quite volatile, ranging from slightly negative correlations to figures above 70 percent over rolling two-year periods.

Figure 15-6 demonstrates that risk arbitrage funds earned positive returns in 78.9 percent of the months over the last 10 years, with a maximum monthly loss for the CSFB/Tremont Risk Arbitrage Index of −6.15 percent. Of course, this maximum loss was experienced during the worst month for stock prices over the same period. This is logical, as deals are likely to fail when stock prices are extremely weak.

Finally, Figure 15-7 shows us that risk arbitrage funds are able to post profits in nearly all stock market environments. Of course,

FIGURE 15-5

CSFB/Tremont Risk Arbitrage Index: 24-month rolling correlation to traditional investments.

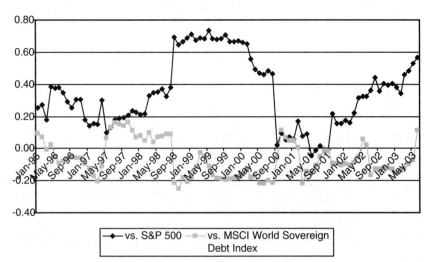

FIGURE 15−6

CSFB/Tremont Risk Arbitrage Index versus S&P 500:
monthly return pairs, January 1994 to June 2003.

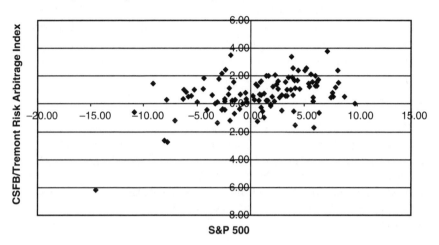

FIGURE 15−7

CSFB/Tremont Risk Arbitrage Index versus S&P 500: monthly
returns sorted by quintiles, January 1994 to June 2003.

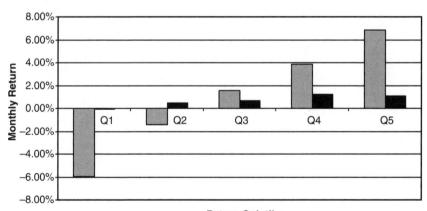

as mergers tend to be announced more frequently during times of rising stock prices, the returns to deal arbitrage generally improve in the most robust equity markets.

Because of the relatively low risk profile of risk arbitrage funds, their managers can afford to use a significant amount of leverage. Ineichen estimates that risk arbitrage hedge fund managers can control 2 to 5 times the assets contributed by their investors.[3]

ENDNOTES

1. This chapter benefits from the discussions in J. G. Nicholas, *Market Neutral Investing: Long/Short Hedge Fund Strategies*, Chapters 4, 7, and 10.
2. J. Paulson, "The 'Risk' in Risk Arbitrage," in V. R. Parker (ed.), *Managing Hedge Fund Risk*. London: Risk Waters Group, 2000.
3. A. M. Ineichen, 2003, *Absolute Returns: The Risk and Opportunities of Hedge Fund Investing*. Hoboken NJ: John Wiley & Sons, 2003.

CHAPTER 16

Distressed Investing and Event-Driven Hedge Fund Strategies

Managers in the distressed investing category will typically trade debt and equity securities of companies in financial distress. Distressed companies may currently be in default on some debt obligations, they may be close to default and negotiating with creditors to restructure their obligations, or the firm may already have declared bankruptcy. The vast majority of these firms will have below-investment-grade credit ratings. Hedge funds can often buy these securities at reduced prices, as many other investors are unable to own these securities. Many institutional investors are prohibited from owning securities of companies with below-investment-grade ratings or companies in default. Investors in distressed securities have been called the ultimate-value investors, as they purchase the securities of firms that no one else wishes to own.

Figure 16-1 illustrates that the opportunities to invest in distressed companies vary widely over the course of the business cycle, with a −43.8 percent correlation between default rates and stock prices. From 1981 to 1998, the annual amount of announced defaults on U.S. corporate bonds ranged from $100 million to $11.3 billion in most years, according to Standard and Poor's. However, the recession years of 1990 and 1991 saw defaults rise to $21.2 billion and $23.6 billion. Each year, from 1999 through 2002, the market experienced new records for the face value of corporate bond defaults, rising from $40.4 billion to $44.0 billion in 1999 and 2000, before exploding to $118.8 billion and $177.8 billion in 2001 and 2002. These record default rates coincided with the weakest stock markets

FIGURE 16-1

Distressed activity by year: U.S. corporate defaults ($ billions) versus % return to the S&P 500. *(Standard and Poor's.)*

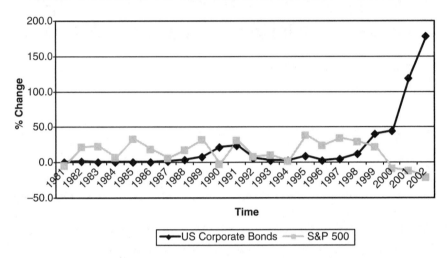

in decades and the popping of the bubble valuations in the technology and telecommunications sectors.

Investors in distressed securities must have special skills to understand the bankruptcy process. In the United States, a firm may file for protection from its creditors under Chapter 7 or Chapter 11 of the U.S. bankruptcy code. Typically, a bankrupt firm has assets that are valued at less than its liabilities, or it owns insufficient liquid assets to pay its short-term liabilities. If a firm fails to negotiate successfully with its creditors, the creditors may force the firm into involuntary bankruptcy proceedings.[1]

Chapter 7 is a liquidation process, where the operations of the firm are closed and all assets are sold as quickly as possible to satisfy the creditors of the firm. All bankruptcies in Europe are liquidations, as the European bankruptcy codes do not allow firms to continue operating after bankruptcy. If a company is liquidated, it is clear that stockholders in the firm will receive nothing, as the life of the firm is ended and there are no continuing operations to provide cash flows to the equity holders.

A Chapter 11 bankruptcy allows the firm to reorganize its operations, with the goal of changing the composition of the liabilities of the firm in a way that will allow the firm to continue as an operating company. The bankruptcy court has broad powers to restructure the obligations of the firm. The options include canceling debt or negotiating partial settlements, canceling leases, changing the terms of labor contracts, and declaring the previous equity of the firm to be worthless.

A vital trait of an investor of distressed securities is the understanding of all debt and equity securities of the firm. There are many ways to invest in a distressed firm, ranging from low-risk to high-risk securities. The lowest-risk investments are the purchase of senior bonds or collateralized bank debt. The holders of these debt obligations have the highest claim on the assets of the firm. All collateralized debt holders have the ability to take a specific asset of the firm, typically real estate or high-value equipment such as aircraft, and sell the asset to satisfy the remaining obligation on the note. Of course, employees, attorneys, and trade credit extended after the bankruptcy is declared are paid first, or the firm could not operate during the bankruptcy process. Senior debt holders have the highest claim on the assets of the firm after all collateralized debt holders and post-bankruptcy obligations have been satisfied. Less senior claims on assets include subordinated debt, leaseholders, trade creditors, and stockholders. In many cases, the private debt, such as bank loans and trade credit, is much larger than the amount of the outstanding publicly traded bonds. Distressed investors may be able to purchase this private debt at discounted prices.

The choice of how to trade a distressed situation depends on whether the firm is liquidating or restructuring, and the trader's view of the value of the assets and the value of the firm. Owning the senior debt or collateralized obligations of the firm is the safest way to invest in a distressed firm, especially in liquidation. If the proceeds of the liquidation are insufficient to completely repay these senior debt holders, all junior claims and equity holders will see their claims expire worthless, while senior debt holders will receive only a partial recovery of their investment. Therefore, subordinated debt holders and stockholders will always prefer a restructuring over a liquidation, especially when the assets of the firm are significantly smaller than the liabilities.

In a restructuring, traders may prefer to purchase the subordinated claims. While the senior debt holders may earn a complete recovery of their investment, the subordinated debt holders often see their debt reorganized into new debt or equity claims on the new firm. Clearly, equity claims on a restructured firm have the opportunity to be more valuable than a straight debt obligation. In most bankruptcies, the owners of common stock see their holdings declared worthless as the stock is canceled and their equity stake is transferred to the debt holders.

Many distressed investors will simply buy-and-hold the securities in the distressed firm, hoping to profit when the court and other investors negotiate the proceeds of the liquidation or restructuring. All retail investors and small hedge funds will have to invest in this passive manner, as their holdings are not significant enough to have any say in the court proceedings. They will simply have to wait months, or even years, before the courts and large creditors decide on the distribution of value to each class of security holder.

However, many large hedge funds, or funds with very concentrated positions, may take an active role in the legal proceedings. Once an investor owns more than one-third of the outstanding debt, or can organize a group of investors to vote with his or her position, the investor can petition the court with his or her version of the restructuring plan. While there are rules about the priority of claims in the bankruptcy process, there is evidence that they are not always strictly followed. The plan filed by activist investors will either seek to bias the distribution of assets toward the security class that they own or try to expedite the court proceedings to earn their distribution in a timelier manner. This one-third threshold is important, as two-thirds of creditors must vote to approve the restructuring plan. Once an investor controls more than one-third of the votes, he or she will be able to block any plans that do not favor his or her holdings. Activist investors may be subject to special liquidity risks, especially if the court blocks them from buying or selling securities of the firm once they file a restructuring plan.

The vast majority of investors in distressed companies will only purchase securities of the firm, and their usual focus is on debt, rather than equity, securities. Managers may hedge the interest rate risk in these positions by shorting Treasury bonds. They may also short the stocks of other firms in the industry to hedge the risk that business conditions will deteriorate and cause a decline in the liquidation values of the assets of the firm.

Other investors will practice capital structure arbitrage, creating spreads between the various securities of the firm. A popular spread is to purchase the debt securities while selling short the common stock of a firm. Typically these investors will purchase the debt and short the equity of the firm, or trade spreads between bonds of different seniority. This strategy may be especially profitable if the short stock position is initiated before the bankruptcy filing, as the stock price declines dramatically when the firm announces its need for reorganization or liquidation.

Kopin Tan, *Barron's* options columnist, describes how capital structure arbitrage can be implemented using equity options.[2] This trade can be quite successful when the bond market and the equity options markets have different views on the company's future. For example, consider a firm whose junk bonds trade at very high yields, while the equity options market prices the put options on the company's stock at low implied volatility levels. A fund manager may choose to purchase the junk bonds to earn the high yield, while buying the equity put options to insure against a continued decline in the stock price. If the company declares bankruptcy, the price of both the junk bonds and the stock will fall significantly. If the trade is structured correctly, the gains from the equity put options will more than offset the losses from the declining bond position. Some managers will buy large numbers of deep out-of-the-money puts, such as $10 puts on a $25 stock. This ensures that the options will have a relatively small dollar price, yet still have a significant payoff if the company declares bankruptcy before the expiration of the option.

This trade may work especially well in market environments such as summer 2003, as bond yields and stock prices were both increasing rapidly. Rising yields on fixed-income securities make bond prices cheaper and more attractive to investors, while rising stock prices are often accompanied by options priced with lower implied volatility. Hedge fund managers who feel that the bond yields on distressed companies are higher than warranted given their expected risks, while put option prices are low, could earn large profits on this trade if their forecasts prove correct.

When creating hedges, it is important that the two securities are highly correlated. The investor must realize that this type of trade only works with distressed securities. Companies with low credit ratings often have bonds whose prices are highly correlated to the stock price. Firms with investment grade debt will often see their bond prices more strongly influenced by interest rates than by the stock price.

If the stock price and the bond price are moving independently, this trade may act more like two separate positions than a coherent hedge.

There are several risks that are unique to distressed investing, and many of those risks are related to the court proceedings and the bankruptcy process.

As with all other investment strategies, hedge fund managers can estimate the return to an investment in distressed securities. For example, a manager may purchase bonds for 60 percent of face value, hoping to receive 80 percent of that value back at the end of the bankruptcy proceedings. If the process takes three months, the fund has earned a 132 percent annualized return on investment. If the proceedings take much longer than expected, such as three years, that annual return falls to 11 percent. The hedge fund manager will need to understand how complicated and controversial the proceedings will be and estimate the time that the legal process will take to reach completion. An active investor may add value to the process simply by expediting the proceedings, as the annualized returns to creditors may be higher the more quickly a settlement is reached.

Investors should also anticipate the value of the firm after the restructuring process. In many cases, the firm will be more valuable after the restructuring, as it has higher cash flows and less risk as a result of the cancellation of debt and leases and more favorable employee contracts. Some firms, however, may never recover from the negative publicity surrounding a bankruptcy announcement. A retail chain or a consumer products company may be especially vulnerable, as its customers need to have confidence that the firm will remain in business and be able to adequately support and maintain its products.

In the vast majority of bankruptcies, the court will cancel the residual claims of the original stockholders, leaving them with no share in the restructured firm. This can be an opportunity for short sellers, who can literally see the stock drop to zero. Unfortunately, the stock trades until the bankruptcy is completed and the stock is canceled, so it can take over one year for the stock to drop from $1 to zero. Many brokerage firms have special margin requirements for short stocks below $5 that can make a short sale less profitable than previously anticipated. If there is a surprising development that allows the original stock to survive the bankruptcy process, the price can rise quickly and cause large losses for short sellers.

Junior, or subordinated, debt holders are often able to exit the restructuring process with a new class of equity in the new, less risky firm. Empirically, new equity issues of previously bankrupt firms dramatically outperform the market during their first year as a new company. This return may be explained by neglect, where most sell-side analysts drop coverage of a company in bankruptcy and only initiate coverage months or years after the new class of stock is created. For all types of stocks, there are generally positive excess returns as the stock grows from no sell-side coverage to a following of three or more analysts. There may also be a large return to shareholders in the new equity, as there may be little public information about the firm, and all of the news about the firm during the bankruptcy process was negative. Investors who understand that the new firm has less debt and lower expenses have a much more realistic, and more positive, view of the firm than most other investors. Once the firm has reported some strong earnings in their first few quarters, public sentiment can change and send the stock price sharply higher.

When a firm is liquidated, investors will anticipate the value of the assets of the firm, and estimate how that value will be distributed to each class of investors in the firm. Assets will receive higher prices when sold to willing bidders, when time is taken to sufficiently market the assets, and when the demand for that type of asset is strong. Assets will sell for lower prices when they must be sold quickly, when their sale is not well publicized, or when there is an excess supply of that type of asset. After the Enron bankruptcy at the end of 2001, many electric and gas utilities simultaneously decided that they needed to sell assets to reduce their debt. Unfortunately, other utilities are the natural buyers for these assets. When all of the natural, or strategic, buyers are selling, it can be difficult to sell your assets at a high price. At this point, financial buyers step in. A financial buyer such as Warren Buffet's Berkshire Hathaway, who does not have significant utility operations, will only buy when these assets are offered at prices that are low enough to generate very high rates of return. Obviously, the price that financial buyers will pay is lower than that offered by strategic buyers, so analysts should estimate the strength of the industry in forecasting the value of the liquidated assets.

Edward Altman, in his book *Distressed Securities* estimates that historic recovery rates, the portion of the face value of bonds returned to investors after a liquidation, have averaged around 40 percent. Secured and senior debt will have higher recovery rates and subordinated debt will have lower recovery rates. These recovery rates have fallen dramatically in recent years, as bankruptcies have been concentrated in industries with less salable assets and more intellectual capital, as well as assets with rapid obsolescence.

Technology, Internet, and telecommunications bankruptcies after the year 2000 had much lower recovery rates. Some fiber optic or telecomm networks that were built with billions of dollars in debt were sold for tens of millions of dollars in liquidation sales, as the technology aged rapidly and the industry was already drowning in excess capacity.

The CSFB/Tremont Distressed Investing Index averaged annual returns of 13.34 percent between January 1994 and June 2003, with a risk of 7.15 percent and a Sharpe ratio of 1.25. (See Fig. 16-2.) The year 2002 was weak for funds investing in distressed securities, as increased bankruptcies and falling credit quality left the sector with a total return of -0.69 percent for the year. Distressed investing is a less popular strategy, estimated at about 2.6 percent of hedge fund assets at the end of 2001.

Distressed investing strategies have a high correlation of 0.55 to the S&P 500, as companies are better able to sell assets or return to profitability when business conditions are favorable. Figure 16-3 shows that this correlation can be quite volatile, averaging 0.54 when stocks are falling, and 0.09 when equities are in a bull market.

The scatter plot of returns to the CSFB/Tremont Distressed Index and the S&P 500 shows that distressed funds post positive returns in 77.2 percent of all months, with a maximum monthly loss of -12.45 percent. (See Fig. 16-4.) This dramatically demonstrates the high kurtosis of 16.24, as this monthly loss is nearly 4 annual standard deviations below the mean. The loss that should happen once in 100 years happened once in just over 100 months. Clearly there is significant event risk and liquidity risks in distressed investing, as the legal proceedings can take a dramatic turn and award advantages to tranches of securities that you do not own.

FIGURE 16-2

CSFB/Tremont Distressed Index performance, 1994 to 2003. (MSCI, reprinted by permission; TASS, CSFB/Tremont, http://www.hedgeindex.com.)

The CSFB/Tremont Distressed Index measures the return to hedge funds that invest in the securities of companies that are approaching, or have declared, bankruptcy. These funds take substantial liquidity and credit risk, and are expected to fully understand the legal processes of bankruptcy proceedings. While these funds typically purchase bonds or bank loans of distressed firms, they may also choose to trade the equity or equity options of the firm.

CSFB/Tremont Distressed Index

Legend: S&P 500 — MSCI World Sovereign Debt Index — CSFB/Tremont Distressed Index

	CSFB/Tremont Distressed
1994	0.66
1995	26.13
1996	25.54
1997	20.74
1998	−1.68
1999	22.18
2000	1.94
2001	20.01
2002	−0.69
Annual Return	13.34
Annual Standard Deviation	7.15
Skewness	−2.80
Kurtosis	16.24
Sharpe Ratio	1.25
Sortino Ratio	1.96
Alpha vs. S&P 500	9.94
Beta vs. S&P 500	0.24
Alpha vs. MSCI World Debt	13.29
Beta vs. MSCI World Debt	−0.11
Best Monthly Return	4.10
Worst Monthly Return	−12.45
Best Annual Return	26.13
Worst Annual Return	−1.68
% Winning Months	77.2%

FIGURE 16-2

Continued. *(MSCI, reprinted by permission; TASS, CSFB/Tremont, http://www.hedgeindex.com.)*

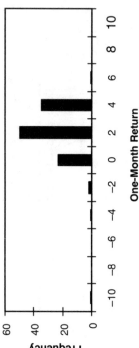

Distribution of one-month returns

Correlation to	CSFB/Tremont Distressed
TASS Fund of Funds	0.65
CSFB/Tremont Hedge Fund Index	0.57
CSFB/Tremont Convertible Arbitrage	0.51
CSFB/Tremont Ded Short Bias	−0.63
CSFB/Tremont Emerging Markets	0.59
CSFB/Tremont Equity Mkt Ntrl	0.35
CSFB/Tremont Event Driven	0.94
CSFB/Tremont Distressed	1.00
CSFB/Tremont E.D. Multi-Strategy	0.75
CSFB/Tremont Risk Arbitrage	0.56
CSFB/Tremont Fixed Inc Arb	0.31
CSFB/Tremont Global Macro	0.31
CSFB/Tremont Long/Short Equity	0.57
CSFB/Tremont Managed Futures	−0.17
CSFB/Tremont Multi-Strategy	0.09
MSCI Discretionary Trading	0.49
MSCI Systematic Trading	−0.11
3 mo Tbills	0.02
S&P 500	0.55
MSCI World Sovereign Debt	−0.10
Average to Hedge Fund Strategies	0.34
Average to Traditional Investments	0.16
Conditional Correlations	
S&P 500 Up Markets (71 mo)	0.09
S&P 500 Down Markets (43 mo)	0.54
MSCI Debt Up Markets (65 mo)	−0.13
MSCI Debt Down Markets (49 mo)	0.04

FIGURE 16-3

CSFB/Tremont Distressed Index: 24-month rolling correlation to traditional investments.

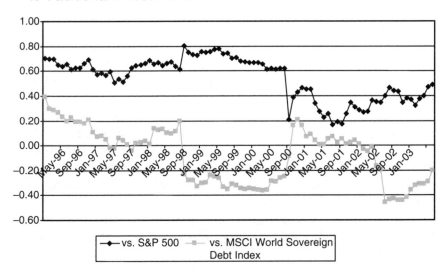

FIGURE 16-4

CSFB/Tremont Distressed Index versus S&P 500: monthly return pairs, January 1994 to June 2003.

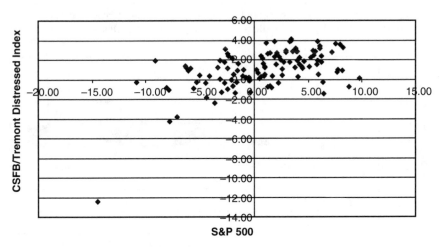

When sorting returns to distressed investments relative to the equity market environment, we note that the largest returns to distressed investments come in average to strong equity markets. (See Fig. 16-5.) When stock prices fall, distressed investments are much less profitable, as there may be less of a demand to buy the assets of the distressed firm, or a recessionary environment reduces the cash flows of the wounded company.

The opportunities for investing in risk arbitrage and distressed investments follow opposite cycles, as we can see in Figure 16-6. The percentage change of the dollar value of announced mergers (provided by Mergerstat) has a −50.4 percent correlation to the dollar value of defaults on U.S. corporate debt (according to Standard and Poor's). Merger activity is strong when stock prices rise, and distressed investments are more prevalent when stock prices are weak. Therefore, we would expect that a hedge fund that trades both risk arbitrage and distressed situations would have a more steady deal flow that funds that specialize in just one of these areas.

The CSFB/Tremont Event-Driven Multi-Strategy Index measures the returns to hedge funds that invest in many types of corporate events, including mergers, bankruptcies, spinoffs, and warrant

FIGURE 16−5

CSFB/Tremont Distressed Index versus S&P 500: monthly returns sorted by quintiles, January 1994 to June 2003.

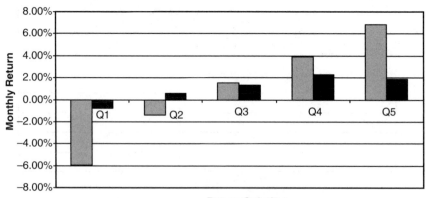

FIGURE 16-6

Merger activity versus distressed activity.

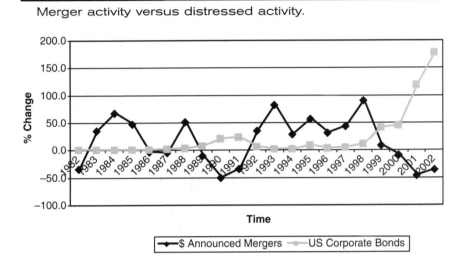

arbitrage. The risk-return relationship of event-driven funds fits squarely between that of the risk arbitrage and distressed investing funds. The multistrategy index offers an annual return of 10.34 percent with a risk of 6.52 percent and a Sharpe ratio of 0.92. (See Fig. 16-7.)

The correlation between the multistrategy funds and the S&P 500 averages 0.48, with 0.59 correlation in falling stock markets and 0.15 correlation in rising markets. This correlation has always been positive in rolling two-year periods since 1994, but has ranged from 0.03 to 0.80 over the last nine years. (See Fig. 16-8.)

As expected, event-driven funds have significant event risk, as shown by the kurtosis of 16.28 and the minimum monthly return of −11.52 percent. Figure 16-9 also illustrates that event-driven multistrategy funds have earned profits in 76.3 percent of all months in our sample.

Figure 16-10 demonstrates that event-driven funds are most profitable, on average, when equity markets are strong. We can expect to experience losses when stock prices are falling, as this sentiment often causes them to flee the risky assets traded in event-driven funds.

This flight-to-quality nature of event-driven funds is illustrated in Figure 16-11. In quintile 5, world sovereign debt prices are rising

FIGURE 16-7

CSFB/Tremont Event-Driven Multi-Strategy Index performance, 1994 to 2003. (MSCI, reprinted by permission; TASS, CSFB/Tremont, http://www.hedgeindex.com.)

The CSFB/Tremont Event-Driven Multi-Strategy Index tracks investments in hedge funds that maintain flexibility in their trading style. These funds typically focus on distressed securities and merger arbitrage trades, changing their style mix based on the relative opportunities currently offered in each type of trade. Managers may also participate in spinoffs, reorganization or options and warrants trading.

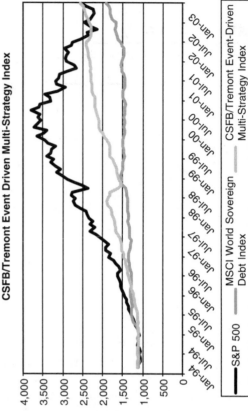

CSFB/Tremont Event Driven Multi-Strategy Index

	CSFB/Tremont Event-Driven Multi-Strategy
1994	0.63
1995	12.91
1996	22.71
1997	20.53
1998	–8.97
1999	23.01
2000	11.83
2001	6.81
2002	1.23
Annual Return	10.34
Annual Standard Deviation	6.52
Skewness	–2.68
Kurtosis	16.28
Sharpe Ratio	0.92
Sortino Ratio	1.39
Alpha vs. S&P 500	7.78
Beta vs. S&P 500	0.19
Alpha vs. MSCI World Debt	11.52
Beta vs. MSCI World Debt	–0.26
Best Monthly Return	4.66
Worst Monthly Return	–11.52
Best Annual Return	23.01
Worst Annual Return	–8.97
% Winning Months	76.3%

FIGURE 16-7

Continued. (MSCI, reprinted by permission; TASS, CSFB/Tremont, http://www.hedgeindex.com.)

Correlation to	CSFB/Tremont Event-Driven Multi-Strategy
TASS Fund of Funds	0.75
CSFB/Tremont Hedge Fund Index	0.68
CSFB/Tremont Convertible Arbitrage	0.60
CSFB/Tremont Ded Short Bias	−0.55
CSFB/Tremont Emerging Markets	0.68
CSFB/Tremont Equity Mkt Ntrl	0.36
CSFB/Tremont Event Driven	0.93
CSFB/Tremont Distressed	0.75
CSFB/Tremont E.D. Multi-Strategy	1.00
CSFB/Tremont Risk Arbitrage	0.65
CSFB/Tremont Fixed Inc Arb	0.44
CSFB/Tremont Global Macro	0.42
CSFB/Tremont Long/Short Equity	0.63
CSFB/Tremont Managed Futures	−0.28
CSFB/Tremont Multi-Strategy	0.18
MSCI Discretionary Trading	0.63
MSCI Systematic Trading	−0.17
3 mo Tbills	0.07
S&P 500	0.48
MSCI World Sovereign Debt	−0.25
Average to Hedge Fund Strategies	0.40
Average to Traditional Investments	0.10
Conditional Correlations	
S&P 500 Up Markets (71 mo)	0.15
S&P 500 Down Markets (43 mo)	0.59
MSCI Debt Up Markets (65 mo)	−0.15
MSCI Debt Down Markets (49 mo)	0.14

Distribution of one-month returns

FIGURE 16-8

CSFB/Tremont Event-Driven Multi-Strategy Index: 24-month rolling correlation to traditional investments.

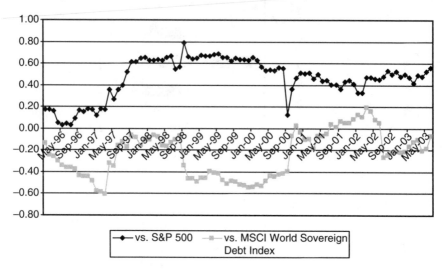

FIGURE 16-9

CSFB/Tremont Event-Driven Multi-Strategy Index versus S&P 500: monthly return pairs, January 1994 to June 2003.

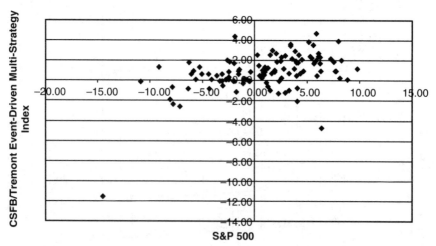

FIGURE 16−10

CSFB/Tremont Event-Driven Multi-Strategy Index versus S&P 500: monthly returns sorted by quintiles, January 1994 to June 2003.

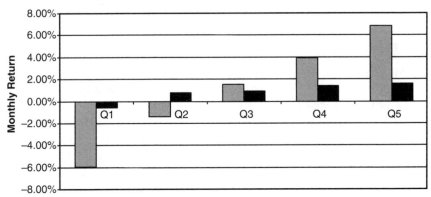

FIGURE 16−11

CSFB/Tremont Event-Driven Multi-Strategy Index versus MSCI World Sovereign Debt Index: monthly returns sorted by quintiles, January 1994 to June 2003.

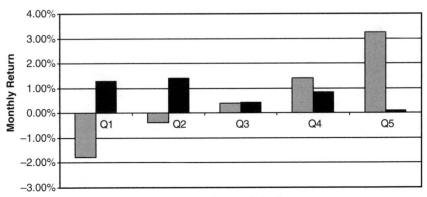

and yields are falling, clear examples of turmoil in the markets that cause investors to seek refuge in government-issued bonds. Beyond this flight-to-quality scenario seen in quintile 5, event-driven funds are solidly profitable in all other scenarios for changes in government bond yields.

ENDNOTES

1. This chapter benefits from the discussions in J. G. Nicholas, *Market Neutral Investing: Long/Short Hedge Fund Strategies*, Chapters 4, 7, and 10.
2. Kopin Tan, "Credit Counts," *Barron's*, August 18, 2003.

Convertible-Bond Arbitrage and Relative-Value Hedge Fund Strategies

Convertible-bond arbitrage is another category of event-driven strategies. With nearly $5 billion in assets, convertible-bond hedge funds may suffer from significant liquidity risk, as these bonds are in high demand and investors often buy these bonds and hold them until maturity or conversion. This high level of demand may leave the prices too high to always present profitable buying opportunities.

Convertible bonds are a relatively small asset class. KBC Financial Products estimated in 1999 that the U.S. market had about $180 billion in outstanding convertible bonds, while Japan and Europe had $124 billion each, and the rest of Asia had a much smaller market of $31 billion. This is a global convertible-bond market of only $460 billion, which is smaller than the combined market capitalization of General Electric and Microsoft at the end of 2002.[1] The Bond Market Association estimates that U.S. convertible-bond issuance exceeded $140 billion over the last three years, leaving the size of the U.S. market at about $285 billion at the end of September 2003.[2]

Traditionally, yield-hungry equity managers liked to invest in convertible bonds, as the coupon income of the bonds generally exceeded the dividend yield of the stock. After the 2003 dividend tax cuts, this strategy is less attractive, as the tax rate on stock dividends has fallen, whereas the tax on bond interest has remained steady at the investor's marginal rate.[3]

It is clear that hedge funds have had a strong influence on the liquidity and pricing of the convertible-bond market. As the assets managed by convertible-bond hedge funds grow, the demand for new convertible issues also rises. This strong demand leads to higher prices and lower yields, which helps corporate issuers, but makes convertibles less attractive to long-only convertible-bond investors. Hedge funds are estimated to purchase 60 percent of new convertible-bond issuance, up from 20 percent in 1998. Because hedge funds care more about the return these bonds could create in an arbitrage situation, new deals are more attractive to these players than the traditional buy-side convertible-bond investors. Longtime convertible-bond investor John Calamos has been buying smaller amounts of the new issues for his mutual funds, as he finds the pricing unattractive.[4]

There are several new structures that are likely to appeal to hedge fund investors but may elicit a colder reception from typical stock and bond buyers. Due to falling interest rates and an increased appetite from hedge fund buyers, companies are able to issue "no-no" convertible bonds. These bonds are priced at par and pay a zero coupon, meaning that they also have no yield. The investors who buy these bonds are simply accepting a call option on the price of the stock instead of the interest that would be paid on an option-free bond of the same firm. Investors are more likely to accept the option instead of a standard bond yield for companies with the most valuable options. In most cases, this means that the most volatile stocks, especially in the technology sector, are able to issue no-nos, as stocks with the highest expected stock price volatility have the most valuable options.[5]

Stock investors must be careful to understand the terms of new convertible-bond issues. Traditionally, new convertible-bond issues were expected to be eventually converted to stock and were counted as potential dilution to the common stock. For example, if the bonds could be converted into the equivalent of 10 percent of the outstanding shares of stock, many stock investors would reduce their earnings per share EPS estimates by 10 percent to offset the increase in the number of shares likely to be eventually issued. However, a 2000 ruling by the Financial Accounting Standards Board (FASB) opened the door to the issuance of contingent convertibles. Contingent convertible bonds have no immediate dilution, which makes the company's stock look stronger than it actually is.

Dilution only occurs after the stock price rises to a predetermined price target, triggering convertibility of the bonds and an increase in the number of shares outstanding.[6]

Convertible bonds fit squarely between stocks and bonds. From 1973 to 2000, the S&P 500 had an average annual return of 13.0 percent with a standard deviation of 17.0 percent, while long-term corporate bonds returned 9.0 percent with a volatility of 11.9 percent. Ibbotson Associates estimates the returns to convertible bonds as 11.9 percent, with a risk of 12.7 percent over the same time period.[7]

It makes sense that the risk-return relationship of convertibles is between stocks and bonds, as convertibles are a hybrid of the two asset classes. When a company issues convertible bonds, it is borrowing funds and agreeing to pay the owner of the security an annual interest payment. This coupon rate is lower than the rate on other bonds of the same company, as the company has sold a call option on its stock to the buyer of the convertible bond. If the stock of the issuer rises significantly over time, the owner of the convertible bond may be repaid in stock instead of cash. While some convertible bonds may have very complicated structures, a plain vanilla convertible bond can be priced as a corporate bond plus an equity call option.

Convertible bonds have some very attractive properties, acting like defensive bonds in equity bear markets and like more aggressive stocks in equity bull markets. As you can see in Figure 17-1, convertible bonds offer 70 percent of the up side of the equity markets, as the embedded call option on the stock becomes more sensitive to stock prices as the market rises. As stock prices fall, this asset class suffers only 52 percent of the downside, as the straight bond feature protects investors as stock prices fall.[8] As the stock moves significantly higher, the delta of the call option increases, causing the convertible bond to have a higher correlation to the stock and the general level of the stock market. When the call option is slightly out of the money, the price of the convertible bond will act more like a bond and increase its correlation to interest rates. Bonds are called "busted convertibles" when the stock option is deep out of the money and has little chance of being exercised, such as when the stock price and the credit quality of the firm has rapidly declined. Trading busted convertible bonds is like trading junk bonds, where it is important to analyze the credit quality of the firm to determine

FIGURE 17−1

Price graph: convertible bonds versus stock price. (*Aswath Damodaran, Investment Valuation, 2d ed., John Wiley & Sons, 2002. Reprinted by permission.*)

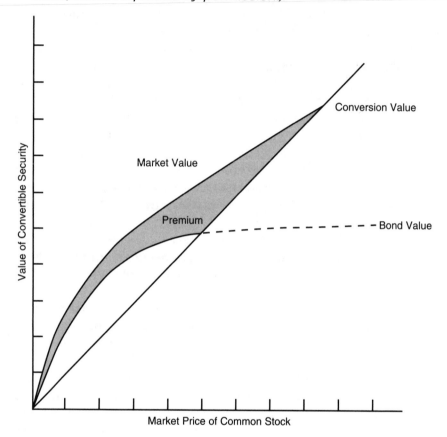

if the firm will be able to pay the principal and interest stated on the bond on a timely basis. The correlation between the stock and the convertible bond increases again as the company experiences distress, as both the bond and the stock could trade down to zero after a default or bankruptcy of the firm.

Convertible bond = bond + equity call option
Option strike price = convertible face value / number of shares per convertible bond

Conversion value = current stock price × number of shares per convertible bond

Conversion premium = convertible-bond price / conversion value

A plain vanilla convertible bond is priced as the sum of a straight bond of the firm and a call option on the firm's stock price. We can find the strike price of the option by dividing the par value of the bond by the conversion ratio. If a $1000 bond can be converted into 50 shares of stock, we can value this as 50 stock options with a strike price of $20 each. Typically the convertible bond will trade at a higher price than the conversion value, which is the conversion ratio multiplied by the stock price. A bond may be issued at par with a $20 strike price when the stock price is trading at $15. This $750 conversion value is found by multiplying 50 shares by the current stock price of $15 per share.

The percentage difference between the price of the bond and the conversion value is called the *conversion premium.* As we move to higher stock prices and to the right of the graph, the conversion premium is falling and the bond is becoming more sensitive to the price of the stock. As we move to lower stock prices and to the left of the graph, the conversion premium is rising and the bond is becoming more correlated to the straight bonds of the firm.

Pricing a convertible bond is as simple as valuing a straight bond and a stock option. The cash flows of the bond should be discounted at the rate which the firm, or companies with similar credit ratings, can issue new debt. If the company's estimated cost of debt capital is 8 percent—that is, the discount rate of the convertible bond's cash flows—even though the convertible may have a lower coupon, such as 3 percent. The convertible bond will have a lower coupon than other types of debt issued by the same firm, as investors will pay for the stock options imbedded in the convertible bond. There are many ratios that can be used in the credit analysis of the firm to determine the appropriate discount rate. Generally a firm with higher sales, assets, cash flows, profits, and stock market value will have a higher credit rating and a lower cost of debt capital. As the face value of the debt and the interest costs of the firm rise relative to these variables, the credit rating will fall and the cost of debt will increase.

There are a number of variables that affect the price of call options on a stock: maturity, strike price, stock price, interest rates, and stock price volatility. The price of the call option will increase with an increase in the stock price, volatility, maturity, and interest rates. We also know that call options decrease in value as the strike price rises. Unfortunately, the Black-Scholes model may not be appropriate for modeling the options imbedded in convertible bonds, as it may be difficult to accept the model's assumptions of constant volatility and interest rates over a 5- to 10-year period, which is the typical maturity of newly issued convertible bonds. It is much easier to ignore these assumptions for the typical maturity of a listed stock option, which is often less than six months.

To implement a convertible-bond arbitrage, the manager will purchase the convertible bonds of the firm and hedge the stock price risk with a short stock position. The hedge ratio will be the delta of the option, which is derived using the implied volatility of the option. If managers have a different view of volatility, they may each implement their hedges in different ratios. Most managers will have a zero delta position for their portfolio of convertible bonds, making their fund insensitive to the direction of the equity market. Some managers may hedge all bonds to a delta-neutral position, while other managers may estimate which stocks will outperform or underperform the market. Managers who are bullish on a stock may hedge with light deltas, selling short fewer shares of stock than required by the delta, leaving exposure to the upside of the stock. Managers who are bearish on a stock may hedge with heavy deltas, selling short more shares of stock than required by the delta, leaving exposure to the downside of the stock. Once the delta risk is hedged, managers are left with a long bond position and a long volatility position. Traders with long volatility positions earn more profits when the stock becomes more volatile, as each time they rebalance their delta hedge they are profiting from trading the stock. As stock prices and volatilities change, deltas also change; you have more opportunities for profitable rebalancing trades.

Managers may or may not hedge the interest rate risk of the convertible-bond portfolio. As interest rates rise, you lose money on the bond position but earn profits from higher options prices and a higher short-stock rebate. As rates fall, the gains on the long bonds will be offset by lower interest income and options prices. Treasury bond futures may not be a good way to hedge the interest rate risk in the portfolio, as this hedge can be very expensive in a flight-to-quality market, when Treasury yields fall and the yields on illiquid convertible bonds increase. The best hedge is to short corporate bonds, either in the same firm, the same industry, or the futures market.

Current income = convertible yield − stock dividend yield
+ short stock rebate

Arbitrage return = current income + stock hedging profit/loss
+ change in straight bond price
+ change in volatility value of the stock option

The return to a convertible-bond arbitrage fund can be separated into a number of influences. The income component of a convertible-bond arbitrage is the coupon on the convertible bond minus the dividend yield on the stock plus the short-stock rebate. During times of lower interest rates, the income to arbitrageurs is likely to fall as the short-stock rebate is correlated to falling Treasury bill rates. The second component of profits is the change in the straight bond price of the firm. Managers will profit when the market level of interest rates and the credit spread of the firm both decline. Should the credit quality of the firm deteriorate when interest rates are rising economywide, this component can show significant losses. Finally, managers can profit from rebalancing the stock hedges relative to the changes in the value of the embedded equity call option. The manager is likely to profit if the implied volatility of the option increases after the bond is purchased, as the volatility price of the option will increase, as well as the large number of profitable rebalancing opportunities that this volatility provides. Conversely, if volatility falls after the bond is purchased, the manager will show a loss on the option component, as well as suffer from a lack of profitable rebalancing opportunities.

The hedge fund manager will attempt to find undervalued convertible bonds by searching for convertibles that either have undervalued bonds or undervalued options. Undervalued bonds offer a higher yield than is required for your estimate of the bond's risk, while undervalued options will have a lower implied volatility than you estimate. If managers have a way to find undervalued bonds or options, they are likely to succeed as a convertible-bond arbitrage hedge fund manager. Managers may also be successful if they can predict stock price direction and bias their delta hedges in the proper direction.

The manager should also know the proper time to unwind a trade, which is accomplished by selling the bond and covering the short position on the stock. If you believe that the volatility of the stock or the credit rating will fall, it would be wise to unwind the trade. You must also decide whether to keep the stock position created when the bond is converted, either at maturity or an earlier date should the company force the conversion of the bonds.

One of the best ways to reduce the risks of convertible arbitrage is to have a diversified portfolio. Ideally, your portfolio would have a large number of positions that would be diversified by credit rating, industry or sector, high versus low implied volatility, and high versus low conversion premiums. If your portfolio was skewed toward lower-rated technology and telecomm bonds with low conversion premiums and high implied volatility during the year 2000, you are likely not a convertible-bond manager today, as each of these risks have created losses in your portfolio.

One of the biggest risks to a convertible arbitrage strategy is illiquidity. Corporate bonds, especially convertibles and high-yield issues, suffer from falling liquidity and falling prices in a flight-to-quality market. The smaller the bond issue, the more difficult it may be to sell. During the Long-Term Capital crisis of 1998, it was nearly impossible to sell high-yield or convertible-bond positions, as traders would not even bid on these risky issues. Convertible-bond managers must estimate the cost if they are forced to liquidate their positions in a difficult market. Illiquidity can also cause managers to unwind the trade if they have their short-stock position recalled due to a difficulty in borrowing the stock.

Before traders open a position, they must estimate the liquidity of both the bond and the stock. While a trade may look good on paper, it may not be possible to trade if the bonds are in limited supply or if it is not possible to borrow and short the stock.

Two of the largest risks facing convertible-bond arbitrageurs are a decline in the credit quality of the bond or the volatility of the stock. The attraction of convertible bonds is that the bond will provide a floor value to the value of the investment when the price of the stock is falling. This relationship typically holds true, as long as the credit quality of the bond does not decline. As the company is downgraded and starts showing signs of distress, the price of the bond can fall as quickly as the stock, creating significant risk for the fund manager. While this risk can be hedged by shorting other bonds of the same firm or through the purchase of credit default swaps, these hedges can be quite expensive and can reduce the profitability of the arbitrage strategy. The best defense against declines in the credit quality in your portfolio is a careful analysis of the credit of the firm and the condition of the industry. The best investment you can make as a convertible-bond manager is to buy bonds with high credit spreads, and see these spreads decline through an improvement in the market view of credit risks or strengthening fundamentals of the firm. It can be extremely risky to own convertible bonds when credit spreads are very low, as you may not be getting paid enough yield to compensate for the increasing risk that inevitably arises in the next market cycle.

Convertible-bond arbitrage funds are naturally long options, which is long volatility. Options traders make money when they buy options for a price that implies lower volatility than is actually experienced over the life of the option. If markets are extremely quiet, volatility can fall, dramatically reducing the value of the option portion of the convertible bond. The best markets for convertible-bond managers are ones with increasing levels of volatility, which makes their options more valuable and their rebalancing trades more frequent and more profitable. Unfortunately, higher market volatility is often experienced during times of increased credit risk, which reduces the value of the bond portion of the investment.

There may also be risks related to the complexity of the bonds. The manager may have to model forced conversions, early call dates, put features, and call-spread features. Other convertibles may be priced in one currency and converted into a stock that trades in another currency. If managers are very sophisticated and can add value in these areas, they may be very successful as fund managers. If other investors attempt to trade complex bonds without thoroughly understanding these features, they may be the source of excess returns for a successful fund manager.

The CSFB/Tremont Convertible Bond Arbitrage Index averaged annual returns of 10.70 percent between January 1994 and June 2003, with a risk of 4.83 percent and a Sharpe ratio of 1.31. (See Fig. 17-2.) This is one of the lowest-risk hedge fund strategies. The year 2002 was weak for convertible-bond arbitrageurs, as low interest rates, declining credit quality and falling stock prices left

FIGURE 17 – 2

CSFB/Tremont Convertible Arbitrage Index performance, 1994 to 2003. (MSCI, reprinted by permission; TASS, CSFB/Tremont, http://www.hedgeindex.com.)

The CSFB/Tremont Convertible Arbitrage Index measures the return to hedge funds investing in convertible bonds. These funds purchase convertible bonds and sell short the stock to create a delta neutral position. Although these investments have little short term correlation to stock prices, they typically retain substantial risk to the stock price volatility and the credit quality of the firm. These funds earn coupon income and the short stock rebate, but are responsible for paying dividends due on their short stock positions.

CSFB/Tremont Convertible Arbitrage Index

Legend: S&P 500 — MSCI World Sovereign Debt Index — CSFB/Tremont Convertible Arbitrage Index

	CSFB/Tremont Convertible Arbitrage
1994	–8.06
1995	16.55
1996	17.87
1997	14.48
1998	–4.42
1999	16.03
2000	25.65
2001	14.58
2002	4.04
Annual Return	10.70
Annual Standard Deviation	4.83
Skewness	–1.70
Kurtosis	4.47
Sharpe Ratio	1.31
Sortino Ratio	2.23
Alpha vs. S&P 500	9.78
Beta vs. S&P 500	0.04
Alpha vs. MSCI World Debt	11.02
Beta vs. MSCI World Debt	–0.13
Best Monthly Return	3.57
Worst Monthly Return	–4.68
Best Annual Return	25.65
Worst Annual Return	–8.06
% Winning Months	82.5%

FIGURE 17-2

Continued. (MSCI, reprinted by permission; TASS, CSFB/Tremont, http://www.hedgeindex.com.)

Correlation to	CSFB/Tremont Convertible Arbitrage
TASS Fund of Funds	0.45
CSFB/Tremont Hedge Fund Index	0.40
CSFB/Tremont Convertible Arbitrage	1.00
CSFB/Tremont Ded Short Bias	−0.23
CSFB/Tremont Emerging Markets	0.32
CSFB/Tremont Equity Mkt Ntrl	0.31
CSFB/Tremont Event Driven	0.59
CSFB/Tremont Distressed	0.51
CSFB/Tremont E.D. Multi-Strategy	0.60
CSFB/Tremont Risk Arbitrage	0.41
CSFB/Tremont Fixed Inc Arb	0.54
CSFB/Tremont Global Macro	0.29
CSFB/Tremont Long/Short Equity	0.26
CSFB/Tremont Managed Futures	−0.23
CSFB/Tremont Multi-Strategy	0.34
MSCI Discretionary Trading	0.37
MSCI Systematic Trading	−0.06
3 mo Tbills	0.15
S&P 500	0.13
MSCI World Sovereign Debt	−0.17
Average to Hedge Fund Strategies	0.29
Average to Traditional Investments	0.04
Conditional Correlations	
S&P 500 Up Markets (71 mo)	0.09
S&P 500 Down Markets (43 mo)	0.30
MSCI Debt Up Markets (65 mo)	−0.03
MSCI Debt Down Markets (49 mo)	−0.06

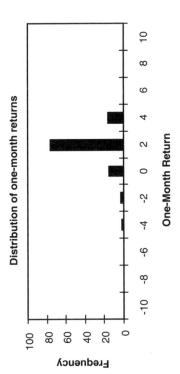

Distribution of one-month returns

these funds with a total return of 4.04 percent for the year. This strategy is growing in popularity among hedge fund managers, increasing from 0.5 percent to 3.4 percent of hedge fund assets between 1990 and 2001. (See Fig. 1-6.)

Over the last 10 years, convertible-bond hedge funds have had an average correlation of 0.13 to the S&P 500. However, we can see from Figure 17-3 that this correlation can change dramatically during turbulent times in the U.S. stock market. For example, we can see that the correlation rose to over 0.60 during the LTCM crisis, as investors sold both stocks and convertibles during this stressful period. However, we can see that convertible-bond arbitrage managers profited handsomely during late 2000, despite losses in the underlying stock market.

Figure 17-4 graphically shows the low correlation between this strategy and stocks by mapping the monthly returns of the CSFB/Tremont Convertible Bond Arbitrage Index to the S&P 500.

Convertible-bond hedge fund managers have been able to show a remarkable consistency of returns that is relatively uncorrelated to returns on traditional investments. From Figure 17-5 we see that

FIGURE 17–3

CSFB/Tremont Convertible Arbitrage Index: 24-month rolling correlation to traditional investments.

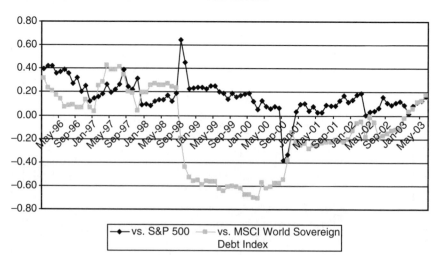

FIGURE 17 – 4

CSFB/Tremont Convertible Arbitrage Index versus S&P 500:
monthly return pairs, January 1994 to June 2003.

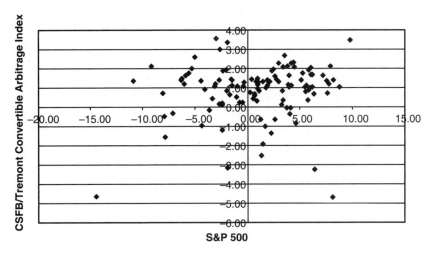

FIGURE 17 – 5

CSFB/Tremont Convertible Arbitrage Index versus S&P 500:
monthly returns sorted by quintiles, January 1994 to June
2003.

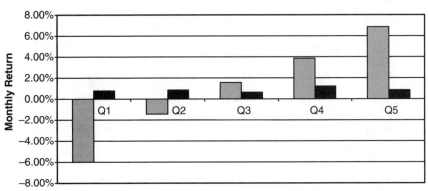

convertible-bond arbitrage managers are able to post positive returns in any stock market return regime. Similarly, Figure 17-6 shows that the returns to this hedge fund strategy is generally not related to the return to fixed-income investments. Interestingly, the lowest returns to convertible-bond hedge funds come during the periods of strongest performance for the MSCI World Sovereign Debt Index. This likely shows the impact of a flight-to-quality market, where investors seek the safety of safe government bonds and sell risky or illiquid securities, such as stocks and convertible bonds.

Because of the relatively low risk profile of convertible-bond arbitrage funds, their managers can afford to use a significant amount of leverage. Ineichen estimates that convertible arbitrage hedge fund managers can control 2 to 10 times the assets contributed by their investors.[9]

FIGURE 17−6

CSFB/Tremont Convertible Arbitrage Index versus MSCI World Sovereign Fixed Income Index: monthly returns sorted by quintiles, January 1994 to June 2003.

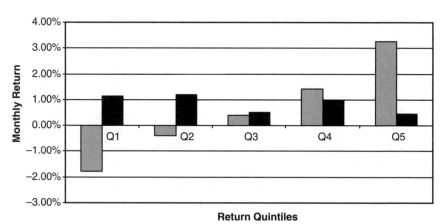

RELATIVE VALUE (MULTIPLE STRATEGY) FUNDS

Relative-value, or multiple-strategy, funds are designed to allow a hedge fund manager the flexibility to trade in a wide variety of long-short strategies. These managers may invest in a number of strategies that we have previously discussed, including merger arbitrage, long-short equity and pairs trading, convertible-bond and fixed-income arbitrage. These funds may also invest in several other strategies, many of which may not have the capacity or liquidity to support funds in a dedicated style but are a good fit in a multiple strategy fund. This includes warrant and options trading, capital structure arbitrage, and structured discount convertible arbitrage.

This shows that there is some value to having the flexibility to opportunistically change strategies and asset allocations between relative-value strategies over time. Not only are the average returns higher, the minimum returns to multiple-strategy funds are smaller than the minimum returns to other single-strategy, market-neutral funds. Because many of these strategies have limited opportunities for trades based on market cycles, it makes sense for a fund to widen its trading styles from one event-driven strategy to the whole range of market-neutral strategies. Similarly, a manager may be forced to invest in a specific strategy given his or her style box, even when he or she believes that returns will be below average for that strategy.

If a manager has the opportunity to reallocate assets to relative-value strategies with higher expected returns or lower expected risks, then it is reasonable to believe that multiple-strategy funds may be able to generate higher expected returns than a single strategy fund. While this value proposition may seem compelling, funds have been pushed toward more style purity in recent years, so we have seen relative-value strategies fall from 10 percent of assets to only 2 percent of assets over the last 10 years. Managers must be careful with such wide latitude to trade relative-value strategies, as it may be easy to stray into specialized trades where they may not have the knowledge or the liquidity to successfully invest their client funds.

One strategy that may appear in multiple-strategy funds that we have not previously discussed is options and warrants trading. Most options trading will be done on a delta-neutral basis, typically buying options and warrants and trading stock to eliminate the risk of moves in the stock price. This trade will isolate the volatility in the derivatives, typically leaving traders profitable opportunities if volatility increases over the life of the options. If the markets suddenly become quiet and volatility falls, this long-volatility strategy can incur significant losses. Other traders may create volatility arbitrage spreads, buying and selling options betting that the volatility between stocks or between stocks and equity indices will converge.

While the term *capital structure arbitrage* is often applied to trading spreads between securities of a distressed firm, there are other strategies that can fit under this definition. Many firms will have different shares of classes, often A shares or B shares, which may offer different voting rights. As the spreads between different share classes of the same firm widen, traders may bet that this spread will tighten.

Funds may also wish to create spreads between stocks that may be related by cross-holdings. For example, Loews Tobacco Corporation (LTR) owns 89 percent of the publicly traded insurance company (CNA), 53 percent of oil well equipment maker Diamond Offshore (DO), and 97 percent of the shares of the Bulova watchmakers (BULV), in addition to its tobacco business. If the difference between the sum of these publicly traded holdings and the stock price of Loews falls below the value of the operating companies fully owned by the parent company, traders would buy LTR and short the publicly traded holdings. If they believed that the parent firm is overvalued and subject to significant litigation risk from their tobacco business and that they would have to spin off their holdings, they may buy the three stocks and short Loews.

While these cases are rare, sometimes they bring true arbitrage profits. For some time in 2000 and 2001, the Limited (LTD) was valued below the market value of its holdings in Intimate Brands (IBI), the holding company of the Victoria's Secret clothing retailer. Buying LTD and shorting IBI was a great trade, but it may have been difficult to borrow the shares of IBI, given their limited float.

The final strategy traded by relative-value managers is structured-discount convertible arbitrage. These Regulation D securities are private placements offered to investment managers by the issuing firms. Small firms may issue these private placements, while other firms will offer discounted prices on these securities to offset their lack of liquidity. While these securities are eventually converted into stock, it may be years before those shares may be publicly traded. Managers who can buy the Reg D securities at discounted prices and short the publicly traded stock can earn profits after the restricted shares become publicly traded and the liquidity premium collapses to zero.[10]

ENDNOTES

1. N. Safaty, "The $460 Billion Global Convertible Bond Market," *KBC Financial Products*, July 25, 2001.

2. L. Rappoport, "Convertibles Poised for Growth?" *Wall Street Journal*, October 12, 2003.

3. A. B. Colter, "Hedge Funds Loved Convertibles, But Now They Could Get Jilted," *Wall Street Journal*, July 16, 2003.

4. A. Lucchetti and T. Lauricella, "These Funds Are Marking a Conversion of Sorts," *Wall Street Journal*, June 27, 2003.

5. K. Brown and S. Thurm, "Companies Find 'No-Nos' Are Very Hard to Resist," *Wall Street Journal*, June 2, 2003.

6. D. Henry, "The Latest Magic in Corporate Finance," *Business Week*, September 8, 2003.

7. S. Lange et al., Convertibles as an Asset Class—2000 Update," Goldman Sachs, March 6, 2001.

8. Ibid.

9. A. M. Ineichen, 2003, *Absolute Returns: The Risk and Opportunities of Hedge Fund Investing.* Hoboken, NJ: John Wiley & Sons, 2003.

10. This chapter benefits from the discussions in Chapters 4, 7, and 10 of J. G. Nicholas, *Market Neutral Investing: Long/Short Hedge Fund Strategies.*

CHAPTER 18

Mutual Fund
Market-Timing Strategies

While many hedge fund strategies trade illiquid securities in hopes of earning excess returns, mutual fund market-timing funds are very different. These strategies are invested in the liquid shares of mutual funds, or at least the funds that allow short-term investments.

Many mutual funds can be traded at the net asset value (NAV) without any loads or transactions costs being charged to the investor. The liquid nature, and low trading costs, of mutual funds make them ideal for hot-money traders, who may exit a trade only days after entering.

Mutual fund market-timing strategies may be more appropriately termed time zone arbitrage. The vast majority of the fund timers focus their trading on international mutual funds. Many open-ended mutual funds managed by U.S. investment managers are priced and traded once each day, at the 4:00 p.m. New York close. Many fund companies allow investors to trade the shares in their international mutual funds at stale prices. This means that when the Asian markets close at 1:00 a.m. or the European markets close at 11:00 a.m., the closing prices in the foreign markets set the NAV for the fund that can be traded until 4:00 p.m. in New York. This asynchronous trading can allow investors to purchase Asian shares up to 15 hours, and European shares up to 5 hours, after the foreign markets have closed. Of course, U.S. markets are open for nearly an entire trading day before the investors need to submit their trades, giving them a tremendous time and information advantage.

In recent years, worldwide stock market returns have become more highly correlated. If good news in the United States leads to sharply higher stock prices today, those prices are very likely to be reflected in the prices of the foreign shares the next day. The asynchronous trading allowed in many mutual funds owning international stocks could be the closest thing to a true arbitrage that the U.S. financial markets allow.

Let's start with an example. Assume that the Nikkei index of Japanese stocks closes unchanged at 10,000 early Tuesday morning. At 8:30 a.m. New York time, over seven hours after the Tokyo close, a bullish U.S. employment report is announced that promises to send U.S. stocks higher. At 2:00 p.m., the S&P 500 index of large U.S. stocks has increased by 2 percent. We can also find direct evidence of an expected increase in Japanese stock prices as futures on the Nikkei index of large Japanese stocks trade at the Chicago Mercantile Exchange during U.S. trading hours. Before 4:00 p.m. New York time, traders or investors are allowed to purchase many mutual funds owning Japanese stocks at their Tuesday morning closing prices, even though the Nikkei futures may indicate that Japanese stocks should open 1.5 percent higher when trading begins in Tokyo on Wednesday morning.

A near arbitrage can be created by selling short the Nikkei futures at around 10,150 while buying the underlying stocks in a mutual fund at the previous day's closing price, at a level equivalent to Nikkei 10,000. This guarantees a profit of 1.5 percent before transactions costs, assuming that the price of the mutual fund shares is highly correlated to the Nikkei index. Some funds may choose to hedge the currency risk, which can slightly increase the Sharpe ratio without significantly reducing returns. Some funds may choose not to hedge either market or currency risk and simply wait until they can sell the fund at the next day's higher closing price. While many mutual fund timers will exit their trade the next day, others may adopt a trend-following strategy, holding the fund for a number of days, only exiting the trade when the markets are expected to turn lower.

A recent *Financial Analysts Journal* article describes the trading and profit opportunities available from mutual fund market-timing strategies.[1] A trader may choose to buy shares in a Japanese mutual fund at stale prices at the end of the U.S. trading day when they expect the fund to increase in value by at least 0.5 percent or 1.0

percent the next day. While the Nikkei futures at the CME are an excellent signal for entering this trade, the S&P 500 futures provide additional information. Traders are expected to hold the position for a number of days, only selling when they receive a signal that the Japanese market is likely to decline. Long-term holders of Japanese funds have a 50 percent probability of profiting in any given day, and experience Sharpe ratios below 1.0. Traders who follow a market-timing system can increase their percentage of profitable days to over 75 percent, while earning a Sharpe ratio over 6.0. Timers using Japanese funds are likely to own the market in 5 to 35 percent of all trading days, making between 8 and 35 round-trip trades per year.

Similar profits are available in trading European funds, but the overlapping trading day between Europe and the United States and the smaller time lag of stale prices reduces the frequency of trading opportunities. Even though it would seem that there is less opportunity to time European funds, timers are expected to earn a Sharpe ratio in excess of 6.0 in this strategy.

In September 2003, a scandal engulfed the mutual fund and hedge fund world. Eliot Spitzer, the New York attorney general, alleged that Canary Capital Partners engaged in illegal activity.[2] Canary was a $730 million hedge fund that implemented a mutual fund market-timing strategy. In 1999, the fund manager, Edward Stern, delivered returns of 110 percent, admittedly on a small capital base. In 2000, 2001, and 2002, Canary delivered gains of 50 percent, 29 percent, and 15 percent, despite a strong bear market in worldwide stock markets.[3] Mutual fund timing strategies are not illegal, but Stern is accused of several illegal maneuvers in pursuit of these lucrative gains.

The first task of a potential mutual fund timer is to read the prospectuses of mutual funds that may offer lucrative timing opportunities. Mutual funds must always follow their prospectus, which is a requirement of the Investment Company Act of 1940. Many funds trade in asset classes that are subject to stale prices, including international stocks and bonds, small-capitalization stocks, and illiquid bonds, such as high-yield bonds and convertibles. Funds that believe that investors may place market-timing trades in their funds may handle the issue in their prospectus in one of three ways: specifically prohibit market timers, discourage market timers, or remain silent on the issue.

Short-term traders who would like to implement a market-timing strategy are advised to avoid funds that specifically prohibit market timing or short-term trading. Many funds specifically outline the discipline meted out to violators, typically a loss of trading privileges to traders who close three trades within a six-month period. The first allegation of illegal activity was that several large banks and mutual fund companies allowed Canary to frequently implement short-term trades in funds where the prospectus specifically outlawed the practice. This can create a double standard, where retail investors may be punished for their market-timing activities while a large investor like Stern was encouraged to trade in this manner, for which he may have compensated the fund managers with large balances deposited in other funds.

Even worse, it is reported that Stern may have engaged in late trading. Not content to earn profits from the asynchronous trading, Canary is alleged to have habitually traded after the close of the New York market, when the hedge fund could take advantage of market-moving news. This backdating of trades is highly illegal under SEC rules and can get traders in big trouble in any U.S. market. Unfortunately, it appears that some large banks and clearing firms may have facilitated Canary's late trading, which may lead to civil and criminal liability for some of the biggest names in the industry.

Mutual fund market timing, of course, is not illegal if it is not prohibited by the fund's prospectus. If the fund does not specifically prohibit market timing, hedge fund managers can assume that it is legal to place timing trades before the New York close of 4:00 p.m. In fact, several fund families actively market to short-term traders, most notably Rydex and Pro Funds.

By the time this book is published, I would expect that mutual fund timing strategies have largely become extinct. This gives us a good lesson in transparency and the idea that many hedge fund strategies are based on very small inefficiencies. When the strategy of these hedge funds was not transparent or widely known, traders were able to earn large profits from these short-term timing strategies. However, as soon as the SEC and retail investors learned that the gains to these strategies generally reduced the returns of most mutual fund investors, banks and mutual funds moved quickly to curtail the practice. Banks and mutual fund firms accused of participating in the market-timing schemes contrary to their prospectuses are expected to repay their mutual fund investors for the gains earned by the short-term traders.

How are the gains to fund timing firms expected to reduce the returns of long-term shareholders? First, we need to remember that the short-term traders may buy mutual fund shares after today's close in the foreign market and sell those same shares the next trading day. Because these traders are buying at yesterday's price, there is no way for the mutual fund to buy more shares in that stock market at the stale prices. If the hedge fund sells the shares the next day at a profit, it is unlikely that the mutual fund has ever bought shares in foreign companies on their behalf. The situation becomes even worse if the mutual fund invested the cash from the hot-money investors, as they will incur transactions costs to buy and sell stocks that the short-term traders never intended to own. Eric Zitzewitz, a professor at Stanford University, calculates that short-term market-timing trades can cost buy-and-hold mutual fund investors in international mutual funds between 1 and 2 percent per year. With estimates that market-timing schemes cost long-term mutual fund shareholders up to $5 billion a year, it is unlikely that any banks or mutual fund companies will continue to allow this short-term trading, as retail investors are unlikely to keep their assets in funds that can provide arbitrage profits to hedge fund managers. [4]

Of course, mutual fund managers will not close all of their funds that may be subject to stale prices. They will simply have to make it less profitable and more difficult for short-term traders to profit at the expense of long-term shareholders. Many funds will move to specifically prohibit short-term trading, with language in the prospectus that threatens to punish market-timing activities. There are three major ways to discourage short-term trading, many of which have long been practiced by shareholder-friendly mutual fund providers.

The most obvious way to discourage time zone arbitrage is to reduce the time lag between the close of the foreign market and the deadline for buying mutual fund shares at that closing price. Instead of the typical deadline of 4:00 p.m., the closing time for the New York exchanges, many fund companies have imposed a 9:30 a.m. deadline. You can only buy foreign stocks at yesterday's price before the opening of the New York markets. An even more appropriate deadline may be 8:30 a.m. New York time, as this is the time when many major announcements are made, including unemployment and inflation rates, are made that can dramatically move the bond markets and set the tone for the day in U.S. stocks.

A second way to make funds friendlier to long-term mutual fund investors is to penalize traders with short holding periods. Many mutual funds will charge short-term redemption fees. A typical fee may cost the trader between 1 and 2 percent of the value of the investment if the mutual fund shares are owned for a period of less than three to six months. Given that the profits from these timing activities are often less than 1 percent per trade, these fees will deter short-term investors from arbitraging all but the largest and least frequent opportunities. These short-term redemption fees are paid not to the mutual fund manager, but to the mutual fund investors, in an attempt to reimburse them for the trading losses and transactions costs incurred by the market timers.

Unfortunately, the short-term redemption fees are not always enforced, giving the timers the ability to trade funds without getting penalized for their rapid turnover of fund shares. It can be especially difficult to detect timing strategies if the trading activity is commingled with other trades in a retirement plan or brokerage firm. It is much more difficult to detect this activity when looking at aggregate data, but single trader data may not always be available to the fund firm if the trades are executed by a third party.

Perhaps the most controversial way to deter market-timing activity is for a mutual fund to institute a policy of fair-value pricing. During most trading days, the fund will price shares at an NAV equal to the closing price in the foreign market, even as late as the closing time in the New York market. However, during market conditions where the NAV is unlikely to reflect the full value of the fund assets, the fund reserves the right to sell new shares in the fund at a fair-value price, which is different than the NAV. Of course, fair-value prices are likely to prevail during volatile days when market timers may perceive the best trading opportunities.

For example, if Nikkei futures trading at the CME are trading within 0.5 percent of the Tokyo close, the fund is likely to price shares at the price prevailing at the Tokyo closing NAV. However, if the mutual fund has a reason to believe that the Japanese market is likely to move by more than 2 percent during the next trading day, fair-value pricing may be invoked, given the large size of the predicted move. If the Nikkei futures are up 2 percent during the U.S. trading day, the mutual fund shares for a Japanese stock fund will be priced at the Tokyo closing NAV plus a markup of 2 percent. Certainly this will reduce market-timing activity, as the stale price arbitrage has been eliminated. Because most open-end mutual fund shares can only be purchased and not sold short, fair-value pricing is most frequently implemented when the NAV is below the next day's expected price.

Imposing fair-value pricing may be more controversial when the NAV is reduced based on an expected decline in the value of foreign stocks. Because most mutual fund shares cannot be sold short, this restriction is expected to impact owners of the fund who are trying to sell at precrash prices. If the U.S. stock market fell by 5 percent in one day, many long-term holders of foreign stock funds may attempt to sell at the stale price, thereby saving these assets from the crash. If fair-value pricing were implemented by this fund, shareholders would be selling at a price lower than yesterday's closing prices. Should the Japanese market not closely follow the U.S. sell-off, it is conceivable that investors could have sold at prices lower than those ever traded in the foreign market.

Fair-value pricing can be a very complicated process. Rather than simply adjusting prices by the change in a related futures contract, many fund companies have very sophisticated pricing algorithms. In order to predict the fair-value NAV, the fund may look at the last trade time of each of their holdings, the change in futures markets, historical correlations to U.S. stocks, and returns to stocks in the same sector.

Unfortunately, fair-value pricing is not frequently used at the present time. Deloitte and Touche reports that while 81 percent of mutual fund companies have the ability to implement fair-value pricing, only 30 percent had made any pricing adjustments to their international funds over the last year. Most funds repriced shares less than seven times a year, probably enforcing this policy less frequently than would be necessary to fully repel market-timing activity.[5]

While market-timing activity is most prevalent in international funds, there are also opportunities to implement this strategy in any illiquid asset class. By definition, if an asset is illiquid, it trades infrequently. Any asset that does not trade frequently is subject to the opportunities and risks that come from stale pricing. Illiquid asset classes may also be more likely to trend, as pricing models may tend to make large price mark-ups in a series of small steps instead of in one large jump. Hot-money flows in asset classes such as small capitalization stocks, high-yield bonds, or convertible bonds can be very disruptive. If large asset flows rush into an illiquid asset class, the resulting investment pressure can cause excess volatility and trading costs for the long-term shareholders.[6]

The fastest-growing mutual fund product does not have any exposure to stale pricing. Examples of exchange-traded funds (ETFs) include the wildly popular QQQ that tracks the NASDAQ stock market and the Spiders, SPY, that track the value of the S&P 500 index. There are dozens of other ETFs that track sectors of the U.S. market, such as biotechnology or semiconductor stocks, or style indices such as the Russell 1000 value index. ETFs may also trade on foreign stock indices, including those in emerging markets.

While exchange-traded funds act like index mutual funds in many respects, they are also very different. When investors buy shares of an open-end mutual fund, such as Fidelity Magellan, they purchase newly created shares directly from the fund manager. When investors buy shares in an ETF, they make the trade on a stock exchange, buying existing shares from another shareholder. As with any trade on a stock exchange, the investor must pay a brokerage commission and a bid-ask spread when buying ETFs, costs not typically associated with the purchase of mutual fund shares. If the demand for a certain ETF increases, the fund will create more shares by trading with large institutional investors.

The *Wall Street Journal* publishes a regular list of the largest ETFs in their monthly mutual funds section. As of August 31, 2003, there were 22 funds that had attracted over $1 billion in investor assets. While the Spiders held nearly $35 billion in assets, the Nasdaq 100 trust controlled over $20 billion. Other large funds include a $6.3 billion iShares S&P 500 fund, a $5.7 billion fund based on the Dow Jones Industrial Average, and a $5.4 billion fund based on the S&P Midcap 400 index. The largest foreign funds included a $3.1 billion fund based on the MSCI EAFE® index of international stocks, and a $1.7 billion fund based on the MSCI Japan stock index. In total, there are 114 U.S. based ETFs, managing over $117 billion in assets as of July 2003.[7]

The two most important differences between ETFs and open-ended mutual funds are real-time pricing and short selling. Traders are allowed to sell short ETF shares, a practice typically not allowed with open-end mutual funds. This means that ETF traders can bet on either an increase or a decrease in a stock index, a dramatic change from the long-only view of the typical mutual fund investor. Next, open-end mutual funds are usually priced once each day at the New York close, which can lead to the stale price arbitrage opportunities. Because ETFs trade on a stock exchange, the prices are always moving during the U.S. trading day. As the expected price of markets move, the ETF shares will closely follow those movements, leading to a much smaller probability of trading on stale prices. Because ETFs may be more difficult to arbitrage than shares in open-end mutual funds, they may be more attractive for investors who want to discourage other market participants from profiting from their investments.

ENDNOTES

1. J. Boudoukh et. al., "Stale Prices and Strategies for Trading Mutual Funds," *Financial Analysts Journal* (July/August 2002) 58:53–71.

2. R. Frank, "Highflying Hedge Fund Crashes," *Wall Street Journal,* September 4, 2003.

3. I. McDonald, "Will Funds Disclose More—Publicly?" *Wall Street Journal,* September 9, 2003.

4. C. Oster and K. Damato, "How Market Timers Can Drain Returns for Some Investors," *Wall Street Journal,* September 8, 2003.

5. J. Hechinger, "Fund Industry Takes Its Time Instituting Fair-Value Pricing," *Wall Street Journal,* September 11, 2003.

6. N. Bullock, "Junk-Bond Funds Get Timed Too," *Wall Street Journal,* September 22, 2003.

7. K. Damato, "Here's a Mutual Fund Timers Can Call Home," *Wall Street Journal,* September 12, 2003.

CHAPTER 19

Funds of Funds

By this point in the book, you should understand the job of a hedge fund manager. Typically, fund managers will spend their time scouring the world for mispriced stocks, bonds, futures, and options. Their trading opportunities will likely fall within a consistent style or a carefully defined group of several styles. While many funds will have a strong risk management orientation, we know that individual hedge funds can be prone to bouts of volatility, either due to market conditions, poor security selection, weak risk management, or a lack of managerial skill. When investors choose to invest in an individual hedge fund, they place faith in the manager and the manager's style and they accept the fee structure, risks, returns, and liquidity offered by that specific fund. The median single-manager hedge fund requires a minimum investment of $500,000, and the returns to the investment may or may not be closely correlated to other funds trading in the same style.

A fund of funds places assets with a manager who will allocate investments over a variety of hedge funds. A typical fund of funds product will invest in 10 to 30 different hedge funds, while some managers may be even more diversified. The most important benefit of investing in a fund of funds is the diversification across hedge fund managers and strategies. When your assets are placed in dozens of different hedge funds, you have reduced your reliance on any single-fund manager. If a single hedge fund fails, your losses are limited to only a portion of the investment value of the fund of funds.

In recent years, we have seen the number of funds of funds grow more quickly than the number of individual hedge funds. We have also seen that the assets invested in funds of funds are growing faster than the assets controlled by individual fund managers.

While the vast majority of the number and assets of all hedge funds are still run by single managers, funds of funds are now growing more quickly. As you can see in Figure 1-1, TASS estimated in March 2003 that there were 1400 funds of funds and 4600 single-manager hedge funds, for a total of 6000 hedge funds. Figure 1-3 shows the growth in single-manager hedge fund assets from $325 billion in December 1998 to $625 billion in December 2002. Funds of funds are growing assets more quickly than single-manager hedge funds, growing from $45 billion to $95 billion over the same time period (Figure 19-1). The total hedge fund community is estimated at 6000 funds managing approximately $720 billion.

As institutional investors continue to increase their allocations to hedge funds, funds of funds are likely to continue growing more quickly than single-manager hedge funds. Many institutions may perform a buy-versus-build analysis before hiring a fund of funds

FIGURE 19−1

Growth of fund of funds assets, number of funds. *(TASS, CSFB/Tremont, http://www.hedgeindex.com.)*

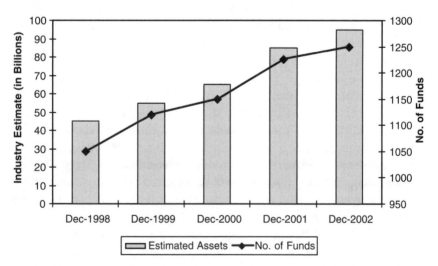

manager, due to the fee structure of these diversified hedge fund investments. Once the institution has more than a $50 million commitment to hedge funds, it may be more cost-effective to hire an employee to structure its hedge fund portfolio.

We can explain the popularity of the fund of funds concept in several ways. First, we may want to compare single hedge funds to actively managed mutual funds, while comparing funds of funds to indexed or passively managed mutual funds.

In any time period, we are guaranteed to see actively managed mutual funds and single-manager hedge funds at both the top and the bottom of the performance tables. By definition, many of these funds will concentrate their investments in a specific sector or style, which may come in and out of favor at different points in the market cycle. While some managers may have well-diversified portfolios within their style, others will have their assets concentrated in a relatively small number of positions. The most volatile funds are likely to have very concentrated portfolios. This volatility, which comes from a willingness to trade in a very different manner than other managers, can lead to either astounding profits or heart-wrenching losses. These funds also rely heavily on manager skill, as a failure to properly analyze trading opportunities or manage risks can lead to the demise of the fund and the investor's net worth. Investors with high return goals and high levels of risk tolerance are those most likely to invest in single-manager funds. Investors who place assets with the managers of single hedge funds are typically searching for alpha, where they earn higher returns than they deserve for the risks they are taking.

Index mutual funds and funds of hedge funds will rank near the middle of the return distribution. It is unlikely that either type of fund will ever reach the top or bottom of the performance tables due to their highly diversified nature. Both an index fund and a fund of hedge funds will be invested in a wide variety of sectors or a number of styles, which smoothes out the volatility found in specific areas of the market. While a concentrated fund can post dramatic losses, it is unlikely that an investor will ever lose the majority of his or her investment in an index fund or a fund of hedge funds. The best fund of funds will underperform the best individual hedge funds but will outperform the worst single hedge funds. Funds of hedge funds are not designed to be "home run" investments, but instead deliver returns close to the average of all hedge funds at reasonably low levels of single style or manager risk. Fund of funds investors are not seeking high levels of alpha, as they are more focused on risk management and diversification.

There are several trends in the hedge fund world that can explain the rise in the prominence of the fund of funds manager. Historically, the majority of hedge fund investors were high-net-worth individuals seeking to earn the dramatic gains that could result from investing in volatile styles such as global macro. When the performance of traditional investments is strong, hedge fund investors are likely to demand relative returns. Because absolute returns of 12 percent per year seem unattractive when stock prices are growing at 20 percent per year, low-risk hedge funds are likely to attract fewer assets during these times. However, the pursuit of relative returns demanded investments in high-volatility hedge fund strategies. After the 1998 failure of the large hedge funds run by Long-Term Capital Management, investor focus on relative returns became less important than the desire for principal protection.

In the summer of 2000, we saw a collapse of the U.S. equity markets, which culminated in the NASDAQ stock market index declining by 80 percent over the next two years. As stocks crashed, investors started to look more toward absolute-return strategies, which result in a significantly smaller return volatility. Returns of 12 percent seem quite attractive when stock markets worldwide are falling precipitously.

Finally, institutional investments in hedge funds are now growing more rapidly than the investments of high-net-worth individuals. Institutional investors are more likely to invest in portfolio diversifiers than return enhancers, as they are usually more focused on minimizing the volatility or maximizing the Sharpe ratio of their portfolios rather than on seeking the largest possible returns. Because these investors are sophisticated enough to understand efficient frontiers and portfolio theory, they will focus on the lower-risk and lower-correlation funds that will most reduce the standard deviation of their portfolio returns without sacrificing much return. Institutional investors, usually pension plans or university endowments, also have a fiduciary responsibility to their stakeholders. These investors have the goal of producing returns over long, perhaps infinite, time periods, so they will never invest in a way that will risk the entire principal of their fund.

A fund of funds manager has a very different job than the manager of a single hedge fund. While the manager of an individual hedge fund is constantly seeking trading opportunities involving individual securities, the fund of funds manager takes more of a macro view, seeking to build a diversified portfolio of hedge fund investments. Managers of individual hedge funds need to be experts in their particular trading style, but fund of funds managers need to be conversant in all types of hedge fund trading strategies. Ideally, fund of funds managers will also have a strong knowledge of portfolio theory, as they seek to build the most efficient, least volatile portfolio of hedge funds.

There are several advantages that a fund of funds manager can offer investors. First, a fund of funds can offer exposure to a wide diversity of hedge fund styles with a low minimum investment. In order to be an accredited investor, an individual only needs to have $1 million in investment capital or an annual income of $200,000. You may remember that nearly 90 percent of accredited investors have a net worth of less than $5 million. If the median hedge fund requires a minimum investment of $500,000, we can see that most high-net-worth individuals will not be able to afford the minimum investment required to build a diversified portfolio of 10 hedge funds. Instead of investing in 10 hedge funds with a combined minimum investment of $5 million, an individual could purchase a highly diversified fund of funds investment with as little as $100,000. Nearly two-thirds of funds of funds can be purchased with a minimum investment of $250,000 or less, while 37 percent of funds of funds require an allocation of $100,000 or less. Clearly, fund of funds managers are selling this low-cost diversification, as only 3.5 percent of funds of funds require a minimum investment of over $1 million.[1]

An individual investor may also appreciate the due diligence services that a fund of funds manager provides. With around 4600 single-manager hedge funds scattered across a wide variety of trading styles, the due diligence process can be intimidating for an investor. Many hedge funds are secretive, and the best information on fund histories is contained in expensive or proprietary hedge fund databases. A fund of funds manager with access to this information can select the most appropriate funds in a short amount of time. Not only will the manager have ready access to quantitative information on hedge fund investments; he or she may also have close relationships with a large number of hedge fund managers.

Of course, we know that quantitative due diligence does not tell the whole story about a hedge fund. Fund of funds managers meet with managers of each hedge fund before an investment is made. This qualitative due diligence considers the design of the hedge fund, including systems and legal documentation. Special attention is paid to the trading strategy, as the tendency to sell options or trade at high levels of leverage can lead to high future risks that may not be caught in the quantitative due diligence of a fund.

A well-connected fund of funds manager will be able to invest in new hedge funds before the track record is included in the return databases. Ideally, the relationship with hedge fund managers would be so close that the fund of funds manager could tell when a fund or style will face declining returns in the near future. This manager due diligence is a constant process. The hedge fund community is quite dynamic, as new funds open and existing funds close or liquidate, while styles come in and out of favor. Unfortunately, the best funds in the past are not guaranteed to be the top funds in the future, so the fund of funds manager is constantly on the watch for managers with declining or rising profitability.

Some individual fund managers may choose to delegate their fundraising duties to a fund of funds manager. While the hedge fund can focus on trading, the fund of funds acts like a third-party marketer, constantly seeking to attract new assets to the hedge fund. Both parties can benefit greatly from this relationship. The hedge fund may be able to attract many more assets with the marketing assistance, and the funds may be invested for a longer period of time than if they were raised directly from individuals. Fund of funds assets may be stickier than investments from high-net-worth individuals. The fund of funds has raised assets from a large number of investors, so the withdrawal of one investor in the fund of funds is not likely to have a large impact on the assets of a single hedge fund, and is often offset by the contributions from other investors. In return for this fundraising assistance, the hedge fund manager will be loyal to the fund of funds manager. A best-case scenario for a fund of funds would be when the hedge fund closes its doors to new investors while continuing to allow the fund of funds to place new assets in the lucrative, yet low-capacity fund.

Some fund of funds managers may choose to act like venture capital investors. In an incubator-like setting, the fund of funds will search for promising young managers. In exchange for start-up costs, such as legal and accounting fees, as well as an initial investment of $20 million or so, the new fund manager will give the fund of funds an equity stake in his or her management firm. The fund of funds can profit from owning a piece of the company and will also have a close relationship with the hedge fund manager. Should the new hedge fund post some impressive performance numbers, the fund of funds will be able to continue to invest in the fund, even after it is closed to new investors. Fund of funds are providing significant value to their investors when they are able to maintain guaranteed capacity to invest in closed funds. This is valuable to investors, as funds are closed to new investors in response to strong investor demand, which likely resulted from a strong track record at the hedge fund.

Hedge fund managers may be more willing to share their portfolio details with fund of funds managers than with other investors. There are many reasons that hedge fund managers may desire to keep the details of their fund a secret. While individual investors may not understand the details, institutional investors may be tempted to replicate the hedge fund manager's trades or trading style. Hedge fund managers may feel safe in discussions with the fund of funds manager. Not only does the fund of funds provide capital for them to trade, the manager is more likely to understand the hedge fund's trading style, while being less likely to replicate the trades. Fund of funds managers generally only make investments in hedge funds and are not seeking to start trading in competition with their hedge fund managers.

Why is it important for fund of funds managers to have detailed position data from each of their hedge fund managers? First, the fund of funds managers want to have a deep understanding of the correlation between their hedge fund investments. If they see that a number of their managers are trading the same stocks, fund of funds managers know that the fund is not as fully diversified as they hoped to be. Second, the fund of funds may choose to add leverage to increase its returns or to increase its liquidity to provide investor redemptions. A strong knowledge of the underlying positions will help managers understand the appropriate amount of leverage to apply to their fund investments. Finally, many fund of funds managers will act as risk managers. Once all of their positions are aggregated, a detailed risk analysis can be performed. Managers can then choose to place overlay trades, making currency, options or futures trades in the fund of funds account to reduce the risks their investors face from investing in this portfolio of hedge funds.

Perhaps the most important job of fund of funds managers is to determine the asset allocation of the fund. How many funds should be included in the portfolio? Which styles should be over-weighted and which styles should be underweighted or removed from the portfolio?

The EACM 100 index diversifies among five different styles, allocating 30 percent of assets to relative-value strategies, 30 percent to equity hedge funds, 20 percent to the global macro style, 5 percent to short sellers, and 15 percent to event-driven funds.[2] Some fund of funds managers may choose to closely follow this strategic asset allocation. Under strategic asset allocation, the investors decide to maintain their portfolio at fixed style weights over long time periods and many market conditions. When one style outperforms the others, its weight will increase in the fund. When the investors rebalance the fund, they return all positions to the strategic target allocation, selling a portion of the funds that have outperformed and adding to their positions in styles with lower returns.

Some fund of funds managers will be able to add value through tactical asset allocation. Under this method of allocating investment funds, the managers may be given wide latitude to vary the weights between different types of hedge funds. Managers may choose to implement their views, either as a market timer or a style timer.

Top-down managers will allocate funds based on their view of the market environment. If they anticipate a strong equity market and falling interest rates, they will focus on more volatile relative-return funds, such as long-short equities or emerging markets. If stocks are likely to fall, managers could increase their allocations to absolute-return funds, such as relative value, and short sellers. Of course, managers may drastically change the portfolio as their view of market conditions change. If managers properly anticipate the market environment, their fund of funds will provide excellent returns with lower levels of risk.

Bottom-up managers will build their fund by focusing on the attributes of each fund manager and hedge fund. This fund of funds manager will invest in what they believe to be superior fund managers. Once they have reached their target number of, say, 20 top managers, their fund of funds is fully invested. The asset and style allocation that results from this bottom-up process is driven by the manager selection process and may not resemble a fully diversified portfolio if the fund manager favors managers from one specific style.

Before investing in, or building, a fund of funds, it is important to understand the objectives. Will the fund be designed to be a high-return, high-volatility fund that will focus its investments in a diversified group of managed futures, global macro, emerging markets, and long-short equity funds? Is the manager planning to focus on one style, promising to fully diversify and manage the risk of owning a number of managed futures funds? Will the fund focus on a specific geographical area, concentrating its investments only in European- or Asian-based hedge funds? These objectives are very different from the description of most funds of funds, where the manager seeks to diversify across a wide variety of hedge fund styles in search of a low-risk, absolute-return strategy.

Institutional investors are likely to prefer funds of funds that focus on absolute returns, especially when the fund is designed to have the lowest possible correlation to the traditional investments that dominate the institution's portfolio. These investors are more closely focused on portfolio diversification rather than return enhancement.

When building the lowest risk, lowest correlation fund possible, managers have several types of correlations to consider. First, we must consider the correlation between hedge funds in the same style. Due to the limited number of trading opportunities, risk arbitrage and distressed managers are likely to have returns that are highly correlated to other funds trading the same style. If the funds within a style are correlated to each other, an investment in only a few funds will closely track the style index. Commodity trading advisers have a very low correlation to each other, so a fund may need to invest in 15 to 25 CTAs to replicate the risk and return characteristics of managed futures indices.

Next, the manager should consider the correlation between the returns to different styles of hedge funds. We can best reduce the volatility of our fund of funds by selecting hedge fund investments that prosper in different market environments and have different return drivers.

Finally, we must also seek to minimize the correlation of the fund of funds to the return of traditional portfolios, which own significant long-only investments in equity and fixed-income securities. Relative-return hedge fund strategies are generally more volatile than absolute-return strategies and have higher correlations to traditional investments. Relative-value and managed futures funds not only have lower volatility, but also have much lower correlations to traditional investments. Special attention should be paid to styles that provide positive returns when traditional investments are performing poorly. Event-driven strategies, emerging markets, global macro, and long-short equity funds have their lowest returns when the S&P 500 is falling, so these funds don't provide much hedging ability in weak equity markets. Managed futures, convertible arbitrage, short bias funds, equity market–neutral, and fixed-arbitrage funds seem like the best hedge, as these styles have traditionally offered positive returns during the times of the most negative returns to U.S. stocks.

The ideal portfolio produces returns that have a low correlation to traditional investments, as well as a low standard deviation of returns. This goal is most likely to be achieved when the fund of funds manager carefully diversifies across hedge fund styles that each prosper in a different market environment. Correlations are very important, as portfolio theory explains that we can invest in high-risk, high-return assets without increasing the risk of our fund. It is only possible to increase returns without increasing standard deviation when the correlation between that fund and our portfolio return is low enough to offset the high volatility of the additional investment.

What differences can we see between the TASS Fund of Funds Index and the CSFB/Tremont Hedge Fund Index? From 1994 to June 2003, the TASS Fund of Funds Index offered an average annual return of 7.55 percent, with a standard deviation of 6.08 percent and a Sharpe ratio of 0.52. (See Fig. 19-2.) Over the same time period, the CSFB/Tremont Hedge Fund Index earned a return of 11.35 percent, with a risk of 8.69 percent and a Sharpe ratio of 0.80. The correlation between these two indices is 91 percent, so we can see that fund of funds managers are attempting to closely track the performance of

TASS Fund of Funds Index performance, 1994 to 2003. (MSCI, reprinted by permission; TASS, CSFB/Tremont, http://www.hedgeindex.com.)

The TASS Fund of Funds Index measures the return to investments in a diversified pool of hedge funds. These funds allow investors to quickly purchase a diversified hedge fund portfolio with a very low minimum investment. Large investors may choose to build their own hedge fund portfolio to avoid the additional fees charged by fund of funds managers.

	TASS Fund of Funds
1994	−5.54
1995	12.81
1996	15.15
1997	16.66
1998	−3.26
1999	22.25
2000	3.69
2001	2.81
2002	2.85
Annual Return	7.55
Annual Standard Deviation	6.08
Skewness	−0.17
Kurtosis	2.23
Sharpe Ratio	0.52
Sortino Ratio	1.06
Alpha vs. S&P 500	5.20
Beta vs. S&P 500	0.19
Alpha vs. MSCI World Debt	7.51
Beta vs. MSCI World Debt	−0.03
Best Monthly Return	5.76
Worst Monthly Return	−6.30
Best Annual Return	22.25
Worst Annual Return	−5.54
% Winning Months	65.8%

TASS Fund of Funds Index

S&P 500 — MSCI World Sovereign Debt Index — TASS Fund of Funds Index

FIGURE 19-2

Continued. (MSCI, reprinted by permission; TASS, CSFB/Tremont, http://www.hedgeindex.com.)

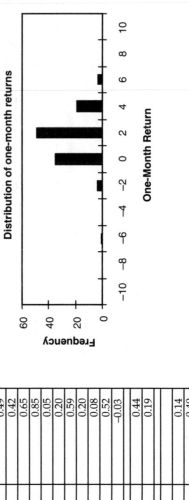

Distribution of one-month returns

One-Month Return

Correlation to	TASS Fund of Funds
TASS Fund of Funds	1.00
CSFB/Tremont Hedge Fund Index	0.91
CSFB/Tremont Convertible Arbitrage	0.45
CSFB/Tremont Ded Short Bias	-0.61
CSFB/Tremont Emerging Markets	0.74
CSFB/Tremont Equity Mkt Ntrl	0.45
CSFB/Tremont Event Driven	0.74
CSFB/Tremont Distressed	0.65
CSFB/Tremont E.D. Multi-Strategy	0.75
CSFB/Tremont Risk Arbitrage	0.49
CSFB/Tremont Fixed Inc Arb	0.42
CSFB/Tremont Global Macro	0.65
CSFB/Tremont Long/Short Equity	0.85
CSFB/Tremont Managed Futures	0.05
CSFB/Tremont Multi-Strategy	0.20
MSCI Discretionary Trading	0.59
MSCI Systematic Trading	0.20
3 mo Tbills	0.08
S&P 500	0.52
MSCI World Sovereign Debt	-0.03
Average to Hedge Fund Strategies	0.44
Average to Traditional Investments	0.19
Conditional Correlations	
S&P 500 Up Markets (71 mo)	0.14
S&P 500 Down Markets (43 mo)	0.40
MSCI Debt Up Markets (65 mo)	0.13
MSCI Debt Down Markets (49 mo)	0.14

the hedge fund universe. However, we can tell that fund-of-funds managers have historically invested in funds with less volatility than the average hedge fund. Comparing Figure 19-2 to Figure 3-1 shows us that while funds of funds underperform the hedge fund index in the strongest equity markets, they make up some of this difference by outperforming the average hedge fund in the weakest equity markets.

The correlation between the TASS Fund of Funds Index and the S&P 500 has averaged 0.52 over the last 10 years, but this correlation is volatile, ranging from 20 percent to 80 percent. Unfortunately, this correlation is much larger (0.40) when stock prices are falling than when stock prices are rising (0.19). Similarly, as we can see in Figure 19-3, the correlations to the MSCI World Sovereign Bond Index averaged −0.03 over the same time period, ranging from −0.44 to +0.36. The correlation between funds of funds and sovereign bonds is consistent, 0.13 in times of rising bond markets and 0.14 when interest rates are rising. Figure 19-4 shows the scattered monthly return pairs between the fund of funds index and the S&P 500. Here we can see that the TASS Fund of Funds Index profits in

FIGURE 19-3

TASS Fund of Funds Index: 24-month rolling correlation to traditional investments.

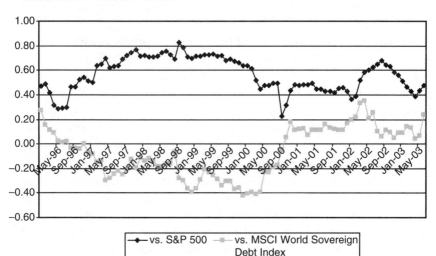

FIGURE 19−4

TASS Fund of Funds Index versus S&P 500: monthly return pairs, January 1994 to June 2003.

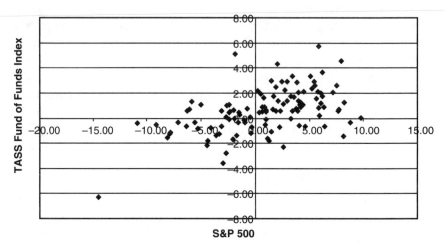

S&P 500

65.8 percent of all months, with the largest losses coinciding with periods of falling stock prices.

Figure 19-5 illustrates the low correlation between fund of funds investments and the MSCI World Sovereign Debt Index. While funds of funds are likely to be profitable in all types of bond markets, periods of rising interest rates seem to produce slightly higher returns to fund of funds products.

Figure 19-6 demonstrates that fund of funds returns increase with the return to the S&P 500 index. When stock prices crash, funds of funds have the highest probability of negative returns. In normal equity markets, however, funds of funds are likely to offer investors positive returns.

Unfortunately, the 3.8 percent annual return difference between the hedge fund index and the fund of funds index seems to be a large price to pay for the risk reduction services provided by fund of funds managers. While the standard deviation of fund of funds returns is much lower than that of the hedge fund index, the annual draw-down, Sharpe, or Sortino ratio or the percent winning months don't seem to illustrate that fund of funds managers are providing superior risk reduction. Each of these statistics suggests that the hedge fund index provides lower risk, or at least a higher risk that is well

FIGURE 19-5

TASS Fund of Funds Index versus MSCI World Sovereign
Debt Index: monthly returns sorted by quintiles, January
1994 to June 2003.

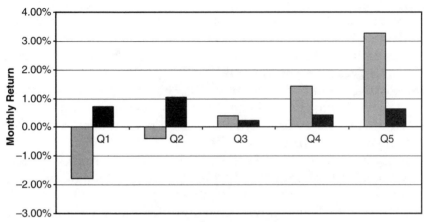

FIGURE 19-6

TASS Fund of Funds Index versus S&P 500: monthly returns
sorted by quintiles, January 1994 to June 2003.

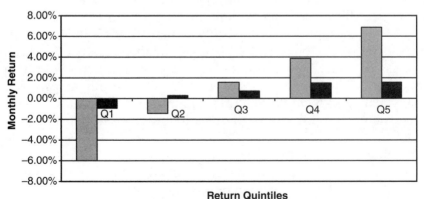

compensated by the additional return. In either case, we can see the rationale for investing in a diversity of hedge fund styles, as both the fund of funds index and the hedge fund index provide much lower return volatilities than the average volatility over all hedge fund styles.

The additional fees charged by fund of funds managers can explain a significant portion of this return difference and are the primary source of criticisms of funds of funds. The average fund of funds charges a 1.4 percent annual management fee, in addition to an incentive fee of 10 percent of profits.[3] Ineichen calculates that the most common fund of funds fee structure is 1 percent plus 10 percent. However, fees vary widely, from a simple 1 percent management fee with no incentive structure to a fee-heavy 2 percent plus 25 percent. Fully 22.7 percent of funds of funds have hurdle rates built into their fee structure, higher than the 18 percent of single-manager funds with hurdle rates. The probability and the size of the hurdle rate grows with the incentive fee, so the difference between 1 percent plus 10 percent and 2 percent plus 25 percent may not be as large as we might initially think. If the 1 percent plus 10 percent fund has no hurdle rate, while the 2 percent plus 25 percent has a hurdle rate based on a minimum 10 percent return, the net fees may be quite similar between the two funds.[4]

Besides performance, fund of funds investors may want to ask several other questions before making an allocation to a fund. First, what is the background and the motivation of the fund of funds manager? While the investor may desire that the manager spend the majority of his or her time making investments, monitoring investments, and managing risk, the reality at many funds is that the manager focuses more on attracting new capital than on any other task.

As with any type of fund, we don't know if the fund of funds manager has the necessary skill to add value to our investment. Many managers have started funds of funds simply because of their access to capital or a desire to diversify away from their management of long-only investments in traditional asset classes. While attracting capital is a vital skill, it can be very different from the skills needed to evaluate managers, manage risk, or predict which fund styles will outperform in the coming year.

An investor should also investigate the transparency and liquidity structure of the fund of funds investment. While some fund of funds managers will disclose which hedge funds they have relationships with, other funds of fund managers will simply state the percentage of assets invested in each hedge fund style.

While fund of funds investments are not as liquid as investments in mutual funds or traditional assets such as equity or fixed-income securities, they can be significantly more liquid than the underlying hedge fund investments. Fothergill and Coke estimate that 88 percent of fund of funds offer monthly liquidity, while 3 percent allow weekly redemptions and 9 percent can be liquidated on a quarterly basis.[5]

Most hedge funds will offer quarterly redemption periods, while some trading the most illiquid strategies may only offer semi-annual or annual opportunities to redeem assets. Fund of funds managers will design their redemption policies to be more liquid than the least liquid hedge funds, but less liquid than the most generous hedge fund withdrawal policies. Ideally, fund managers will design fund of funds liquidity to be the average liquidity of the underlying funds.

One of the most recent product introductions is that of the investable hedge fund index. In the summer of 2003, several well-known investment firms (S&P, MSCI, CSFB/Tremont) offered low-cost, highly liquid investable hedge fund index products. While these funds may closely resemble a fund of funds, they offer several differences.[6] First, these investments allocate funds to a relatively static pool of between 40 and 60 hedge fund managers, diversified across 9 to 11 styles. Initially, these funds will be equal weighted across managers, with the idea that the selected managers will be a relatively permanent part of the investment as long as their performance is acceptable. Standard and Poor's seems to have a very successful product, as its fund attracted over $500 million in investments in the first six months of operation. With fees at the index level of less than 75 basis points and the publication of a daily net asset value, this product carries several important advantages over traditional fund of funds investments. Some market participants predict that these products don't offer the promised value added, citing the heterogeneity of funds within a given style and the potential value added to fund of funds through style timing or the opportunity to replace the underlying managers. It also seems difficult for some to believe that these funds are an index, given that they invest in less than 1 percent of the available hedge funds.[7] Finally, the success of these products may cause the selected hedge funds to become overwhelmed with assets, which could add the necessity of adding more managers as the investable hedge fund index program becomes more popular.

Now that the daily liquidity genie is out of the bottle, it may only be a matter of time until exchange-traded funds start to track hedge fund strategies. Once ETFs start to track hedge funds, the next logical step is to trade options on these securities. Concerns abound about retail investor access to hedge fund type strategies. However, with daily liquidity and a published prospectus, we may soon see the retailization of absolute-return strategies.

Merrill Lynch introduced total return asset contracts in 2002, which looks like the first step in this direction. Five funds have already started trading, focusing on commodities, currencies, and even a long-short technology stock fund. While acting like futures, they require full payment at purchase, similar to buying a stock. While these funds are low-fee and tax-efficient, they are not yet very liquid, as you must contact Merrill to purchase them.[8] The wave of the future is low-cost, highly liquid funds. It is only a matter of time.

ENDNOTES

1. A. M. Ineichen, *Absolute Returns: The Risk and Opportunities of Hedge Fund Investing*. Hoboken, NJ: John Wiley & Sons, 2003.
2. M. Fothergill and C. Coke, "Funds of Hedge Funds: An Introduction to Multi-Manager Funds," *Journal of Alternative Investments* 4 (2001): 7–16.
3. Ibid.
4. A. M. Ineichen, 2003, *Absolute Returns*, op. cit.
5. M. Fothergill and C. Coke, "Funds of Hedge Funds," op. cit.
6. P. Taylor, "Fund of Funds in Drag," *Absolute Returns*, April 2003.
7. Ibid.
8. L. Braham, "Back to the Futures, with Less Risk," *Business Week*, November 3, 2003.

GLOSSARY

ABS Asset-backed securities. These debt securities are backed by the principal and interest cash flows from automobile or credit card loans.

absolute returns Returns that are not relative to a benchmark. Most appropriate for funds that have little correlation to established market indices.

alpha A measure of excess return above a standard benchmark, such as the S&P 500.

Association for Investment Management and Research (AIMR) A professional association that sponsors the CFA exam program, while promoting ethics and proper performance presentation standards for investment fund managers worldwide.

beta Measures an asset's risk with respect to a market benchmark, usually the S&P 500. A security with a beta of 1.5 will, on average, be 1.5 times as volatile as the benchmark index.

bond basis trading The basis is the difference between a cash price and (usually) a near-term futures price. Trading the basis spread takes advantage of the underlying future's discount or premium to the cash instrument.

capital account Measures the net flows of investment capital between countries. and is expected to balance the currency supply-and-demand situation caused by current account transactions.

Chartered Alternative Investment Analyst (CAIA) An educational program that concentrates on alternative investments. See http://www.caia.org.

Chartered Financial Analyst (CFA) An educational program sponsored by AIMR. See http://www.aimr.org.

Collateralized fund obligation (CFO) An asset-backed security that is used by funds of funds to raise capital.

collateralized mortgage obligation (CMO) A security backed by a pool of mortgages, where principal and interest is passed through to the investor. They consist of several tranches (pieces) and maturities.

commodity pool operator (CPO) A fund that diversifies investments between a number of commodity trading advisers.

commodity trading adviser (CTA) CTAs manage separate futures accounts.

conditional correlation A correlation statistic that focuses on a specific period of time, such as those months when equity markets post negative returns.

conversion premium Is equal to the convertible bond price divided by the conversion value.

conversion ratio A stated number of common shares that are received when a conversion occurs. The conversion ratio is determined at the time of issuance of the convertible bond.

conversion value Is equal to the current stock price multiplied by the conversion ratio or the number of shares per convertible bond.

convertible bond   A hybrid security that is composed of a straight bond plus an equity call option.

convertible bond option strike price   Is equal to the convertible bond's face value divided by the conversion ratio or the number of shares per convertible bond.

convexity   The difference between the actual price change of a bond and the linear price change estimated by duration.

credit spread trading   A spread that contains long and short fixed-income products, such as long an AAA bond and short an A-rated bond.

CSFB/Tremont   A hedge fund index published by Credit Suisse First Boston. See http://www.hedgeindex.com

current account   The net flows of goods, services, and transactions between countries. This is commonly compared to the capital account balance to determine the future direction of a currency price.

delta   Measures the rate of change in an option's price relative to its underlying security.

downside deviation   Measures the square root of the downside semivariance.

downside semivariance   a version of the standard deviation or variance calculation that only counts returns below a stated level, usually zero.

drawdown   The maximum percentage loss from the high-water mark.

duration   Measures the price sensitivity of a fixed-income instrument relative to a change in interest rates.

efficient frontier   A combination of securities or portfolios that maximizes returns for any level of risk or minimizes expected risk for any level of expected return.

Evaluation Associates Capital Markets (EACM)   The EACM 100 is an index of 100 large, extremely successful hedge funds, diversified over several strategies.

extreme value theory   A statistical method used to describe unusual events. EVT is used to analyze tail events and risk.

gamma   Measures the rate of change for an option's delta.

Goldman Sachs Commodity Index (GSCI)   An arithmetic index, weighted by the world production levels of commodities, including agricultural and energy products, industrial and precious metals, and livestock

Hedge Fund Research (HFR)   Publishes three hedge fund indexes. See http://www.hfr.com.

high-water mark   A minimum threshold measured by net asset value where incentive fees start. The high-water mark is measured monthly. A manager must attain the high-water mark before any incentive fees are paid out. If a manager fails to meet the high-water mark, then no incentive fees are paid.

hurdle rate   The minimum return required before a manager can earn incentive fees.

IO   An interest-only security based on the interest payments from a pool of mortgages or other bonds. Once the principal payments of a bond are repaid, the interest-only strip stops collecting interest and terminates.

kurtosis A measure of the flatness or peakedness of a distribution curve.

leptokurtotic distribution A symmetrical distribution with a higher than normal center peak and fat tails.

managed futures Funds that are managed by CPOs and CTAs.

Managed Account Reports (MAR) An index that tracks performance of individual CTAs, as well as CTA funds and pools. MAR computes returns on both an equal-weighted and a dollar-weighted basis. See http://www.marhedge.com.

mean reversion A statistical description of how underlying instruments such as interest rates and commodities move away from and toward a long-term average (mean).

mean-variance optimization A quantitative method used to build efficient portfolios using the mean and variance of each asset, as well as the correlation between asset returns.

Morgan Stanley Capital International (MSCI) Publishes several indexes, including the MSCI European Index, MSCI Fixed Income Index, MSCI Emerging-Markets Global Index, and the MSCI World Index. See http://www.msci.com.

mortgage-backed securities (MBS) Securities backed by the interest and principal payment cash flows from underlying mortgages.

negative carry trade This occurs when the cost of financing a bond position exceeds the coupon income earned from the purchased securities.

option adjusted spread Measures the yield spread of a fixed-income instrument after adjusting for the price of imbedded options.

PPS AIMR's Performance presentation standards are used to ensure fair and full representations and disclosures on returns and risk. PPS requires that returns be calculated on the total investment amount, including the use of borrowed funds. See http://www.aimr.org.

PAC bonds Planned amortization class (PAC) bonds are similar to these sequential pay CMOs, but with a support bond structure. PAC bonds are built to create a stable amortization schedule similar to a fixed-maturity bond, one that is relatively insensitive to prepayments in an assumed range. They have the most stable cash flows and lowest prepayment risk of any mortgage backed security.

pairs trading A trading strategy that purchases a security and short sells another security. The instruments in the pair will have either a statistical or a relative value relationship.

PO A principal-only security based on the collateralized principal payments from a pool of mortgages or other bonds.

positive carry trade This occurs when the cost of financing a bond position is less than the coupon income earned from the purchased securities.

relative returns A return that is benchmarked against an index such as the S&P 500 or the EACM 100. Most appropriate for funds that are designed to track or beat an established market index.

repo market Repurchase agreement market. A financing trade where fixed-income securities are pledged for a fixed term (under one year) in exchange for cash. At the end of the term, the fixed-income securities are repurchased, paying the lender of the funds a stated interest rate.

scenario analysis   A statistical analysis that estimates a fund's gains and losses given changes in market activity. This usually requires analyzing hundreds of market scenarios and their potential impact on the value of a fund's positions.

Sharpe ratio   A measure of risk-to-reward trade-off; calculated as past excess returns divided by the volatility of the portfolio's return:

$$\text{Sharpe ratio} = (\text{return}_{actual} - \text{return}_{risk\text{-}free}) / \text{standard deviation}_{return}$$

short stock rebate   Interest earned on the proceeds of short sales.

skewness   A statistical measure of a distribution curve's asymmetry. Right-skewed distributions have positive skewness, and left-skewed distributions have negative skewness.

Sortino ratio   A variation of the Sharpe ratio that substitutes volatility of return with downside deviation of the return:

$$\text{Sortino ratio} = (\text{return}_{actual} - \text{return}_{risk\text{-}free}) / \text{downside deviation}_{return.}$$

TASS   A research division of the Tremont company. TASS calculates a dollar-weighted index of the performance of individual CTAs, as well as an index of fund of funds managers.

TED spread   TED spread terminology was traditionally used to denote the spread between the yield on Treasury bills and Eurodollars. Today, TED spread can be applied to the spread between government and corporate yields in any currency.

Treynor ratio   Another measure of risk-reward trade-off. This ratio uses the portfolio's beta in the denominator:

$$\text{Treynor ratio} = (\text{return}_{actual} - \text{return}_{risk\text{-}free}) / \text{beta}_{portfolio}$$

Undertakings for Collective Investments in Transferable Securities (UCITS) standards   Mutual funds that abide by UCITS standards have one set of regulations in all European Union countries.

value-at-risk (VAR)   A methodology that attempts to quantify market risk or event risk to estimate the potential losses of a fund.

vega   The change in the price of an option given a change in implied volatility.

Anson, M. J. P. 2002. *Handbook of Alternative Assets*. New York: John Wiley.

Anson, M. J. P. 2001. "Hedge Fund Incentive Fees and the 'Free Option,'" *Journal of Alternative Investments* 4: 43–48.

Altman, E. I. 1999. *Distressed Securities: Analyzing and Evaluating Market Potential and Investment Risk*, 2nd ed. Washington, DC: Beard Books.

Asensio, M. P. 2001. *Sold Short: Uncovering Deception in the Markets*. New York: John Wiley & Sons.

Black, K. H. 2000. "Desperately Seeking Alpha," *Journal of Global Financial Markets* 1: 17–20.

———. 2001. "Life after Debt," *Journal of Global Financial Markets* 2: 15–18.

———. 2003. "Reaching for Yield? Try the European Convergence Trade," *Journal of Global Financial Markets*.

———. 2001. "Short Selling around the World," *Journal of Global Financial Markets* 2: 16–19.

———. 2002. "Why Didn't We All Short Enron?" *Journal of Global Financial Markets* 3: 8–12.

Boudoukh, J., et. al. 2002. "Stale Prices and Strategies for Trading Mutual Funds," *Financial Analysts Journal* (July–August) 58: 53–71.

Brooks, C., and H. M. Kat. 2002. "The Statistical Properties of Hedge Fund Index Returns and Their Implications for Investors," *Journal of Alternative Investments* (Fall) 5: 26–44.

Burghardt, G. D., and T. M. Belton. 1993. *The Treasury Bond Basis: An In-Depth Analysis for Hedgers, Speculators and Arbitrageurs*, 2nd ed. New York: McGraw-Hill.

Burstein, G. 1999. *Macro Trading and Investment Strategies: Macroeconomic Arbitrage in Global Markets*. New York: John Wiley & Sons.

Coker, D., 1999. *Mastering Microcaps: Strategies, Trends and Stock Selection*. Princeton, NJ: Bloomberg Press.

Fabozzi, F. 1993. *Bond Market Analysis and Strategies*, 2nd ed. Englewood Cliffs, NJ: Prentice Hall.

Fothergill, M., and C. Coke. 2001. "Funds of Hedge Funds: An Introduction to Multi-Manager Funds," *Journal of Alternative Investments* 4: 7–16.

Fung, W., and D. A. Hsieh. 1999. "A Primer on Hedge Funds," *Journal of Empirical Finance* 6: 309–331.

———. 1997. "Empirical Characteristics of Dynamic Trading Strategies: The Case of Hedge Funds," *Review of Financial Studies* 10: 275–302.

Herzberg, M., and H. Mozes. 2003. "The Persistence of Hedge Fund Risk: Evidence and Implications for Investors," *Journal of Alternative Investments* 6: 22–42.

Ineichen, A. M. 2001. "The Search for Alpha Continues: Do Fund of Fund Managers Add Value?" *UBS Warburg Global Equity Research*.

———. 2003. *Absolute Returns: The Risk and Opportunities of Hedge Fund Investing*. Hoboken, NJ: John Wiley & Sons.

Jaeger, L. 2002. *Managing Risk in Alternative Investment Strategies*. London: Prentice Hall Financial Times.

Jaeger, R. A. 2002. *All About Hedge Funds: The Easy Way to Get Started*. New York: McGraw-Hill.

Jaffer, S. 2003. *Funds of Hedge Funds for Professional Investors and Managers*. London: Euromoney Books.

Jorion, P. 2000. "Risk Management Lessons from Long-Term Capital Management," *European Financial Management* 6: 277–300.

Lake, R. 1999. *Evaluating and Implementing Hedge Fund Strategies*. London: Euromoney Publications.

Lange, S., et. al. 2001. "Convertibles as an Asset Class: 2000 Update," Goldman Sachs (March 6).

Lederman, J., and Klein, R. A. 1996. *Market Neutral: Long/Short Strategies for Every Market Environment*. New York: McGraw-Hill.

Lowenstein, R. 2000. *When Genius Failed: The Rise and Fall of Long-Term Capital Management*. New York: Random House.

McCrary, S. 2002. *How to Create and Manage a Hedge Fund: A Professional's Guide* Hoboken, NJ: John Wiley & Sons.

Mahadevan, S., and Schwartz, D. 2002. "Hedge Fund Collateralized Fund Obligations" *Journal of Alternative Investments* 5: 45–62.

"Millionaire Has-Beens" 2003. Viewed at http://www.cnnmoney.com, June 12.

Moore, K. M. 1999. *Risk Arbitrage: An Investor's Guide*. New York: John Wiley & Sons.

Nederlof, M. L. 2003. "Balancing the Interests of Managers and Investors in Hedge Fund Disclosure," *Managing Today's Investment Firm*. Charlottesville, VA.: AIMR.

Nicholas, J. G. 2000. *Market Neutral Investing: Long/Short Hedge Fund Strategies*. New York: Bloomberg Press.

———. 1999. *Investing in Hedge Funds*. New York: Bloomberg Press.

"The Original Turtle Trading Rules." 2003. Viewed at http://www.originalturtles.org/docs/turtlerules.pdf.

Parker, V. R. 2000. *Managing Hedge Fund Risk*. London: Risk Waters Group, Ltd.

Reverre, S. 2001. *The Complete Arbitrage Deskbook*. New York: McGraw-Hill.

Safaty, N. 2001. "The $460 Billion Global Convertible Bond Market," *KBC Financial Products*, July 25.

Schilit, H. 2002. *Financial Shenanigans: How to Detect Accounting Gimmicks and Fraud in Financial Reports*, 2nd ed., New York: McGraw-Hill.

Schneeweis, T., Kazemi, H., and Martin, G. 2002. "Understanding Hedge Fund Performance: Research Issues Revisited—Part I?" *Journal of Alternative Investments* 5: 6–22.

———. 2002. "Understanding Hedge Fund Performance: Research Issues Revisited—Part II?" *Journal of Alternative Investments* 5: 8–30.

——— and Pescatore, J. F. 1999. *The Handbook of Alternative Investment Strategies*. New York: Institutional Investor.

Schwager, J. D. 1989. *Market Wizards: Interviews with Top Traders*. New York: Harper & Row.

————. 1992. *The New Market Wizards: Conversations with America's Top Traders*. New York: HarperCollins.

Shapiro, A. C. 2003. *Multinational Financial Management*, 6th ed. Upper Saddle River, NJ: Prentice Hall.

Staley, K. A. 1997. *The Art of Short Selling*. New York: John Wiley & Sons.

Strachman, D. A. 2000. *Getting Started in Hedge Funds*. New York: John Wiley & Sons.

Tan, K. 2003. "Credit Counts," *Barrons*, August 18.

Tuckman, B. 1996. *Fixed Income Securities: Tools for Today's Markets*. New York: John Wiley & Sons.

Warwick, B. 2000. *Searching for Alpha: The Quest for Exceptional Investment Performance*. New York: John Wiley & Sons.

INDEX

ABOUT THE AUTHOR

Keith Black is a chartered financial analyst and a chartered alternative investment analyst. He is currently an assistant professor of Finance at the Illinois Institute of Technology. Previous to his academic life, he worked in various financial analyst positions for a variety of financial institutions, including the Chciago Board of Trade, Hull Trading Company, and First Chicago Capital Markets. He has written numerous articles for many industry and academic journals and has appeared on many media outlets, including WebFN, National Public Radio, the *Financial Times*, and the *Chicago Tribune*.